Housesteads Roman Fort, Hadrians Wall
Photo © Skyscan Photolibrary / Alamy

Key to map pages

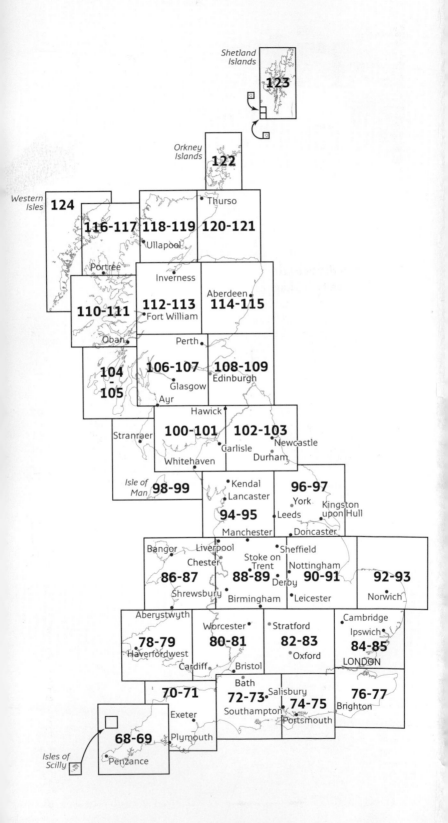

Shetland Islands **123**

Orkney Islands **122**

Western Isles **124**

116-117

118-119 Ullapool

120-121 • Thurso

Portree •

Inverness

Aberdeen •

110-111

112-113 Fort William

114-115

Oban •

Perth •

104 - 105

106-107 Glasgow •

108-109 Edinburgh •

Ayr •

Hawick •

Stranraer •

100-101 Carlisle • Whitehaven •

102-103 • Newcastle Durham •

Isle of Man **98-99**

Kendal • Lancaster •

96-97 York •

Kingston upon Hull

94-95 Leeds • Manchester •

Doncaster •

Bangor • Liverpool • Chester •

Sheffield • Stoke on Trent

Nottingham • Derby •

86-87 Shrewsbury •

88-89 Birmingham •

90-91 Leicester •

92-93 Norwich •

Aberystwyth •

Worcester •

Stratford • Oxford •

Cambridge • Ipswich •

78-79 Haverfordwest •

80-81 Cardiff •

Bristol •

82-83

84-85 LONDON

Bath •

70-71

72-73 Salisbury • Southampton •

74-75 Portsmouth •

76-77 Brighton

Exeter •

Isles of Scilly

68-69 • Penzance

Plymouth •

Discovering
Britain's
Heritage

Contents

Published by Collins
An imprint of HarperCollins Publishers
77-85 Fulham Palace Road, Hammersmith, London W6 8JB

www.collins.co.uk

Copyright © HarperCollins Publishers Ltd 2007

Collins® is a registered trademark of HarperCollins Publishers Limited

Mapping generated from Collins Bartholomew digital databases

The grid on this map is the National Grid taken from the Ordnance Survey map with the permission of the Controller of Her Majesty's Stationery Office.

Printed in China

ISBN-13   978 0 00 725666 2
ISBN-10   0 00 725666 3   Imp 001   UC12294 / MDR

e-mail: roadcheck@harpercollins.co.uk

② Britain's heritage

Great Britain comprises three nations, England, Scotland and Wales, all with an amazing wealth of heritage. This atlas and guide lists over 500 sites to visit for an insight into the best of this national heritage.

Skara Brae

From ancient monuments to royal palaces

From Stone Age dwellings, Roman baths and the humble cottages of agricultural and industrial workers to manor houses and royal palaces, Britain has a rich and varied heritage spanning many thousands of years. There is the glory and grandeur of many stately homes – Blenheim, Chatsworth, Castle Howard, to name just a few. In contrast, but of no less significance, is the settlement of Skara Brae in Orkney which was in continuous use between 3100 BC and 2500 BC and is now the best preserved prehistoric village in Northern Europe.

Ecclesiastical buildings

Small churches, ruined abbeys right up to vast cathedrals; Britain has an impressive and rich ecclesiastical heritage reflected in buildings still standing today. Most cathedrals are architectural masterpieces. Other religious buildings have had great significance in the history of the nation and many have an incredible story to tell.

Fortifications

With a military history spanning over 2500 years, Britain has sites ranging from Iron Age forts, Roman defences and medieval castles to later fortifications built to defend the coast or border country.

Transport

Britain was paramount in the early development of railways and aviation, canals and maritime ventures. The world's first steam locomotive was built by Richard Trevithick in Britain in 1830 and in the 19th century the British shipbuilding industry was the largest in the world.

Birch Grove steam locomotive, built in 1899 and based at the Bluebell Railway

Mining & industry

The Industrial Revolution in 18th and 19th century Britain changed the economy of the nation and made way for the industrialisation of Europe and America. Britain forged the way ahead with technologies in mining, iron foundries, potteries and brickworks and the landscape is still rich with the legacy of this revolution. The sites that remain commemorate the people and places that pioneered this development.

Big Pit & Blaenavon Industrial Landscape in the 1950s

Photo © Big Pit

World Heritage Sites

In 1972 the United Nations Educational, Scientific and Cultural Organization (UNESCO) adopted a treaty for the preservation of outstanding examples of cultural and natural heritage sites around the world. Cultural heritage sites may be single buildings or monuments, groups of buildings and sites or even a landscape of special significance. Each year a committee evaluates proposals for new sites to be included. By 2007 there were 830 sites listed worldwide of which 27 were in the United Kingdom. Four of these are in overseas territories (Henderson Island, Gough Island and Bermuda) or Northern Ireland but the other 23 are highlighted in yellow on the maps on pages 68-124 and in the guide section of this atlas. Together they represent the finest examples of Britain's heritage from the ancient monuments of Neolithic times to the Regency splendour of Bath.

Tower of London

Orkney Islands

Heart of Neolithic Orkney
★ (Maes Howe, Stones of Stenness, Ring of Brodgar & Skara Brae)

★ St Kilda

★ Old & New Towns of Edinburgh

★ New Lanark

Frontiers of the Roman Empire
(Hadrian's Wall)

★ Durham Castle & Cathedral

Studley Royal Park
★ including the ruins of
Fountain Abbey

Isle of Man

Saltaire ★

★ Liverpool - Maritime Mercantile City

★ Derwent Valley Mills

Castles & town walls of
King Edward in Gwynedd
(castles of Beaumaris,
Harlech, Caernarfon
& Conwy)

★ Ironbridge Gorge

Blenheim
Palace

Westminster Palace,
Westminster Abbey &
St Margaret's Church

Blaenavon Industrial
Landscape ★

Tower of London

Royal Botanic ★★★
Gardens, Kew

Maritime ★ Canterbury Cathedral,
Greenwich   St Augustine's Abbey
              & St Martin's Church

City of Bath ★

Stonehenge, Avebury ★
& associated sites

Dorset & East Devon Coast
(the 'Jurassic Coast')

Isles of Scilly

Cornwall & West Devon
Mining Landscape

World Heritage Sites are highlighted in yellow.

Abbotsford House, *Sc.Bord.* 108 C6
☎ 01896 752043 www.scottsabbotsford.co.uk
Sir Walter Scott, the novelist, bought a farmhouse
here in 1811, replacing it with a castellated and
turreted mansion in the Scottish Baronial style
and naming it Abbotsford in memory of the
Melrose Abbey monks who forded the River Tweed
here. He gleaned architectural ideas from many
sources, including Melrose Abbey, Linlithgow
Palace and Rosslyn Chapel, while internally the
house is little altered and visitors can see the
author's personal possessions, 9000 volume
library and eclectic collection of historic relics such
as a lock of Bonnie Prince Charlie's hair and Mary,
Queen of Scots' crucifix.

Aberdour Castle, *Fife* 108 A3
☎ 01383 860519 www.historic-scotland.gov.uk
Overlooking the harbour is a 13th century fortified
residence. There are also the ruins of the 14th
century keep along with other buildings built and
extended in later centuries. One of these is still
roofed and contains a gallery on the first floor,
complete with painted ceiling, illustrating how it
was furnished in 1650. There is also a restored
walled garden with a fine circular dovecot and
terraced garden.

Alfriston Clergy House (NT), *E.Suss.* 76 B5
☎ 01323 870001 www.nationaltrust.org.uk
A thatched, half-timbered 14th century Wealden
Hall House with a pretty cottage garden. It was
the first historic building acquired by the National
Trust in 1896, purchased for a nominal £10. The
house is oak framed and infilled with wattle and
daub. One of the beams has a carving of an oak
leaf which some believe gave rise to the adoption
of the National Trust's famous logo.

Alnwick Castle & Garden, *Northumb.* 103 D1
☎ 01665 510777 www.alnwickcastle.com;
www.alnwickgarden.co.uk
Just to the north of Alnwick town centre and
rising impressively above the River Aln, the castle
has been home to the Percys, the ancestral family
of the Duke of Northumberland, since 1309. It is
the second largest lived-in castle in England (after
Windsor). The exterior view of this austere and
striking medieval fortress, with its life-size stone
figures standing guard on the battlements, is in
stark contrast to the sumptuous state rooms
furnished in Italian Renaissance style. Adam
ceilings and fireplaces are the legacy of
restoration by the first Duke of Northumberland in
the 18th century and there are fine paintings and
porcelain. The Regimental Museum of the
Northumberland Fusiliers is housed in the Abbots
Tower. Archaeological exhibits, the Percy coach,
dungeon, gun terrace and landscaped grounds by
Capability Brown are among other attractions.
Often used as a film location, scenes from the
'Harry Potter' films have been filmed at the castle.
The Alnwick Garden (separate charge) is a project
underway to transform the former 18th century
sloping walled garden into a modern, innovative
garden and, notably, features The Grand Cascade.

Alnwick Castle & Garden

Ancient High House, *Staffs.* 89 D4
☎ 01785 619131
Built in 1595 by John Dorrington, this Tudor
building is the largest timber-framed town house
in England. King Charles I and his nephew Prince
Rupert stayed here in 1642 at the beginning of
the Civil War and, when overrun by the
Parliamentarians the following year, it became a
prison for Royalist prisoners. Extensive renovation
by the Borough Council has enabled the building
to be opened to the public, and exhibits of period
furniture, wallpapers and costumes can be
enjoyed. It is also home to the Staffordshire
Yeomanry Museum.

Ancient High House   Photo © Stafford Borough Council

Anderton Boat Lift, *Ches.* 88 B2
☎ 01606 786777 www.andertonboatlift.co.uk
The boat lift is the only one of its kind in the UK,
and when it was built in 1875 it was the first
anywhere in the world. Boats enter one of two
counterbalanced water-filled tanks which then
pass each other mostly by the process of gravity.
The rise is 50ft (15m) between two sections of the
Trent and Mersey Canal. A visitor centre explains
the processes fully and there are trips up and
down the lift on a specially built glass-bottomed
boat.

Anglesey Abbey (NT), *Cambs.* 84 B1
☎ 01223 810080 www.nationaltrust.org.uk
This attractive Jacobean house was built on the
site of an earlier Augustinian priory. Much of what
visitors see today is the legacy of Huttleston
Broughton, 1st Lord Fairhaven, who bought the
house in 1926 and, over the next thirty years,
accumulated a large collection of paintings,
books, furniture, tapestries and clocks. He also
landscaped the superb gardens which extend to
98 acres (40ha), and comprise both formal and
informal designs. The lawns and avenues of trees
combine with more structured planting to provide
colour all year round and are enhanced by Lord
Fairhaven's fine collection of statuary. Within the
grounds is Lode Mill, an 18th century working
watermill.

Anne Hathaway's Cottage, *Warks.*   82 A2
☎ 01789 292100
The pre-marital home of the wife of William
Shakespeare, and of her descendants until the late
19th century. It is a Tudor 12-roomed thatched
farmhouse, parts of which date back to the 15th
century. Recent additions to the lovely garden are
the Shakespeare Tree Garden, which has many of
the trees mentioned in his plays, and a maze, the
design of which dates from the Elizabethan era.

Antonine Wall, *Falk.*   107 D4
☎ 0131 668 8800   www.historic-scotland.gov.uk
This Roman fortification stretched 38 miles
(61km) from Bo'ness on the Forth to Old Kilpatrick
on the Clyde. Built circa AD142–3, it consisted of
a turf rampart on stone foundation behind a ditch
12ft (3.7m) deep and 40ft (12m) wide. Forts were
positioned approximately every 2 miles (3km) and
linked by a cobbled road. It was probably
abandoned around AD163. Remains are best
preserved in the Falkirk/Bonnybridge area.

Arbeia Roman Fort & Museum, *T. & W.*   103 E3
☎ 0191 456 1369
In a commanding position at the mouth of the
River Tyne, the Roman stone fort of Arbeia was
the supply base for Hadrian's Wall. Reconstructed
buildings, including the impressive West Gate, and
a varied display of archaeological finds from
weapons to jewellery, present a picture of life on
the northern frontier of Roman Britain.

Arbroath Abbey, *Angus*   114 C6
☎ 01241 878756   www.historic-scotland.gov.uk
The substantial ruins of a Tironesian monastery
founded by William the Lion in 1178. The Abbey
is most notably associated with the signing of the
Declaration of Arbroath in 1320, which asserted
Scotland's independence from England. There is
also a herb garden, exhibits about life in the
Abbey and the Declaration, and a visitor centre.

Arbury Hall, *Warks.*   89 F6
☎ 024 7638 2804
The original house is Elizabethan but it was
transformed in the 18th century into one of the
finest examples of Gothic Revival architecture in
the country. Home to the Newdegate family since
the 16th century, many of the superb rooms are
open to the public. There are superb vaulted
ceilings and displays of art, glass, porcelain and
antique furniture. The house is surrounded by fine
landscaped gardens with lakes and woodland
walks.

Arlington Court (NT), *Devon*   70 C1
☎ 01271 850296   www.nationaltrust.org.uk
An early 19th century house on the site of two
previous buildings. The 3000 acre (1200ha) estate
was home to the Chichester family for over 500
years, and the house contains many of the diverse
and exotic acquisitions of the last owner, Miss
Rosalie Chichester. There are extensive formal and
informal gardens, delightful woodland walks, a
small carriage museum and a bat cave where a
large colony of Lesser Horseshoe bats can be
observed by closed-circuit television.

Arundel Castle, *W.Suss.*   75 D4
☎ 01903 882173   www.arundelcastle.org
Arundel Castle is the ancestral home of the Dukes
of Norfolk, who have played an important role in
English history, the third duke being the uncle of
Anne Boleyn and Catherine Howard, two of Henry
VIII's wives.
  Situated on a hill with views over the River Arun
and out to sea, the castle is an impressive sight,
dominating the nearby town with its towers and
battlements. It dates from the end of the 11th
century with the building of the motte. The
gatehouse dates from 1070, but most of the rest
is 19th century.
  Within the castle there are fine collections of
paintings by Van Dyck, Gainsborough, as well as
16th century furniture, tapestries, clocks and
armour. The magnificent grounds include a
Victorian kitchen and flower gardens. The Fitzalan
Chapel is also worth a visit.

Arundel Castle   Photo © John Braine

Ashmolean Museum, *Oxon.*   64 B2
☎ 01865 278000   www.ashmolean.org
Claiming to be Britain's first museum, the
Ashmolean opened in 1683, displaying a
collection of natural history specimens assembled
by the Tradescant family. Although chiefly famed
for their horticultural expertise, the Tradescants
were wide-ranging and idiosyncratic collectors,
their acquisitions including not only natural
history items but amongst many others a picture
made from feathers, the Passion of Christ carved
on a plum stone and a hat band of snake bones.
The collection was transferred to the ownership of
Elias Ashmole who presented it to Oxford
University. In the late 19th century, it was
rehoused in the magnificent neo-classical building
which is its present home. It was subsequently
merged with the university's art collection.

Athelhampton, *Dorset*   72 C5
☎ 01305 848363   www.athelhampton.co.uk
A splendid 15th century manor house with
impressive Grade I gardens. The central feature of
the house is the Great Hall, built in 1493 by Sir
Robert Martyn, a former Lord Mayor of London.
The 20 acre (8ha) garden was designed by Inigo
Thomas in the late 19th century and, in addition
to the world famous topiary pyramids, there are
eight walled gardens inspired by the Renaissance,
as well as fountains, pavilions and a 16th century
dovecote.

Attingham Park (NT), *Shrop.*   88 B5
☎ 01743 708162   www.nationaltrust.org.uk
A late 18th century mansion with magnificent
interiors, built originally for the 1st Earl of
Berwick, now owned by the National Trust. Guided
tours are available which give an insight into life
up and downstairs, as the kitchens and servants
quarters are open to the public. The picture
gallery was designed by John Nash who
constructed the curved ceiling out of iron and
glass. Surrounding the house are mature gardens,
deer park, woodland and riverside walks.

Audley End, *Essex*   84 B3
☎ 01799 522399   www.english-heritage.org.uk
This magnificent Jacobean mansion was built
between 1603 and 1614 by Thomas Howard, the
1st Earl of Suffolk, on the site of a former abbey.
At the time, it was the largest house in England.
In 1668, it briefly became a royal palace when it
was purchased by Charles II for £50,000, for his
use when visiting the races at Newmarket.
Between 1708 and 1753 a large part of the house
was demolished; the building we see today is just
a small part of the original.
  In the 1760s much of the interior was remodelled
by Robert Adam and, today, visitors can see over
thirty rooms containing attractive period
furnishings. Adam's work can also be seen in the
extensive grounds where he created ornamental
garden buildings to enhance the superb landscape
park laid out by Lancelot 'Capability' Brown in
1762. There are fine Victorian gardens featuring a
parterre, originally laid out in 1830 and re-created
in 1993, a rose garden, as well as a walled garden
of approximately 10 acres (4ha) within which is
an impressive 170ft (52m) long vine house.

Avebury Ring & Alexander Keiller Museum (NT), Wilts. 82 A6

☎ 01672 539250   www.nationaltrust.org.uk;
www.english-heritage.org.uk

Around 4500 years old, this is possibly the largest stone circle in Europe, the surviving sarsen stones being enclosed by a substantial earthwork almost 1 mile (1.6km) in circumference. Within this there were two smaller stone circles, though little remains of the more northerly.

Information about Avebury Ring can be found in the Alexander Keiller Museum (for which there is a charge), named after the former owner of the site who endeavoured to restore the area following the plunder and removal of stones which took place, particularly in medieval times. The museum gives an excellent overview of the site, explains the known history and displays artefacts uncovered during archaeological excavations.

Avebury Ring   Photo © National Trust

Avoncroft Museum of Historic Buildings, Worcs. 81 F1

☎ 01527 831363   www.avoncroft.org.uk

An unusual museum which has over 25 historical buildings from the last 700 years, painstakingly dismantled and rebuilt on a site of 25 acres (10ha). Originally the aim was to rescue and restore only timber-framed buildings, but such has been the success of the venture that all manner of buildings are now on show, including a 1946 prefab, a working windmill, church and gaol.

Baddesley Clinton (NT), Warks. 82 A1

☎ 01564 783294   www.nationaltrust.org.uk

This moated house sits in grounds of 120 acres (48ha) and has been largely unchanged for almost 400 years. The original building dates from the 15th century and stayed in the family of its owner, the Under Treasurer of England, John Broome, until it was acquired by the National Trust in 1981. The house has three priest holes which were installed in the late 16th century by Henry Ferrers, a staunch Roman Catholic. The gardens include ponds and lakeside walks, a walled garden and nature trail.

Balmoral Castle, Aber. 114 A4

☎ 013397 42534   www.balmoralcastle.com

Situated on the south side of the River Dee, Balmoral has been the Highland holiday home of the Royal Family since 1852. The present castle was designed by Aberdeen City architect William Smith under the keen eye of Queen Victoria's husband, Prince Albert, who considered the castle they previously leased on the site too small. The pale colour of the granite stone used in the building is quite distinctive and was quarried from nearby Glen Gelder.

The only part of the castle open to the public is the ballroom which has items from within the castle on display; paintings, porcelain and the Balmoral Tartans and Tweeds collection. In the stables there are carriages on view, while in the carriage hall there is a display of commemorative china and an exhibition about the Balmoral Estate.

Three acres (1ha) of formal gardens include a conservatory and Victorian glasshouses, kitchen garden and water garden, and there are waymarked walks along the river and through the woods. Guided ranger walks, land rover safaris and pony trekking are also available. Balmoral is only open to the public between 1 April and 31 July.

Bamburgh Castle, Northumb. 109 F6

☎ 01668 214515   www.bamburghcastle.com

Formidable Norman castle dominating the seaside village of Bamburgh, much restored in the 18th and 19th centuries but still retaining the original large square keep. The castle is stunningly situated on a rocky outcrop above a long white sandy beach with views seawards of the Farne Islands and Holy Island. Bamburgh withstood many sieges but fell into disrepair after sustaining severe damage during the Wars of the Roses in 1464. The first Lord Armstrong, inventor, engineer and industrialist, carried out major restoration and refurbishment in the 19th century, and Bamburgh is still the home of the Armstrong family today. Paintings, furniture, tapestries, china and glassware are displayed in the fine King's Hall and Cross Hall. The old laundry building houses an Aviation Artefact Museum with many parts from crashed World War II aircraft, while the Armstrong Museum portrays the life of the first Lord Armstrong through his work as an engineer. There is an impressive collection of armour and a dungeon.

Bannockburn 1314, Stir. 107 D3

☎ 01786 812664   www.nts.org.uk

This is the site of the famous battle in 1314 when Robert the Bruce, King of Scots, defeated the English Army of Edward II. The Heritage Centre stages a colourful exhibition, with life-size figures of Bruce and William Wallace, heraldic flags and an audiovisual presentation on the Battle of Bannockburn.

Basildon Park (NT), W.Berks. 82 C6

☎ 0118 984 3040   www.nationaltrust.org.uk

Handsome late 18th century Palladian mansion with impressive classical façade, built of Bath stone and salvaged from neglect in the mid 20th century. The richly decorated interior contains some fine plasterwork, the Shell Room, with its unusual collection of sea shells, and a striking Octagon Room. Waymarked walks can be taken through the 400 acres (160ha) of attractive parkland and there are small but colourful formal gardens.

Bath, B. & N.E.Som. 81 E6

www.visitbath.co.uk

The only hot springs in the country are the source of Bath's name and of its importance as a fashionable resort and tourist attraction. This in turn generated the wealth which enabled the construction of the wonderful Georgian buildings which have helped to give Bath its World Heritage Site status.

Bath Abbey   Photo © www.heritagecities.com

Bath Abbey, B. & N.E.Som. 54 B2

☎ 01225 422462   www.bathabbey.org

Built between 1499 – 1616, this is one of England's last great medieval churches, known by the Elizabethans as the 'Lantern of the West' because of the abundance of stained glass. The most impressive example is the great East Window, illustrating 56 scenes from the life of Christ. Externally, the most remarkable feature is the west front, carved angels commemorating a dream of the founder, Bishop Oliver King. A small but informative museum in the vaults traces the abbey's history.

Battle Abbey, *E.Suss.* 76 C5
☎ 01424 773792 www.english-heritage.org.uk
Partially ruined abbey on the site of the Battle of
Hastings, traditionally said to have been founded
by William the Conqueror in 1070 to atone for the
terrible loss of life incurred during the conquest of
England. The gatehouse, built circa 1338, is the
best preserved part of the abbey. Supposedly, the
altar was located on the very spot where Harold II
died.

Bayham Abbey, *E.Suss.* 76 B4
☎ 01892 890381 www.english-heritage.org.uk
Now an impressive ruin, located in a pretty
wooded valley, Bayham Abbey was founded
around the turn of the 12th century, and built
from local golden sandstone. During the 18th
century the site was landscaped to create the
effect of a 'romantic' ruin.

Beamish, North of England Open Air Museum, *Dur.* 103 D4
☎ 0191 370 4000 www.beamish.org.uk
Celebrating the industrial, rural and social
heritage of the north-east, Beamish shows how
people lived and worked in the 1800s and early
1900s. A town, colliery village and railway station
have been re-created with many authentic
buildings being dismantled elsewhere and brought
to the site. Staff in period costume are a wealth of
information.

Visitors may go shopping in the town shops,
and there is also a bank, dentist and newspaper
office in the main street. Guided tours of the drift
mine take visitors underground. The colliery
village includes tiny pit cottages, a chapel and a
school where playing with traditional toys in the
playground is a popular activity. Cheese is made
on a working farm, nearby is a manor house and,
by way of contrast, there is a Victorian fairground.

Trams link the various areas, and replica buses
and horse-drawn vehicles provide other means of
transport. Covering over 300 acres (120ha),
Beamish provides a full day out for all the family.
Winner of both British and European Museum of
the Year awards.

Beaulieu Abbey, *Hants.* 74 A4
☎ 01590 614604 www.beaulieu.co.uk
The Cistercian abbey was founded here by King
John in 1204 and built with stone brought in from
the Isle of Wight and Caen in Normandy. The
estate of 10,000 acres (4000ha) was a wealthy
one and consequently a magnificent abbey was
built. This was subsequently ruined during the
Dissolution of the Monasteries, the monks'
refectory being converted to form the parish
church. The cloister is the best preserved part of
the abbey, while the Domus, or lay brothers'
dwelling, remained entire and now houses an
excellent exhibition on life in the medieval abbey.

Beaulieu Palace House, *Hants.* 74 A4
☎ 01590 614604 www.beaulieu.co.uk
Following the Dissolution of the Monasteries,
Beaulieu Abbey estate was sold to the Earl of
Southampton, an ancestor of the current owner,
Lord Montagu. The Palace House was built in the
19th century around the abbey gatehouse,
producing a curious combination of 14th century
Gothic, as seen in the fan vaulted ceilings, and
Baronial style Victorian architecture.

Beaumaris Castle , *I.o.A.* 86 C2
☎ 01248 810361 www.cadw.wales.gov.uk
The castle sits in the town of Beaumaris, on the
shores of the Menai Strait, and offers fine views
across to the mountains of Snowdonia. This was
the last and largest of King Edward's edifices,
erected to establish his authority over the Welsh.
Beaumaris Castle was started in 1295 and,
although never fully completed, it remains
remarkably intact and is a designated UNESCO
World Heritage Site.

It is an impressive example of military
architecture, having an outer moat and perfectly
symmetrical double concentric walls within. The
fortified dock had moorings for ships of
considerable size. The high walls, gatehouses and
strong towers were intended as stout defences,
but the castle never came under attack. The inner
buildings accommodated a Great Hall, luxurious
rooms, kitchens, stables and a chapel. Visitors can
also explore the fascinating interior passageways
found inside the walls of the inner ward.

Bede's World, *T. & W.* 103 E3
☎ 0191 489 2106 www.bedesworld.co.uk
Dedicated to the 8th century monk, the Venerable
Bede, who chronicled the ecclesiastical history of
the time, this is an absorbing day out for all the
family. Bede's World incorporates the monastic
site of St Paul's, a museum, an Anglo-Saxon
demonstration farm and herb garden. Many
fascinating archaeological finds are displayed in
the interactive exhibition which explores early
medieval life and Christian heritage.

Beeston Castle (ruins), *Ches.* 88 B3
☎ 01829 260464 www.english-heritage.org.uk
There are stunning views to be seen from this
13th century ruined castle which stands tall on
sandstone crags overlooking the Cheshire Plains –
it is well worth the steep climb to the top. The
Castle of the Rock exhibition outlines the history
of the site, from prehistoric times to the Civil War
when the castle was eventually destroyed by the
Parliamentarians in 1646.

Belton House (NT), *Lincs.* 90 C4
☎ 01476 566116 www.nationaltrust.org.uk
Built in the Restoration style for Sir John Brownlow
in the late 1600s, this sumptuous country house
is well worth a visit for the wealth of elaborate
woodcarving and plasterwork, not to mention the
fine furniture, silverware and tapestries. A
magnificent Orangery graces the formal gardens
and the substantial landscaped parkland includes
a lake; perfect for a leisurely stroll.

Belvoir Castle, *Leics.* 90 B4
☎ 01476 871000 www.belvoircastle.com
For 1000 years Belvoir has been home to the
Dukes of Rutland. Meaning 'beautiful view', the
name is actually pronounced 'beaver' and the
view is right across the glorious Vale of Belvoir.
The present castle was built in the early 1800s
after a fire destroyed the previous one, and it
contains many fine paintings and sculptures
along with French furniture, tapestries and
porcelain. There is also a fascinating museum
dedicated to the history of the Queens Royal
Lancers. Outside, the sloping lawns lead to the
terraced formal gardens and the secluded
Duchess' Spring Gardens.

Beaumaris Castle

Bembridge Windmill (NT), *I.o.W.* 74 B5
☎ 01983 873945   www.nationaltrust.org.uk
Built around 1700 and in use until 1913, this is
the only surviving windmill on the Isle of Wight. It
contains a complete set of restored wooden
machinery, most of it original.

Beningbrough Hall (NT), *N.Yorks.* 96 B4
☎ 01904 472027   www.nationaltrust.org.uk
This grand Georgian mansion was built in 1716. It
now houses numerous 18th century treasures,
including over 100 portraits loaned from the
National Portrait Gallery. Its impressive Baroque
interior boasts outstanding woodcarving and
plasterwork, an unusual central corridor spanning
the entire length of the house, and a fully equipped
Victorian laundry. Outside is a wonderful walled
garden, interesting wood sculptures, potting shed,
wilderness play area and 7 acres (3ha) of parkland
to be enjoyed.

Benthall Hall (NT), *Shrop.* 88 B5
☎ 01952 882159   www.nationaltrust.org.uk
A 16th century sandstone house which was given
a more Gothic look in the 18th century. The
magnificent interior has fine oak panelling and a
carved oak staircase, while the plasterwork is
equally stunning. The 3 acre (1.2ha) grounds
include a restored plantsman's garden as well as a
rock garden, rose garden and terraces There is also
a 17th century Restoration church which holds
services on alternate Sundays.

Berkeley Castle & Gardens, *Glos.* 81 D5
☎ 01453 810332   www.berkeley-castle.com
Completed in 1153, England's oldest inhabited
castle is still home to the Berkeley family after 25
generations. The cell where King Edward II was
held captive for 18 months before his murder in
1327 can be seen, as can the 30ft (9m) deep
dungeon. The extensive grounds feature a
butterfly house, lily pond and the bowling alley
where Elizabeth I played bowls with her courtiers.

Berrington Hall (NT), *Here.* 81 D1
☎ 01568 615721   www.nationaltrust.org.uk
This elegant house was designed and built in the
late 18th century by Henry Holland while the
parkland was designed by his father-in-law
'Capability' Brown. The main feature is a 14 acre
(5.6ha) lake, which has sweeping views down the
valley to the Brecon Beacons. The exterior
sandstone walls from which the house is built give
it a severe first impression, but the interior is
delicate with beautifully detailed ceilings and a
spectacular staircase hall.

Berry Pomeroy Castle, *Devon* 71 D5
☎ 01803 866618   www.english-heritage.org.uk
With a reputation as one of the most haunted
castles in England, this decidedly atmospheric
ruin is splendidly located on a crag above a wooded
valley. The oldest part is thought to date from the
14th century, but the main building, a large
mansion, was built between 1548 – 1613 and was
subsequently abandoned later in the 17th century.

Big Pit National Coal Museum & Blaenavon Industrial Landscape, *Torfaen* 80 B4
☎ 01495 790311   www.museumwales.ac.uk
The industrial landscape around Blaenavon is
designated as a World Heritage Site as it is an
outstanding example of the heritage of South
Wales as the world's major producer of iron and
coal in the 19th century. Evidence of the past can
still be seen in the coal and ore mines, quarries,

primitive railway system, furnaces, and the social
infrastructure of the surrounding community. As
an example, overlooking a traditional mining valley
at Blaenavon, Big Pit had been a working coal mine
for over 200 years until its closure in 1980. The
present tour guides are all former miners. On the
surface are colliery workings, reconstructed
buildings and the old pit-head baths to explore, but
the main attraction is the 300ft (90m) descent in
the pit cage; hard hat and lamp are provided. The
hour-long guided tour recalls life at the coal face
and leads through underground roadways, air
doors and stables to the shafts and coal faces.

Birdoswald (Banna), *Cumb.* 102 A3
☎ 016977 47602   www.english-heritage.org.uk
In a commanding position overlooking the River
Irthing, this well-preserved Roman fort was one of
16 along Hadrian's Wall. Parts of the walls and
gateways remain and the fort is linked to
Harrow's Scar Milecastle by an impressive section
of the Wall. Excavations have revealed a basilica
and granaries, and the site has an interactive
visitor centre and self-guided trail. Birdoswald
continued to be used after the Roman departure
up until the 17th century and a farmhouse dating
to that period remains.

Bishop's Palace, *Hants.* 74 B4
☎ 01489 892460   www.english-heritage.org.uk
The impressive ruins of the medieval seat of the
Bishops of Winchester, set in wooded grounds. The
palace was built in 1136 by Henry de Blois, brother
of King Stephen, and was subsequently enlarged
in the 14th century by William of Wykeham before
being reduced to its present state by Parliamentary
forces in 1644. The remains of the Great Hall can
be seen, together with the three-storey tower. The
ground floor of the Dower House has been
restored as a 19th century farmhouse.

Black Country Living Museum, *W.Mid.* 89 D6
☎ 0121 557 9643   www.bclm.co.uk
A faithful reproduction of a village dating from the
turn of the 20th century is the centrepiece of this
museum which focuses on the industrial heritage
of the West Midlands. There are even caverns and
an underground coal mine. Guides in period
costume are on hand to demonstrate traditional
skills – there is a forge, foundry, colliery, cobbler –
and there is plenty to occupy the children. Most of
the museum is set outdoors but there is also an
interactive exhibition hall, gift shop and tea room.

Blackness Castle, *Falk.* 107 E3
☎ 01506 834807   www.historic-scotland.gov.uk
A 15th century stronghold, once one of the most
important fortresses in Scotland and one of four
castles the Articles of Union left fortified. Shaped
like a ship with three sides surrounded by water, it
has served as a royal castle, a state prison in
Covenanting times and a powder magazine in the
1870s. More recently, it has been a film location
for the BBC production of 'Hamlet'. Visitors can
explore inside, walk the walls and climb the
central tower.

Blackwell The Arts & Crafts House, *Cumb.* 94 B2
☎ 015394 46139   www.blackwell.org.uk
In a beautiful position overlooking Lake
Windermere, Blackwell was designed by M.H.
Baillie Scott between 1897 and 1900 as a holiday
home for a wealthy Manchester brewer. It is a
wonderful example of the architecture of the Arts
and Crafts Movement. Much of the original interior
decoration, including stained glass and carved

Blenheim Palace

panelling, remains intact and is complemented with furniture, paintings, arts and crafts. Changing exhibitions of historic and contemporary applied arts and crafts are held in upstairs galleries.

Blair Castle, P. & K.   113 E5
☎ 01796 481207   www.blair-castle.co.uk
This white turreted baronial castle, set within magnificent grounds, was the traditional seat of the Dukes and Earls of Atholl. The oldest part, Cumming's Tower, dates back to 1269. Over 30 rooms convey more than 700 years of history. Discover fine collections of furniture, portraits, lace, china, costumes, arms, armour, Jacobite relics and Masonic regalia. Explore the deer park, restored 18th century walled garden, woodland, riverside and mountain walks.

Blenheim Palace, Oxon.   82 B4
☎ 01993 811091   www.blenheimpalace.com
A stunning example of English Baroque architecture, Blenheim Palace was built for John Churchill, 1st Duke of Marlborough, following his victory at the Battle of Blenheim and was the birthplace of Sir Winston Churchill. The palace was designed by Sir John Vanbrugh and built between 1705 – 22. The building itself covers 14 acres (5.5ha), whilst the grounds, landscaped by Lancelot 'Capability' Brown in the 1760s, extend to over 2000 acres (800ha). Internally, the palace is sumptuously and elaborately decorated and furnished; there are gold leaf ceilings by Nicholas Hawksmoor, marble and stone carvings by Grinling Gibbons, frescoes by Louis Laguerre and portraits by Reynolds, Romney and Van Dyck. The ceiling of the Great Hall, 67ft (20m) high, has a painting depicting Marlborough's victory at Blenheim and the Long Library, a particularly impressive 183ft (56m), has a magnificent stucco ceiling and there are several impressive state rooms.

The grounds were originally designed by Henry Wise, Queen Anne's gardener, but now only the walled garden remains, and much of the later work, including the splendid lake, was by 'Capability' Brown, while the Italian Garden and Water Terraces were designed by Achille Duchene in the early 20th century. The parkland provides hours of pleasant walking, and there is also a maze, adventure playground and butterfly house.

Blickling Hall (NT), Norf.   92 C4
☎ 01263 738030   www.nationaltrust.org.uk
An impressive sight, Blickling Hall is an early 17th century Jacobean mansion built mainly of red brick and limestone. Highlights within the house include the spectacular 125ft (38m) Long Gallery with its superb plaster ceiling, a library, an oak staircase and fine collections of paintings, furniture and tapestries. The parkland surrounding the house was landscaped in the 18th century and includes an artificial lake and 600 acres (243ha) of woodland. Unusually, within the grounds there is a burial pyramid.

Bluebell Railway, W.Suss.   75 F3
☎ 01825 720800   www.bluebell-railway.co.uk
The Bluebell Railway, named after the profusion of bluebells seen beside the line in spring, is the only all-steam, standard gauge, preserved railway in the country. It extends for 9 miles (14.5km) from Sheffield Park in the south, via Horsted Keynes, to Kingscote in the north. British Railways closed the line in March 1958 as a cost cutting exercise; two years later 4 miles (6.5km) to the north of Sheffield Park were reopened by a group of enthusiasts. Since then, a further 5 miles (8km) have been added. There are plans to extend the track as far as East Grinstead where it will connect with the main line. The railway's headquarters and locomotive department are situated at Sheffield Park station where an impressive selection of engines can be found. Some older locos date from the 1870s, with the newest built as late as the 1950s. There is also a museum of small exhibits, a model railway, a shop, a restaurant and a real ale bar at this station. The restoration and maintenance of carriages and wagons takes place at Horsted Keynes where work in progress can be seen from a viewing gallery.

Bodiam Castle (NT)

Bodiam Castle (NT), E.Suss.   76 C4
☎ 01580 830436   www.nationaltrust.org.uk
Everyone's favourite; a picture book castle with massive sandstone walls and towers rising from a broad moat, spiral staircases, battlement walks and hidey-holes to explore. Today, only a small part of the interior survives.

Bodiam was built in the late 14th century by Sir Edward Dalyngrigge, who had amassed considerable wealth in the wars against France, as a defensive stronghold protecting the Rother Valley from the French. It was intended to be a comfortable home as well as a defensible castle and symbolized the movement from traditional castle to comfortable manor house.

The castle was left partially ruined after attack in 1645 during the Civil War. Repairs to the building commenced in the 19th century, and during the early 20th century the castle was sympathetically restored by its then owner Lord Curzon who bequeathed it to the National Trust in 1926.

Bolling Hall, W.Yorks.   95 F5
☎ 01274 431814
Much of this splendid period house dates back to the 1600s and was once home to the Bolling family. The Hall displays a variety of period furnishings, together with stained-glass windows depicting Coats of Arms in the central hall. The house also contains a medieval tower to the 18th century wing.

Bolsover Castle, Derbys.   89 F2
☎ 01246 822844   www.english-heritage.org.uk
Looking like a 'proper' castle, this 'Little Castle' is really a 17th century mansion house built to represent the romantic ideal of chivalry and elegance. Walking around, an imaginative audiovisual presentation re-creates the atmosphere of the time. The huge Riding House, originally built by William Cavendish to train horses in the art of manege, has been converted into a Discovery Centre and the restored garden boasts a fountain with 23 new statues. There is a visitor centre and café, and picnics are allowed in the grounds.

Bolton Castle, N.Yorks.   95 E2
☎ 01969 623981   www.boltoncastle.co.uk
Bolton Castle is an enormous 14th century fortress, with walls 9ft (3m) deep and towers rising 100ft (30m). In 1568, Mary, Queen of Scots, was imprisoned within its walls and Royalists were besieged here during the Civil War. Within the castle, tableaux portray life here during the 15th century. Outside, there is a medieval garden and walled herb garden, together with a vineyard, rose gardens, a maze and an orchard.

Bonawe Iron Furnace, Arg. & B.   111 F6
☎ 01866 822432   www.historic-scotland.gov.uk
The restored remains of this charcoal fuelled furnace, once used for iron smelting, is the most complete example of its type. Established in 1753, it functioned until 1876. Displays illustrate the iron making process. Open from end of April to September only.

Boughton House

Photograph by kind permission of His Grace The Duke of Buccleuch K.T.

Bothwell Castle, *S.Lan.* 106 C5
☎ 01698 816894　www.historic-scotland.gov.uk
Regarded as the finest 13th century stronghold in the country, Bothwell Castle was much fought over by the Scots and English during the Wars of Independence. Substantial ruins of this red sandstone castle remain today in a picturesque setting alongside the River Clyde.

Boughton House, *Northants.* 90 C6
☎ 01536 515731　www.boughtonhouse.org.uk
The 'English Versailles', so called because of the French-style changes made to the original 1500s Tudor monastic building. Home to the Dukes of Buccleuch, the interior is richly furnished and the ceilings are decorated with delightful mythical scenes. The Buccleuch collection of fine art is world renowned, including works by Van Dyck and Caracci.

There is a superb armoury and ceremonial coach, and the grounds house a tearoom, play area and walled garden with plant centre. The house is open in August only while the grounds are open from May until August.

Bowhill House, *Sc.Bord.* 108 B6
☎ 01750 22204　www.bowhillhouse.co.uk
A splendid Georgian mansion in impressive woodland setting, containing a remarkable collection of French furniture designed by Andre Boulle, paintings by Canaletto, Gainsborough, Reynolds and Van Dyck, tapestries and fine porcelain. There are some interesting historical exhibits including letters from Queen Victoria and proof copies of Sir Walter Scott's books.

There are walks and an adventure playground in the grounds. The house is only open in July; check in advance for opening times of grounds.

Breamore, *Hants.* 73 E4
☎ 01725 512468　www.breamorehouse.com
A red brick Elizabethan manor house, constructed in the characteristic E-shape of the period, set in beautiful parkland in the Avon valley. It is still a family home, and contains fine collections of furniture, porcelain and tapestries, whilst the wood-panelled Great Hall displays 16th and 17th century portraits. A carriage museum in a converted stable block contains the last operational stage coach in England, and there is an informative countryside museum in the old farmyard. An adventure playground and maze provide additional entertainment for children.

Bredon Tithe Barn (NT), *Worcs.* 81 F3
☎ 01684 855300　www.nationaltrust.org.uk
This 14th century Tithe Barn is built of local Cotswold stone and was lovingly restored after a fire in 1980. It is around 140ft (44m) in length with an aisled interior giving it a distinctly ecclesiastical feel. It also features a remarkable stone chimney cowling.

Brighton Pier, *B. & H.* 56 C3
☎ 01273 609361　www.brightonpier.co.uk
Opened on 20th May 1899, this 1722ft (525m) long pier (Grade II* listed) features filigree ironwork arches and some of the original kiosks. Over the years, these basic attractions have been joined by a huge array of modern-day amusements such as a funfair, arcades, night club, bars and restaurants.

Brinkburn Priory, *Northumb.* 103 D2
☎ 01665 570628　www.english-heritage.org.uk
The Augustinian priory of Brinkburn, founded around 1135, is set amongst woodland beside the River Coquet. On a fine day the priory grounds are a lovely place for a picnic. Restored in the 19th century, the church of the original monastery survives intact and contains some striking wooden contemporary sculptures by Fenwick Lawson. Venue for the Brinkburn Music Summer Festival. Standing nearby is a Gothic style manor house.

Bristol Industrial Museum, *Bristol* 81 D6
☎ 0117 925 1470　www.bristol-city.gov.uk
Located in the Floating Harbour in a converted goods transit shed, the museum is home to a wide range of exhibits relating to Bristol's industrial heritage. The port's history is told through models, paintings and memorabilia, and there are exhibitions on the printing and packaging industry, and Bristol's part in the infamous slave trade triangle.

British Museum, *Gt.Lon.* 63 A3
☎ 020 7323 8299　www.thebritishmuseum.ac.uk
This is the oldest public museum in the world and was founded in 1753 when Sir Hans Sloane bequeathed his considerable collection of artefacts, along with his library and herbarium, to the nation in return for paying his heirs £20,000. George II and the Parliament of the time, led by the Speaker, Arthur Onslow, were persuaded to accept the gift and a public lottery was held to raise the necessary funds. The next year Montagu House was acquired in order to house the collection which has since increased to over six million objects. Over the years the building has had to expand to accommodate this huge collection, and the bulk of the neoclassical building which visitors see today, including the impressive south front, dates from 1852.

The museum houses the world's greatest collection of antiquities including the national collections of archaeology and ethnography, with treasures from all over the globe. Highlights include the Rosetta Stone, the Elgin Marbles and the Sutton Hoo treasure. There are also Egyptian mummies, which include not only humans but cats, baboons and even crocodiles, and the 2000 year old peat-preserved Lindow Man. The exhibits are so rich and varied that to attempt to see them all in a single visit would be impossible.

Broadlands, *Hants.*   **74 A3**
☎ 01794 505010   www.broadlands.net
Originally a 16th century house, remodelled in the 18th century to a create a handsome Palladian mansion, Broadlands is beautifully set in sweeping lawns bordered by the River Test and in grounds landscaped by 'Capability' Brown.

A particular feature of the house is the magnificent Saloon with its white and gold plaster ceiling. Many of the fine furnishings, paintings and sculptures were originally acquired by the family of Lord Palmerston, noted Victorian prime minister whose birthplace this was and whose life is remembered in an exhibition here. A more recent resident was Lord Mountbatten of Burma, and an interesting and informative exhibition on his life and times has been staged by his grandson, Lord Romsey, the present owner. Open from end of June to early September.

Brodick Castle (NTS), *N.Ayr.*   **105 E5**
☎ 01770 302202   www.nts.org.uk
An imposing, originally 13th century red sandstone castle on a site occupied initially by Irish and later by Vikings. Extended in the 17th and 19th centuries, the pleasant interior belies the somewhat forbidding exterior. Brodick's greatest treasures are its gardens; the woodland garden, started in 1923, is home to one of Europe's finest rhododendron collections, magnificent in spring, whilst the walled garden contains tender and exotic plants encouraged by the mild climate. Set at the foot of Goat Fell on the Isle of Aran, the estate provides scenic trails, abundant wildlife and an adventure playground.

Brodie Castle (NTS), *Moray*   **113 F1**
☎ 01309 641371   www.nts.org.uk
The oldest parts of Brodie Castle are 16th century, although the Brodie family owned land here as early as the 12th century. The well furnished castle interior contains fine French furniture, porcelain, and a major art collection of modern British and French paintings. There are some impressive ornate plasterwork ceilings, a large library and fully equipped Victorian kitchen. The grounds are famous for the spring display of daffodils, many of them specialist varieties, and there are woodland walks and a four acre (2ha) pond with wildlife observation hides. The park also contains a notable carved Pictish stone.

Brontë Parsonage Museum, *W.Yorks.*   **95 E5**
☎ 01535 642323   www.bronte.info
Formerly home to the famous Brontë family, this Parsonage has been carefully preserved into a museum. On show are eleven rooms furnished as they were in the mid 1850s, including the dining room, the kitchen, Mr Brontë's study, Charlotte's room and the children's study. Throughout are displays of the siblings' books and manuscripts, their letters to friends and their personal possessions.

Broughton Castle, *Oxon.*   **82 B3**
☎ 01295 276070   www.broughtoncastle.com
A medieval manor house built around 1300 and set on an island surrounded by a 3 acre (1ha) moat. Much of the original building remains, but it was greatly enlarged in the late 16th century, adding splendid decorative plasterwork, panelling and fireplaces. The castle was a secret meeting place for Parliamentarians during the Civil War, and at one stage it was besieged and captured by Royalists. There is an interesting display of arms and armour from this period in the Great Hall.

The grounds contain colourful herbaceous borders, roses, climbers and a formal walled garden. Not open every day; it is advisable to telephone in advance.

Broughton House (NTS), *D. & G.*   **100 B4**
☎ 01557 330437   www.nts.org.uk
Delightful 18th century town house, home between 1901–33 to the artist Edward Hornel, who helped establish an artists' colony in Kirkcudbright. Some of his paintings hang in the gallery here, later ones influenced by visits to Japan.

The 2 acre (1ha) garden consists of distinct compartments including Hornel's Japanese-style garden. Check in advance for opening times.

Buckfast Abbey, *Devon*   **71 D5**
☎ 01364 645500   www.buckfast.org.uk
This was originally founded in 1018, but was abandoned after the Dissolution of the Monasteries until 1882 when Benedictine monks took over the site. They rebuilt the abbey in a traditional Anglo-Norman style with some particularly striking stained glass work. There is an informative exhibition on the site and shops selling a variety of produce from Benedictine monasteries across Europe. Physic, Sensory and Lavender gardens have been re-created in the grounds.

Buckingham Palace, *Gt.Lon.*   **62 B2**
☎ 020 7766 7300   www.royal.gov.uk/output/page555.asp
Built in 1705, and originally called Buckingham House, it was purchased by George III for his wife Queen Charlotte in 1761. Over the years it has been remodelled and extended a number of times, firstly by George IV with the assistance of his architect John Nash. A new suite of rooms was added and the north and south wings were rebuilt, with the Marble Arch as a centrepiece to the courtyard. The arch was later removed and now stands near the north east corner of Hyde Park. Queen Victoria made further alterations and additions, most notably the East Front which was designed by architect Edward Blore in 1847. Due to the deterioration of the stone, this was subsequently refaced in 1913 creating the familiar façade that we see today. Soon after Queen Victoria's accession in 1837, it became the monarch's official London residence.

The palace is open during August and September with visitors able to see 19 of the state rooms. These include the Throne Room, the Blue Drawing Room, the impressive White Drawing Room and the 150ft (46m) Picture Gallery. The huge

Ballroom can also be seen; at 122ft (37m) long and 60ft (18m) wide, it is used for State banquets and can accommodate 150 guests. Treasures that can be seen within the palace include paintings by artists such as Rembrandt and superb examples of English and French furniture.

Buckingham Palace   Photo © Visit London

Buckinghamshire Railway Centre, *Bucks.*   **83 D4**
☎ 01296 655450   www.bucksrailcentre.org.uk
This is a working steam museum boasting one of the biggest collections of locomotives, wagons and carriages in the country. As well as the opportunity to ride on steam-hauled trains, there is a good-sized miniature railway and the chance to see restoration work in progress.

Buckland Abbey (NT), *Devon*   **70 B5**
☎ 01822 853607   www.nationaltrust.org.uk
Originally a 13th century monastery overlooking the Tavy valley, this was subsequently converted to a family home, initially owned by the sea-faring Grenville family. In 1581 the property was bought by Sir Francis Drake and it remained in his family until 1942. Features include the fine, oak-panelled Great Hall, exhibitions on Drake's achievements and adventures, Elizabethan gardens and craft workshops.

Buildwas Abbey, *Shrop.* 88 B5
☎ 01952 433274   www.english-heritage.org.uk
Founded by the Savignacs in 1135 and merged with the Cistercian Order soon after, the abbey changed little until the dissolution and is unusual in that the cloister is situated north of the main church. Parts of the original tiled floor of the Chapter House still exist and, apart from the roof, the building is still virtually intact.

Burghley House, *Peter.* 90 C5
☎ 01780 752451   www.burghley.co.uk
This superb Tudor mansion was built between 1565 and 1587 by William Cecil (later Lord Burghley), who was Elizabeth I's Lord Treasurer and principal advisor. It is set in a 300 acre (120ha) deer park landscaped in 1756 by Lancelot 'Capability' Brown. Externally, the mansion remains virtually unchanged and is considered by many to be one of the finest examples of late Elizabethan architecture. The beautiful interiors are a marvellous showcase for the house's impressive collection of art, which was amassed largely by the 5th and 9th Earls of Exeter (Lord Burghley's descendents) who were both avid collectors.

Burns National Heritage Park, *S.Ayr.* 100 A1
☎ 01292 443700   www.burnsheritagepark.com
Set up in 1995, this embraces several sites in the Alloway area closely connected with Robert Burns, considered Scotland's national poet. The whitewashed Burns Cottage is the poet's birthplace, a small, dark, gloomy building giving a good impression of impoverished 18th century rural existence. Adjacent is the Museum, tracing Burns' life and displaying his manuscripts and memorabilia. A short distance away is the modern Tam O' Shanter Experience with entertaining audiovisual presentations on the poet's life and a re-enactment of his famous poem, 'Tam O' Shanter'. The ruined Alloway Kirk across the road is the burial place of Burns' father and one of the settings for 'Tam O' Shanter', as is the nearby stone arch Brig O' Doon. The neoclassical Burns Monument, decorated with characters from the poems, has pleasant, well-tended gardens.

Burton Constable Hall, *E.Riding* 97 E5
☎ 01964 562400   www.burtonconstable.com
On show inside this stately Elizabethan mansion are 30 wonderfully preserved rooms in 18th and 19th century fashion. They are styled with fine furniture, paintings and sculptures. There is a 'Cabinet of Curiosities' containing an intriguing collection of fossils, natural history and scientific instruments and a library containing 5000 books. Within the stable block is a riding centre, and there are 200 acres (80ha) of parkland, landscaped by 'Capability' Brown.

Buscot Park (NT), *Oxon.* 82 A5
☎ 0845 345 3387 or 01367 240786   www.buscot-park.com
An 18th century Palladian mansion with a remarkable collection of paintings and furniture belonging to the Faringdon Collection Trust. Paintings include works by Rembrandt, Rubens, Murillo and Reynolds, some particularly notable Pre-Raphaelite pieces and contemporary items, and there is furniture designed by Thomas Hope and Robert Adam.

Caerlaverock Castle, *D. & G.* 101 D3
☎ 01387 770244   www.historic-scotland.gov.uk
A splendid moated, triangular 13th century castle, with a substantial keep gatehouse at the northern apex, entered by a footbridge. Its impregnable appearance is reinforced by the desolate surroundings of the Solway coast, though the castle was captured on several occasions. Capture invariably resulted in damage, and the castle is consequently a mixture of building styles, both externally and internally. It was finally abandoned in 1640 when it was wrecked by the Covenanters.

Caernarfon Castle, *Gwyn.* 86 B2
☎ 01286 677617   www.cadw.wales.gov.uk
Built on a promontory projecting out into the Menai Strait, this UNESCO World Heritage Site castle dominates the town of Caernarfon and has survived in fine condition. Construction was started by Edward I in 1283 as part of his ring of castles intended to control Welsh uprisings, and it was planned as a royal residence and seat of government. The building was completed by Edward II in 1322. Massive walls run between the 11 great polygonal towers, topped by battlemented wall walks, giving the castle formidable defences. Also incorporated into the scheme were drawbridges, heavy doors and six portcullises. Each of the towers is different and one included a water gate enabling supplies to be brought by sea.

The Queen's Tower houses the regimental museum of the Royal Welch Fusiliers. An audiovisual presentation explains the history and customs associated with the castle. Continuing a tradition established by Edward I, the castle is the venue for the investiture of the Prince of Wales, as was the scene in 1969 when Prince Charles was presented to the people here.

Caerphilly Castle   Photo © Welsh Tourist Board

Caerphilly Castle, *Caerp.* 80 B5
☎ 029 2088 3143   www.cadw.wales.gov.uk
Right in the town centre, Caerphilly is the largest castle in Wales, but was never a royal residence. It was built by Red Gilbert de Clare to defend the territory of Henry III against Welsh Prince Llywelyn the Last. The medieval fortress, started in 1268, occupies a strategically important 30 acre (12ha) site, having a complex design of massive gatehouses, water defences and stout concentric walls. The most unusual feature of the castle is one of the towers which leans outwards at an angle ten degrees from vertical – the result of subsidence.

An extensive water system provided the first point of defence around the castle, followed by a rectangular enclosure with robust outer and inner walls. The latter contain two great gatehouses and the remains of the hall. In the heart of the castle are the living areas, together with kitchens, a chapel and domestic quarters. Over the past 200 years the complex has undergone much restoration. Visitors can watch an audiovisual display and see replica siege engines in the visitor centre.

Calanais Standing Stones, *W.Isles* 124 D3
☎ 01851 621422   www.calanaisvisitorcentre.co.uk
A unique cruciform setting of megaliths, second in importance only to Stonehenge, which were erected about 3000BC. An avenue of 19 monoliths leads north from a circle of 13 stones, with rows of more stones fanning out to the south, east and west. Inside the circle is a small, chambered tomb. Entry to the visitor centre is free but there is a small charge for the audiovisual presentation.

Calanais Standing Stones   Photo © John Gordon

Calke Abbey (NT), *Derbys.* 89 F4
☎ 01332 863822   www.nationaltrust.org.uk
An interesting example of a baroque country house captured in its state of decline. The last baronet died here in 1924 and left splendidly decorated rooms, where the family had lived, along with deserted, run-down areas, abandoned due to lack of servants. Little restoration work has been done, in order to preserve the remarkable social history it portrays. There is an extensive natural history collection, wonderful parkland, café and shop, and a walled garden with Auricula theatre.

Canons Ashby, *Northants.* 82 C2
☎ 01327 861900   www.nationaltrust.org.uk
The house takes its name from an Augustinian Priory, the church surviving on a hilltop in the grounds. Home to the Dryden family since it was built in the mid 1500s, it has remained virtually the same since 1710. The Jacobean plasterwork is exceptional and the Elizabethan wall paintings have been superbly restored. The formal gardens have also been brought back to their 18th century glory.

Canterbury Cathedral, *Kent* 77 E3
☎ 01227 762862   www.canterbury-cathedral.org
The cathedral was founded in AD597 by St Augustine, a missionary from Rome, and has been the centre of the English church ever since. Today, the impressive cathedral, along with nearby St Martin's Church and St Augustine's Abbey, is a World Heritage Site.

The architectural styles of the cathedral range from Norman to Perpendicular. The large crypt is the oldest part of the present building and dates from the 11th century. Rebuilt after a fire, the 12th century Quire features beautiful stained glass windows depicting miracles and stories associated with Thomas Becket. Famously murdered here in 1170, he is one of the cathedral's most notable archbishops. Two years later he was made a saint. As a result of his martyrdom the cathedral became one of the world's most important centres of pilgrimage.

The magnificent nave, comprising tall columns and vaulted arches, was built in the 14th century and took 28 years to complete. Visitors can see medieval tombs within the cathedral including those of King Henry IV and Edward, the Black Prince. To get the most out of a visit to this remarkable building, guided and audio tours are available.

Cardiff Castle & Museum, *Cardiff* 57 B2
☎ 029 2087 8100   www.cardiffcastle.com
The castle dates from 1091 and was elaborately embellished in Victorian times by the 3rd Marquess of Bute in an elaborate neogothic style. Highly decorative, fantasy adornments abound, particularly in the clock tower, fountains and lavish interiors. The Welsh Regiment Museum is situated within the castle grounds.

Cardoness Castle, *D. & G.* 100 B4
☎ 01557 814427   www.historic-scotland.gov.uk
An excellent example of a fortified tower house, this late 15th century stronghold is now a well preserved ruin. The four-storey building still retains the original staircase, vaulted basement and elaborate fireplaces, and has views over the Water of Fleet to Fleet Bay.

Carew Castle, *Pembs.* 78 B4
☎ 01646 651782   www.carewcastle.com
The substantial ruins of Carew Castle stand on river meadows between the village and an ancient tidal mill. The castle was built between the 13th and 16th centuries and was the site of the Great Tournament of 1507. A circular walk links the castle, mill, causeway, millpond, 11th century Celtic cross and medieval bridge.

Carisbrooke Castle & Museum, *I.o.W.* 74 A5
☎ 01983 522107   www.carisbrookecastlemuseum.org.uk
Such an obvious defensive site almost demanded the construction of a castle, and there is evidence that people complied, certainly from Saxon times and probably before. The present castle dates from around 1100, and still retains the typical motte and bailey outline, but was considerably enlarged in the late medieval period. Following the Armada in 1588 it was further fortified, and the wellhouse and its tread wheel were added so that water could be drawn more easily from the 161ft (49m) well in the event of siege.

Carisbrooke's chief claim to fame is as the place of imprisonment of Charles I prior to his trial and execution.

Carlisle Castle, *Cumb.* 101 F4
☎ 01228 591922   www.english-heritage.org.uk
An imposing Norman fortress with a fascinating and eventful history due in no small part to its proximity to the English and Scottish border. Mary, Queen of Scots was imprisoned here in 1568 after her abdication from the Scottish throne, and the castle also featured in the Wars of the Roses and the Jacobite Rising. The impressive 12th century keep still stands, as does the inner gatehouse with portcullis known as the Captain's Tower. 'Licking stones' found in a room used as a dungeon are grim testimony to the conditions of those imprisoned here. The King's Own Royal Border Regiment Museum is located within the castle.

Carlisle Cathedral, *Cumb.* 101 F4
☎ 01228 548151   www.carlislecathedral.org.uk
Originally founded in 1122, the cathedral today is notable for the large east window which contains some 14th century stained glass, the choir with distinctive 14th century barrel-vaulted blue starry ceiling, a 16th century carved Flemish altarpiece (Brougham Triptych) and medieval carving and paintings. Cathedral and diocesan silver is displayed in the Treasury.

Carreg Cennen Castle, *Carmar.* 79 E4
☎ 01558 822291   www.cadw.wales.gov.uk
These old ruins, high on a crag near Trapp in the Black Mountains, were rebuilt in the 13th and 19th centuries. Visitors can explore prehistoric caves, battlements and vaulted passageways, and enjoy the outlook from the grassy hilltop.

Cartmel Priory, *Cumb.* 94 B3
☎ 01524 701178   www.nationaltrust.org.uk
This fine Augustinian priory church, founded in 1188, reflects many periods of ecclesiastical architecture and is still in use today. It contains notable stained glass and carved choir stalls. Also remaining is the original priory gatehouse (National Trust) which is used as the Cartmel Heritage Centre.

Castell Dinas Bran (ruins), *Denb.* 87 F3
☎ 01938 553670   www.castlewales.com
Both a hillfort and medieval castle, the ruins stand high above Llangollen. It is reputedly the final hiding place of the Holy Grail, a treasured Christian relic. Access is by public footpath taking some 20 minutes each way.

Castle Campbell, *Clack.* 107 E3
☎ 01259 742408   www.historic-scotland.gov.uk
Once known as Castle Gloom, the castle is set high on a promontory above Dollar Glen. Built towards the end of the 15th century by the 1st Earl of Argyll, it was burned by Cromwell in the 1650s. The original tower, however, is well preserved along with its courtyard and great hall. The 60 acres (24ha) of woodland in the glen make an attractive walk to the castle.

Castle Drogo (NT), *Devon* 71 D4
☎ 01647 433306   www.nationaltrust.org.uk
Contrary to appearances, this is an early 20th century building designed by Sir Edwin Lutyens and built in an outstanding position above the Teign valley. Constructed of specially quarried granite, the foundations were cut into the hillside, and in some rooms the exposed rock can be seen. Outside, established formal gardens provide a colourful setting in spring and summer, and there are lovely woodland walks, some providing magnificent views over the Teign valley.

Castle Fraser (NTS), *Aber.* 115 D3
☎ 01330 833463   www.nts.org.uk
A magnificent castle completed in 1636 and one of the most sophisticated Scottish buildings of the period. It has a notable Great Hall with tall windows and a high ceiling, striking in its simplicity. Castle Fraser also contains a wealth of historic portraits, curtains, carpets and bedhangings. There is a formal walled garden in the grounds.

Castle Howard, *N. Yorks.* 96 C3
☎ 01653 648444   www.castlehoward.co.uk
A magnificent stately home, built in 1699 by the architect Sir John Vanbrugh. Castle Howard, with its famous dome, can be found in the Howardian Hills, between Malton and Thirsk. The castle continues to be home to the Howard family, where they have resided since it was built. Inside are exceptional collections of art, including paintings by Canaletto, Holbein, Gainsborough and Reynolds, and furniture by Chippendale and Sheraton. There are also impressive antique sculptures and a splendid collection of porcelain and china. Furthermore, costumed characters take on the role of historic personalities to re-enact life as it used to be in this stately home.
    More can be seen outside, in over 1000 acres (400ha) of gardens and parklands. There are also exceptional temples, lead statues and monuments, lakes, waterways and fountains. All of which makes a trip to Castle Howard a wonderful day out.

Castle Menzies, *P. & K.* 113 E6
☎ 01887 820982   www.menzies.org/castle
This imposing 16th century castle presents a fine example of the transition between a Z-plan clan stronghold and a later mansion house. Seat of the clan chiefs for over 400 years, Castle Menzies was involved in a number of historic occurrences, which are recounted in the museum.

Castlerigg Stone Circle, *Cumb.* 101 E5
☎ 0870 333 1181   www.english-heritage.org.uk
Megalithic circle of 38 stones in a beautiful setting surrounded by Lakeland fells. Dating from about 3000 years ago, the circle is 100ft (30m) in diameter and encloses a smaller rectangle of ten stones. The site is thought to have been used as a tribal gathering place, although the precise use is unknown.

Cawdor Castle, *High.* 113 E1
☎ 01667 404615   www.cawdorcastle.com
Cawdor Castle is the name romantically associated with Shakespeare's Macbeth, and dates originally from the 14th century. The medieval tower and drawbridge are still intact and generations of art lovers and scholars are responsible for the eclectic collection of paintings, books, tapestries and porcelain found in the castle. There are three beautiful gardens, five nature trails, nine-hole golf course, putting green, gift, book and wool shop.

Charlecote Park (NT), *Warks.* 82 A2
☎ 01789 470277   www.nationaltrust.org.uk
A 16th century house visited by both Queen Victoria and Elizabeth I – the entrance porch still has the coat of arms of Elizabeth I to commemorate her stay of two nights in 1572. All of the rooms are luxuriously furnished, the dining room and library having particularly exquisite ceilings in the Elizabethan Revival style. The formal gardens open out onto 250 acres (100ha) of parkland designed by 'Capability' Brown where, allegedly, Shakespeare was once caught poaching deer.

Chartwell (NT), *Kent* 76 A3
☎ 01732 868381   www.nationaltrust.org.uk
The family home of Winston Churchill for over 40 years, he purchased it in 1924 because he fell in love with the impressive views over the Weald. The large brick built house is still full of many of his personal possessions. Churchill also left his mark on the attractive gardens, creating lakes, garden walls and rockeries.

Chastleton House, *Oxon.* 82 A3
☎ 01608 674355   www.nationaltrust.org.uk
One of the most outstanding Jacobean properties in England, Chastleton has been continuously occupied by one family since its construction in the early 17th century. Particular treasures include elaborate plasterwork, Florentine tapestries and delightful glassware. Entry is by timed ticket and it is advisable to book in advance.

Chatham Historic Dockyard & World Naval Base, *Med.* 76 C2
☎ 01634 823807   www.chdt.org.uk
The history of the dockyards extends back over 400 years. Nelson's famous flagship The Victory was built here in 1765. Today, on an 80 acre (32.5ha) site, visitors can see vessels including a World War II destroyer HMS Cavalier, a 1962 submarine Ocelot and HMS Gannet which is the last surviving Victorian navy sloop. The site also contains a museum and an exhibition on the Royal National Lifeboat Institution.

Chatsworth House, *Derbys.* 89 E2
☎ 01246 565300   www.chatsworth-house.co.uk
In the heart of the Derbyshire Peak District stands one of Britain's best loved stately homes, the residence of the Duke and Duchess of Devonshire. The magnificent house has over 25 beautifully decorated and furnished rooms, containing some of the finest treasures to be found in a private collection.
    There are over 100 miles (161km) of walks through the 1000 acres (405ha) of Lancelot 'Capability' Brown designed parkland, which includes a lovely 100 acre (41ha) garden and the famous gravity fed waterworks, which power spectacular fountains and a waterfall cascading down a long flight of stone steps. Chatsworth has never rested on its laurels; the estate has been developed to provide a first-class adventure playground, with 'commando' style rope walks down to safe water and sand play areas for tiny tots. A working farmyard allows children to get really close to the animals and a 28-seat trailer provides tours of the woods and parkland. The maze is a challenge, and for shopaholics there is a farm shop selling Estate and local produce as well as one selling everything from furniture to porcelain. There are brass band concerts on a Sunday and events throughout the year. Truly a top-class family day out.

Chatsworth House

Chedworth Roman Villa (NT), *Glos.* 81 F4
☎ 01242 890256 www.chedworthromanvilla.com
Discovered in 1864 and now owned by the
National Trust, the Villa sits at the head of a small
valley overlooking the River Colne. It would have
been one of the grandest houses in the Cotswolds
at the time it was built, with evidence of 32
rooms, and there are still substantial remains
including two Roman baths and some extremely
well-preserved mosaic flooring. There are
audiovisual demonstrations and a museum within
the grounds.

Chepstow Castle , *Mon.* 81 D5
☎ 01291 624065 www.cadw.wales.gov.uk
Strategically set overlooking a Wye Valley gorge,
Chepstow was one of the first stone castles to be
built in Britain. Construction was commenced in
1068 as a stronghold for the Norman conquest of
south-east Wales and is unusual in having no
early timber base. Over successive centuries the
defences were enlarged and in the 12th century
the impressive edifice was divided into four
separate, connecting sections. Towering over the
present-day entrance is the gatehouse containing
a prison in one of its round towers. Further
additions included a second hall, tower, gatehouse
and comfortable living quarters with well-
equipped kitchens and storerooms.
  The castle came under siege twice during the
Civil War and now visitors can see exhibitions on
the history of its construction. Life-sized models of
the medieval lords who occupied the castle, and a
dramatic Civil War battle scene illustrate the
changing role of Chepstow Castle through the
Middle Ages. Outdoor evening theatre is often
performed here in summer.

Chester Cathedral Photo © Joe Wainwright
Cheshire C.C.

Chester Cathedral, *Ches.* 58 B2
☎ 01244 324756 www.chestercathedral.com
There has been Christian worship on the site of
the cathedral since the 10th century, when a
Benedictine monastery dedicated to St Werburgh
was founded. During the 13th century work began
on a new church on the site, built in the Gothic
style. It was constructed around the original
Norman church which was then taken down from
the inside. Parts of this Norman building are still
in evidence, for example in the refectory which
now houses the cafeteria. The Gothic style church
took around 250 years to complete and this long
history of worship has led to all architectural
styles being represented in the building. In 1541,
following the dissolution of the monasteries, the
church was dedicated as the Cathedral Church of
Christ and the Blessed Virgin Mary. Over many
years the church became neglected until, in the
late 19th century, Sir George Gilbert Scott
masterminded a major restoration project. Of
particular note are the intricate medieval carvings
above the choir stalls featuring dragons, angels
and monsters. It was here that Handel first
rehearsed 'The Messiah' and a copy of his
annotated score is on display. Digital audio tours
are available using hands-free equipment.
Admission charges have now been introduced.

Chiltern Open Air Museum, *Bucks.* 83 E5
☎ 01494 871117 www.coam.org.uk
Over 30 historic buildings have been constructed
on this attractive 45 acre (18ha) park and
woodland site. Most of the buildings were rescued
from destruction and have been carefully
dismantled and moved from their original
locations to create this museum. The diverse
display includes re-creations of a Victorian
farmyard, complete with animals, a 1940s fully
furnished 'prefab' and an Iron Age enclosure.
There is even an Edwardian Public Convenience.
  There are also demonstrations of traditional
skills and information on the methods and
materials used to make the buildings as well as
plenty of hands-on activities. It is closed during
the winter months apart from special events
which are held throughout the year.

Chirk Castle (NT), *Wrex.* 87 F4
☎ 01691 777701 www.nationaltrust.org.uk
The castle, to the west of Chirk, has been
continually occupied for over 400 years, although
the high walls and drum towers are still evidence
of its 14th century origins. The state rooms
contain fine items of furniture, tapestries and
portraits. The formal gardens adjoining the castle
contain superb yews, roses and climbing plants,
whilst further away lie a hawk house, rock garden
and shrub garden with pool.

Chiswick House, *Gt.Lon.* 83 F6
☎ 020 8995 0508 www.english-heritage.org.uk
This fine 18th century domed villa, designed by
Lord Burlington in 1728, was modelled on
Palladio's Villa Rotonda at Vicenza. The William
Kent interiors, particularly the reception rooms
which include a domed saloon and velvet room,
are sumptuous. Many have painted ceilings and
gilded decorations, and feature period furnishings.
Kent, alongside royal gardener Charles Bridgeman,
was also responsible for the design of the gardens
where he continued the Italianate theme with Doric
columns, statues and obelisks, plus a cascade.

Christchurch Priory, *Dorset* 73 E5
☎ 01202 488645 www.christchurchpriory.org
Considered to be the longest parish church in
Britain at over 300ft (90m), this splendid medieval
monastic building is noted for its exceptional
interior carvings. Access to the tower, via 120 steps
up a spiral staircase, is sometimes available for a
small charge, and is worth it for the splendid views.

Chysauster Ancient Village, *Cornw.* 68 A5
☎ 01831 757934 www.english-heritage.org.uk
A late Iron Age courtyard village believed to have
been inhabited at least up until the Roman
occupation. The settlement consists of eight oval
stone houses, each with a central courtyard, and
a stone wall enclosing the whole complex. Within
the houses some rooms were for human
occupation, others for animals or food storage.

Clandon Park (NT), *Surr.* 75 D2
☎ 01483 222482 www.clandonpark.co.uk
Impressive Palladian mansion built circa 1731 for
the 2nd Lord Onslow. Notable for its imposing
two-storey marble entrance hall with magnificent
Italian plasterwork ceiling. The house contains the
Gubbay collection of furniture and porcelain,
along with tapestries and the Ivo Forde Meissen
collection of Italian comedy figures. The gardens,
designed by Lancelot 'Capability' Brown in 1781,
include a grotto, Maori house and parterre.

Claydon (NT), *Bucks.* 83 D3
☎ 01296 730349 www.nationaltrust.org.uk
A charming, mainly 18th century house belonging
to the Verney family until the mid 20th century.
The unassuming exterior hides a wealth of
extravagance in interior decoration. This was carved
in the rococo style by Luke Lightfoot and the house
contains some of the most remarkable decorative
carving in the country, seen at its most
outstanding in the Chinese Room. Florence
Nightingale was a frequent visitor after her sister's
marriage to Sir Henry Verney, and there is a display
of memorabilia relating to her life and work.

Corfe Castle (NT)

Cleeve Abbey, *Som.* 71 E1
☎ 01984 640377 www.english-heritage.org.uk
A late 12th/early 13th century Cistercian abbey particularly noted for its well preserved cloisters, considered amongst the finest in England.

Clevedon Court (NT), *N.Som.* 80 C6
☎ 01275 872257 www.nationaltrust.org.uk
Surviving virtually intact from its construction in 1320, the house incorporates parts of older buildings including a 12th century tower and 13th century hall. The contents include fine collections of glass, Eltonware and furniture, and there are sketches by William Makepeace Thackeray who wrote much of 'Vanity Fair' here.

Cobham Hall, *Kent* 84 B6
☎ 01474 823371 www.cobhamhall.com
Large, attractive red brick mansion dating from 1584, set in 150 acres (61ha) of parkland landscaped by Humphrey Repton. The interior features a notable hall by James Wyatt in the Gothic style and a granite staircase dating from 1602. The house is currently an independent school and opening times are therefore restricted to the Easter and summer holidays.

Colchester Castle Museum, *Essex* 85 D3
☎ 01206 282939 www.colchestermuseums.org.uk
Housed in the largest Norman keep in Britain, the museum have a wide range of exhibits spanning 2000 years of British History. There are also Roman vaults beneath the castle.

Commandery, The, *Worcs.* 81 E2
☎ 01905 361821 www.worcestercitymuseums.org.uk
An historic timber-framed building which was the headquarters of Charles II during the Civil War, though its origins date back much further than that, possibly to the 11th century.

Compton Castle (NT), *Devon* 71 D5
☎ 01803 875740 www.nationaltrust.org.uk
Built between the 14th and 16th centuries, this fortified manor house has been the Gilbert family home almost continuously for the last 600 years. The original buildings, dating from 1350 and fortified in Henry VIII's reign, have remained unaltered since.

Conwy Castle, *Conwy* 87 D2
☎ 01492 592358 www.cadw.wales.gov.uk
Occupying an imposing location over the river in the centre of Conwy town, the castle is one of the most important examples of military architecture in Europe. It was built for Edward I in 1283-9 by 1500 craftsmen, with supplies brought in by sea. Eight huge drum towers with pinnacled battlements dominate the two wards of the castle. The large outer ward was accessed from the town, whereas the inner ward, with the royal apartments, was approached only by water. The Middle Gate connected the two sections.

Conwy Castle

Corfe Castle (NT), *Dorset* 73 D5
☎ 01929 481294 www.nationaltrust.org.uk
A hilltop ruin which dominates the surrounding countryside. Built by the Normans in the late 11th century to replace an earlier Saxon structure which had been the site of the murder of King Edward the Martyr in AD978, the castle controlled the route through the Purbeck Hills. It was used as a prison, and subsequently as a treasury and hunting lodge by King John in the early 12th century, whilst Henry III added further walls, towers and gatehouses.

Cornish Mines & Engines (NT), *Cornw.* 68 B4
☎ 01209 315027 www.nationaltrust.org.uk
Local engineer Richard Trevithick developed the high pressure steam system which originally powered these two impressive beam engines. Their purpose was to operate the winding gear to transport men and ore through the mineshafts and to pump out water from depths of around 1800ft (550m).

Cornwall & West Devon mining landscape, *Cornw. / Devon* 69
In the early 19th century Cornwall and West Devon produced two thirds of the world's supply of copper. The industry declined in the 1860s but it left a landscape transformed by the deep mines, engine houses, ports and harbours all associated with the rapid growth of pioneering copper and tin mining. The area was designated a World Heritage Site in 2006 due to the importance of the area to the industrial revolution in Britain and also its significance in the development of mining worldwide.

Cotehele (NT), *Cornw.* 70 B5
☎ 01579 351346 www.nationaltrust.org.uk
On the River Tamar just west of Calstock. Originally a medieval manor house, improved and enlarged by Sir Richard Edgcumbe and his son between 1490 and 1520. Subsequent alterations have not substantially affected their work, making this one of the least altered medieval houses in the country. The gardens provide all year round colour and are crossed by a network of woodland and riverside walks.

Coughton Court (NT), *Warks.* 81 F1
☎ 01789 400777 www.coughtoncourt.co.uk
The house has been in the Throckmorton family since 1409 and has remained relatively unchanged since the Tudor gatehouse was built in 1530. There are exhibits relating to Mary, Queen of Scots, including the chemise she was wearing when she was executed, and also a Gunpowder Plot exhibition – at the time the house was rented out to one of the plotters, Sir Everard Digby. The grounds include one of the country's finest walled gardens and also a lake, riverside walk, bog garden and orchard.

Coventry Cathedral, *W.Mid.* 82 B1
☎ 024 7652 1200 www.coventrycathedral.org.uk
The old Cathedral was famously bombed in November 1940 during the devastation of Coventry and the remains have been incorporated into the new Cathedral which was consecrated in 1962. A new chapel was added to celebrate the millennium, and the visitor centre has many displays showing the history of the Cathedral and the city of Coventry.

Coventry Transport Museum, *W.Mid.* 82 B1
☎ 024 7623 4270 www.transport-museum.com
The largest collection of British vehicles in the world, at the birthplace of the British motor industry. The collection includes cars, vans, trucks, bicycles and motorbikes from the present day back to 1896 when the first factory was established. Famous marques such as Daimler, Maudsley, Triumph, Jaguar, Riley and Humber are represented.

Craigievar Castle (NTS), *Aber.* 114 C3
☎ 01339 883635 www.nts.org.uk
Completed in 1626, Craigievar is an excellent example of Scottish baronial architecture although it was built for a merchant, William Forbes. It is like the castles of fairytales with the seven storeys topped with turrets, gables and corbels.

Craigmillar Castle, *Edin.* 108 A4
☎ 0131 661 4445 www.historic-scotland.gov.uk
The oldest part of the castle is the L-shaped tower built in the early 1400s which was later surrounded by an embattled double curtain wall. By the end of the 16th century it was a comfortable residence and today, partially ruined, the castle still retains a strong sense of the mighty fortress it once was. Mary, Queen of Scots, has close links with the castle. She fled here following the murder of Rizzio, and the murder of her second husband was plotted here.

Crathes Castle (NTS), *Aber.* 115 D4
☎ 0870 118 1951 www.nts.org.uk
An impressive 16th century tower house with remarkable original painted ceilings and a collection of Scottish furniture and family portraits. It was the home of the Burnett family for more than 350 years until it was given to the National Trust in 1951. The walled garden, originally the kitchen garden, was divided in the 20th century into eight separate themed gardens with many herbaceous plants.

Criccieth Castle , *Gwyn.* 86 C4
☎ 01766 52227 www.cadw.wales.gov.uk
Overlooking Tremadog Bay, the ruins include the inner wall, impressive gatehouse and original wall walk dating from the 13th century. A cartoon video shows the story of Gerald of Wales and other Welsh princes.

Crichton Castle, *Midloth.* 108 B4
☎ 01875 320017 www.historic-scotland.gov.uk
A large castle built around a medieval tower house to create an elegant interior courtyard. The arcaded range erected by the Earl of Bothwell between 1581 and 1591 has a façade of faceted stonework in an Italian Renaissance style.

Croft Castle (NT), *Here.* 80 C1
☎ 01568 780141 www.nationaltrust.org.uk
This impressive country manor house has fine Georgian interiors and furniture while the curtain wall and round towers at each corner date from the 14th and 15th centuries. The grounds include an avenue of 350 year old Spanish chestnuts, and adjacent to the castle are the remains of the earthworks of the original fort.

Crossraguel Abbey, *S.Ayr.* 105 F6
☎ 01655 883113 www.historic-scotland.gov.uk
The substantial remains of a 13th century Cluniac monastery founded by the Earl of Carrick. The chapter house and gatehouse are amongst the best preserved and visitors can view the abbey precincts and surroundings from the top of the latter. The abbey was abandoned during the Reformation in the late 16th century.

Culloden (NTS), *High.* 113 E1
☎ 01463 790607 www.nts.org.uk
Site of the fierce battle on 16 April 1746, when the Hanoverian Army defeated the forces of Bonnie Prince Charlie, thereby ending the Jacobite uprising. The Graves of the Clans, the Well of the Dead, the Memorial Cairn, the Cumberland Stone and the Field of the English can also be seen. The visitor centre houses a Jacobite exhibition.

Culross Palace (NTS), *Fife* 107 E3
☎ 01383 880359 www.nts.org.uk
Built in 1597–1611 for local entrepreneur Sir George Bruce, the palace features its original decorative interiors and period 17th and 18th century furnishings. The restored 17th century garden contains rare herbs and perennials of the period. Elsewhere in Culross village, discover the remains of a Cistercian Abbey founded in 1217, the eastern part of which forms the present parish church. The Town House provides an exhibition of the area's history.

Culzean Castle (NTS), *S.Ayr.* 105 F6
☎ 0870 118 1945 www.nts.org.uk
A dramatic clifftop location and splendid design by Robert Adam in the late 18th century makes Culzean (pronounced Cullane) one of the most impressive of Scotland's stately homes. Replacing the original 15th century structure, the exterior, with arrow slits and battlements, evokes the medieval period, but the elegant interior exemplifies the classical designs favoured by Adam. The spectacular Oval Staircase is considered one of his finest achievements, while the sumptuous Circular Saloon makes a striking contrast to the surrounding natural scenery.

Culzean Castle (NTS) Photo © National Trust for Scotland

Cutty Sark, *Gt.Lon.* 84 A6
☎ 020 8858 2698 www.cuttysark.org.uk
This famous tea clipper, built in 1869, was the fastest in the tea race from China and subsequently, when used in the Australian wool trade, she consistently set new speed records. The impressive visitor centre explains the history of the ship and also the plans for its conservation and restoration which is expected to last until 2009. This unfortunately means that there is no access to the ship itself.

Danebury Ring, *Hants.* 74 A3
☎ 01722 334956
An Iron Age hill fort, dating from about 500BC, with substantial defensive earthworks enclosing a 13 acre (5ha) site. Its name comes from 'dun', meaning hill, and 'bury', meaning fort.

The earliest evidence for occupation is Neolithic artefacts but the hill fort itself was not built until around 475BC and was abandoned around 100BC.

The site has been extensively excavated to reveal evidence for 75 roundhouses and many more rectangular storage buildings, and many of the finds can be seen at the Museum of the Iron Age in Andover. The isolated site has magnificent views over the surrounding downland.

Dartmouth Castle, *Devon* 71 D6
☎ 01803 833588 www.english-heritage.org.uk
The first to be designed with specific respect to artillery use, this 15th century castle has a superb location on the narrow entrance to the Dart estuary. A contributor to the coastal defence system over the last 500 years, the building is still in good repair. Informative displays recount the castle's history.

Deal Castle, *Kent*   **77 F3**
☎ 01304 372762   www.english-heritage.org.uk
Coastal defensive fort built in 1539 during the
reign of Henry VIII to protect England from France
and Spain. Constructed in the shape of a Tudor
Rose, the walls were deliberately built low and
rounded to avoid enemy fire from the sea. Visitors
can explore the underground passages and see
the 53 gunports.

Dean Castle, *E.Ayr.*   **106 B6**
☎ 01563 522702   www.deancastle.com
A splendid collection of restored buildings
comprising a 14th century fortified keep with a
15th century palace, dungeon, battlements,
banqueting hall, kitchens and minstrels' gallery.
The museum contains a significant collection of
arms and armour, medieval musical instruments,
tapestries and some Robert Burns' manuscripts.
Entry to the castle is by guided tour only.

The surrounding 200 acre (80ha) country park
provides a variety of attractions including formal
gardens, nature trails and a ranger service offering
guided walks.

Dean Heritage Centre, *Glos.*   **81 D4**
☎ 01594 822170   www.deanheritagemuseum.com
Set around a restored corn mill and millpond, the
centre looks at various aspects of the Forest of
Dean – geology, hunting, crafts, the industrial
heritage including iron and coal mining.

Denbigh Castle , *Denb.*   **87 E2**
☎ 01745 813385   www.cadw.wales.gov.uk
The ruins of this Norman fortification overlook
Denbigh town. It retains a large gatehouse, three
towers, a steep barbican and an ancient,
weathered statue, probably of Edward I.

Denny Abbey & Farmland Museum, *Cambs.*   **84 A1**
☎ 01223 860988   www.dennyfarmlandmuseum.org.uk
Originally founded in 1159, this Benedictine
abbey features superb Norman interiors and
displays telling the story of the abbey through the
centuries. Over the years it has housed the
Knights Templars and the Poor Clares (nuns of the
Franciscan order), eventually becoming a
farmhouse.
  The Farmland Museum looks at the rural history
of the local area and farming over the years.
Attractions include a village shop, a traditional
farmer's cottage and a 17th century stone barn.

Derby Industrial Museum, *Derby*   **89 F4**
☎ 01332 255308   www.derby.gov.uk
The site of the world's oldest factory (the silk
mills, built in the early 1700s) is appropriately the
location for this museum. It tells the story of
Derby's industrial heritage; mining, pottery,
foundry work, railway engineering and a major
exhibition of Rolls Royce aero-engines form the
backbone of the museum. There are regularly
changing displays and events.

Derwent Valley Mills, *Derbys.*   **89 F3**
☎ 01332 255802   www.derwentvalleymills.org
An area of historic mills dating from the late 18th
century stretching 15 miles (24km) from Matlock
Bath to Derby. Designated a World Heritage Site
in 2001, there are numerous sites of historical
importance including the complex of mills,
workshops and warehouses at Cromford which
was the world's first site where water power was
successfully harnessed in textile production. The
later mills at Cromford and also Masson Mill,
which uses a more substantial water source, show
the growing confidence of the developers, in
particular inventor Richard Arkwright, in the
explosion of new technology and techniques that
were becoming available.

Dirleton Castle & Gardens, *E.Loth.*   **108 C3**
☎ 01620 850330   www.historic-scotland.gov.uk
The oldest part of this romantic castle dates from
the 13th century and, although the castle was
destroyed in 1650, there are still large parts of the
original masonry in evidence. The gardens dating
from the 16th century are well worth a look.

Doddington Hall, *Lincs.*   **90 B2**
☎ 01522 694308   www.doddingtonhall.com
This beautiful Elizabethan mansion, gatehouse
and family church were completed in 1600 and
the exterior has remained unchanged. However,
the interior is a surprise, having been completely
redecorated and furnished in the Georgian style in
the mid 1700s.

Outside, the lovely gardens occupy 6 acres
(2.4ha), most of which are walled, with formal
topiary and herbaceous planting. There is also a
wild garden and intriguing turf maze.

Dolaucothi Gold Mine (NT), *Carmar.*   **79 E2**
☎ 01558 825146   www.nationaltrust.org.uk
At Pumsaint, in deepest Wales, the Romans
discovered gold deposits in the river Cothi and
evidence remains of their sophisticated and
ingenious tunnels, aqueducts and caverns. A
second gold rush followed in the late nineteenth
century and now visitors, equipped with miners'
lamps and helmets, can tour the workings, hear
the history and try gold panning for themselves.

Dorney Court, *Bucks.*   **83 E6**
☎ 01628 604638   www.dorneycourt.co.uk
A timber-framed, brick infilled 15th century
building with a magnificent great hall and gallery,
considered to be one of the finest examples of a
Tudor manor house in England. The pleasant
gardens have a particular claim to fame – here
was grown the first pineapple to be cultivated in
England. Opening is limited so it is advisable to
telephone in advance.

Dornoch Cathedral, *High.*   **119 D5**
☎ 01862 810357   www.visitdornoch.com
This small, well maintained cathedral was
founded in 1224 by Gilbert, Archdeacon of Moray
and Bishop of Caithness. Partially destroyed by
fire in 1570 and restored in 1835 – 37, and again
in 1924, the fine 13th century stonework is still
visible.

Dover Castle, *Kent*   **77 F3**
☎ 01304 211067   www.english-heritage.org.uk
Situated 375 feet (114m) above sea level, the
castle has played a key role in the defence of the
realm: William the Conqueror saw its importance
and strengthened the castle shortly after the
Battle of Hastings. However, much of the castle as
we see it today dates from the reign of Henry II
when the impressive four-storey keep, the
distinctive inner bailey and part of the outer walls
were built, creating a concentric fortress. Just prior
to the death of King John the castle was damaged
by a French siege and his son, Henry III, was quick
to carry out strengthening work completing the
outer bailey. The castle maintained its defensive
role right up to and including World War II, when
the tunnels became the headquarters from which
the evacuation of Dunkirk was directed.

Dover Castle   Photo © English Heritage

Drum Castle (NTS), *Aber.*   **115 D3**
☎ 01330 811204   www.nts.org.uk
The 13th century tower of Drum is one of the
three oldest tower houses in Scotland. Jacobean
and Victorian extensions made the house into a
fine mansion and it contains notable portraits and
furniture, much from the 18th century. Drum was
the home of the Irvine family for more than 650

Dunnottar Castle Photo © Grampian Tourist Board

years and a room displays family memorabilia. The extensive grounds include a collection of historic roses, an arboretum and the ancient oak woodland of the 'Old Wood of Drum'.

Drumlanrig Castle, D. & G. 100 C2
☎ 01848 331555   www.drumlanrig.com
A sweeping drive through a wooded avenue leads to an imposing late 17th century castle built of local pink sandstone. Originally a 15th century castle, it was converted, complete with turrets, towers and cupolas, for the 1st Duke of Queensberry. The state rooms have splendid oak panelling, Louis XIV furniture and paintings by Holbein, Murillo, Rembrandt and Brueghel. The 40 acres (16ha) of formal and informal gardens are being restored according to the original plans, and new rhododendron areas are being created using seed collected from the wild. The adjacent Drumlanrig Country Park has waymarked trails, wildlife including red squirrels and otters, and some magnificent specimen trees.

Dryburgh Abbey, Sc.Bord. 108 C6
☎ 01835 822381   www.historic-scotland.gov.uk
Founded in the 12th century in a delightful location on the banks of the River Tweed, the pink sandstone abbey remains showcase several architectural styles as the buildings were frequently assailed by the English, until 1545 when they were abandoned. Even so, Dryburgh is the most complete of the Border abbeys, the barrel vaulted chapter house being particularly impressive. Sir Walter Scott is buried here, as is Field Marshal Earl Haig, the World War I leader.

Duart Castle, Arg. & B. 111 E6
☎ 01680 812309   www.duartcastle.com
This is one of Scotland's oldest inhabited castles and home to the 28th Chief of Clan Maclean. The keep, built in 1360, adjoins the original courtyard. Used as a garrison for Government troops after the 1745 Rising, it then fell into ruin but was restored by Sir Fitzroy Maclean in 1911.

Dudmaston (NT), Shrop. 88 C6
☎ 01746 780866   www.nationaltrust.org.uk
This 17th century house has exhibits of the flower paintings of Francis Derby dating from the same time, as well as modern and botanical art. The grounds include rock, rose and bog gardens and are especially impressive in the spring with collections of rhododendrons and azaleas. There are also woodland and lakeside walks in the 300 acre (120ha) parkland.

Dunfermline Abbey & Palace, Fife 107 E3
☎ 01383 724586   www.dunfermlineabbey.co.uk
The remains of the great Benedictine abbey founded by Queen Margaret in the 11th century. The foundations of her church are under the present 12th century Romanesque style nave. Robert the Bruce is buried in the choir, now the site of the present parish church. Of the monastic buildings, the ruins of the refectory, pend and guesthouse remain.

Dunham Massey Hall, Park & Gardens (NT), Gt.Man. 88 C1
☎ 0161 941 1025   www.nationaltrust.org.uk
An early Georgian manor house that was extensively remodelled in the early 20th century, resulting in sumptuous Edwardian interiors. Over 30 rooms are open to the public, including the refurbished kitchen, laundry and servants'

quarters. Of particular note is the 18th century walnut furniture, the silver collection of the 2nd Earl of Warrington, and some fine paintings. The house is set in 250 acres (101ha) of wooded deer park with formal avenues of trees, an orangery and a working 17th century mill.

Dunnottar Castle, Aber. 115 D4
☎ 01569 762173   www.dunechtestates.co.uk
A spectacular ruin 160ft (48.5m) above the North Sea, recognisable to many film buffs as the setting of Franco Zeffirelli's film 'Hamlet' which starred Mel Gibson. Situated on a flat-topped promontory with sheer cliffs on three sides, and linked to the mainland by a narrow neck of land, Dunnottar's dramatic defensive position ensured a rich and colourful history. Between the 9th and 17th centuries the castle was fought over many times and for over three hundred years was held by the Keiths, who were Earls Marischal of Scotland, the most powerful family in Scotland. In 1297 William Wallace attacked the English garrison and burnt the wooden castle here, and Mary, Queen of Scots was a visitor in 1562 and 1564. Most famously, in 1652 the Scottish crown jewels, the Honours of Scotland, were hidden here safely for eight months during a siege by Cromwell's army. Today several buildings from different periods remain, including the 14th century tower house. Access is by means of a steep path and steps.

Dunrobin Castle, High. 119 E4
☎ 01408 633177   www.highlandescape.com
Overlooking the sea and set within magnificent formal gardens, Dunrobin Castle has belonged to the Earls and Dukes of Sutherland for centuries. It was originally a square keep, built in the 13th century by Robert, Earl of Sutherland, after whom it was named Dun Robin. Its turreted, chateau-style appearance resulted after extensive modifications by Sir Charles Barry during the 1840s, after he had completed the new Houses of Parliament. As Scotland's most northerly great house, the castle is also its largest, with 189 rooms, and it is the oldest continuously-inhabited home. Period rooms display fine paintings, furniture, family memorabilia and even a steam-powered fire engine. The sheltered gardens, with their formal parterres, were first laid in 1850 and were inspired by those of Versailles. There are falconry demonstrations and a Victorian museum includes an exceptional collection of Pictish stones.

Dunstanburgh Castle (NT), Northumb. 109 F6
☎ 01665 576231   www.nationaltrust.org.uk
Extensive and dramatic ruins of a 14th century castle on headland cliffs. Reached by coastal footpath from Craster or Embleton.

Dunster Castle & Gardens (NT), Som. 71 E1
☎ 01643 821314   www.nationaltrust.org.uk
Dating from at least Norman, and possibly Saxon times, the castle has a magnificent site on a wooded hill above the village of Dunster. The chief medieval relic is the 13th century gatehouse, while the main building, dating from 1617, was substantially remodelled for domestic use in Victorian times. The 28 acre (11ha) gardens are equally interesting with unusual and subtropical plants, including the National Collection of Arbutus (strawberry trees), probably England's oldest lemon tree, camellias, magnolias and a fine display of spring bulbs. There are extensive views across Exmoor, the Quantock Hills and the Bristol Channel.

Durham Cathedral & Durham Castle, *Dur.*   59 B2
☎ 0191 386 4266   www.durhamcathedral.co.uk
Dominating the Durham city skyline, this awe-inspiring cathedral, with three massive towers, stands high above and in an almost complete loop of the River Wear. The present cathedral was largely built between 1093 and 1133 and is considered to be the greatest piece of Romanesque architecture in Britain. The nave, however, has pointed arches which makes it unique for this period.

The cathedral contains the tomb of Cuthbert, 7th century Bishop of Lindisfarne, and of the Venerable Bede who wrote about the life of St Cuthbert. Exhibitions tell the story of the cathedral and how it was built and 'The Treasures' in the 13th century undercroft displays St Cuthbert's cross and fragments of his coffin. The medieval Monk's Dormitory has a wonderful hammer-beam oak roof and houses part of the cathedral library. Visitors may climb the 325 steps of the tower. Together with Durham Castle (built 1072), which is now part of the university, the cathedral is designated a World Heritage Site.

Dyrham Park (NT), *S.Glos.*   81 E6
☎ 0117 937 2501   www.nationaltrust.org.uk
Impressive and little altered late 17th century house set in 268 acres (105ha) of deer park, built for William Blathwayt, a minister in William III's government. It contains some fine furnishings, paintings and a collection of Delftware, popular at the time in deference to the king's Dutch origins.

Eastnor Castle, *Here.*   81 E3
☎ 01531 633160   www.eastnorcastle.com
Built by the 1st Earl Somers in 1820, and extensively restored after 1949, the castle is still privately owned by his descendants – the Hervey-Bathurst family. The grounds are magnificent, comprising an arboretum, lake and deer park in which there are mazes and nature trails.

Edinburgh, *Edin.*   108 A4
Edinburgh is a superb city for visitors and with most of the interesting features so close together it is great for exploring on foot. The city grew up around the castle and it still dominates the skyline today. The Royal Mile, consisting of mostly medieval buildings, runs east from the castle to the Palace of Holyroodhouse, through the heart of the Old Town. Numerous narrow streets and alleys lead off it, many with fascinating architecture to explore. The New Town is immediately to the north, separated only by the beautiful Princes Street Gardens. In stark contrast to the Old Town, it is full of spacious terraces and crescents that are some of the finest examples of Georgian town planning in Europe. The Water of Leith walkway takes visitors to the unspoilt Dean Village. To the east of the main city centre is Holyrood Park, a 650 acre (263ha) oasis of peace with hills, crags, moorlands, marshes and lochs. Arthur's Seat, within the park, is the core of an extinct volcano (822ft, 251m high) and it is worth a walk to the top for superb views over the entire city and the Firth of Forth. Each August the city really comes to life as, over a period of three weeks, The Festival takes place. It is a combination of theatre, dance, music and comedy with performances at all hours of the day and night.

Palace of Holyroodhouse

Edinburgh Castle, *Edin.*   60 B1
☎ 0131 225 9846   www.historic-scotland.gov.uk
The castle rises from an extinct volcanic outcrop and dominates the city that has grown up around it. There has been some kind of fortress up on the hill since the 7th century although the oldest part of the present castle, St Margaret's Chapel, was built during the 12th century. In its early years the castle was a royal residence but has assumed an increasingly military role over time, and today still houses an important garrison for the Scottish regiments. The Scottish crown jewels are on display alongside the Stone of Destiny. In the castle vaults, once used as cells for military prisoners, is Mons Meg cannon, a 15th century siege gun which could fire a 500 pound stone a distance of 2 miles (3km). Each day at one o'clock a gun is fired from the castle, a tradition that has continued unbroken since the 17th century. Each August the grounds play host to the Military Tattoo with massed bands, pipes, drums and display teams from around the world.

Eilean Donan Castle, *High.*   111 E1
☎ 01599 555202   www.eileandonancastle.com
Situated on an islet in Loch Duich, this picturesque and inhabited castle dates back to 1214. It passed into the hands of the Mackenzies of Kintail, who became the Earls of Seaforth, was garrisoned by Spanish Jacobite troops in 1715 and blown up by the English. During the 20th century, the castle was fully restored.

Elgin Cathedral (ruins), *Moray*   120 B6
☎ 01343 547171   www.historic-scotland.gov.uk
The magnificent and substantial ruin of the 13th century cathedral known as the 'Lantern of the North' and regarded by many as the most beautiful in Scotland. Interesting features include the 15th century octagonal chapter house with vaulted ceiling and a Pictish cross-slab in the choir. Spectacular views of the cathedral and surrounding area are possible from a platform at the top of one of the massive towers.

Ellesmere Port Boat Museum, *Ches.*   88 A2
☎ 0151 355 5017   www.boatmuseum.org.uk
The canal basin and historic dock where the Shropshire Union Canal meets the River Mersey is home to what claims to be the world's largest collection of traditional canal craft. The museum owns over 5000 items, ranging from large boats to canal company buttons, although not all are on display. Indoors there are exhibits of industrial heritage, waterways objects, working steam machinery and a series of dock workers' cottages recreating scenes from domestic life between the 1840s and 1950s.

Eltham Palace, *Gt.Lon.*   84 A6
☎ 020 8294 2548   www.english-heritage.org.uk
A 1930s mansion constructed around a Great Hall, which was originally built for Edward IV in the 1470s. It had all the latest electrical gadgets including a centralised vacuum cleaner and sound system. The interior exhibits superb examples of Art Deco styling, for example, the dining room has black and silver doors, an aluminium ceiling and maple walls. The bathroom features onyx and gold mosaic. The gardens extend to 19 acres (7.5ha) and include a moat, rose garden and pergola.

Elton Hall, *Cambs.*   90 C6
☎ 01832 280468   www.eltonhall.com
Dating from Tudor times, this romantic house is a combination of medieval, Gothic and classical architectural styles and has been home to the Proby family for over 350 years. The house has superb furniture, porcelain and some outstanding paintings by Constable, Gainsborough and Reynolds. The Library has over 12,000 books including Henry VIII's prayer book, complete with his writing. The beautiful gardens are especially good in the summer; the herbaceous borders are a riot of colour and the rose garden, which includes highly scented old fashioned roses, is stunning. There is also a sunken garden, a knot garden and a Gothic orangery, as well as an arboretum.

Ely Cathedral, *Cambs.*   84 B1
☎ 01353 667735   www.cathedral.ely.anglican.org
This magnificent cathedral dates from the late 11th century and was originally built as a monastic church, gaining cathedral status in 1109. After the Dissolution it continued to exist as a cathedral except for a brief period in the 17th century when Oliver Cromwell used it as a stable for his cavalry horses. The architecture is unusual with a 248ft (75.5m) long Norman nave and a remarkable 14th century Octagon Tower.

Erddig (NT), *Wrex.*   88 A3
☎ 01978 355314   www.nationaltrust.org.uk
Dating from the 18th century, this impressive estate near Wrexham was the home of the Yorke family. The grand 'upstairs' state rooms boast fine collections of furniture and original artefacts, whilst 'below stairs' the servants' quarters give fascinating glimpses into the lives of the workers. An extensive range of outbuildings is also of considerable interest and includes a display of vintage vehicles in the stable yard. There is much to attract all ages, and regular event days are planned throughout the season, including horse-drawn carriage rides. Walks lead through the garden areas into a large park with woodland. The gardens feature an array of speciality fruit trees, the national collection of ivies, a Victorian parterre and yew walks.

Erddig (NT)   Photo © Ellen Webster

Exeter Cathedral, *Devon*   71 E4
☎ 01392 285983   www.exeter-cathedral.org.uk
Miraculously escaping major structural damage during the World War II bombing of Exeter, the cathedral and its close provide an historic retreat amidst the post-war rebuilding of the city centre. Evidence of Christian worship on this site dates from the 5th century, but the oldest features of the current building are the twin Norman towers dating from the early 12th century. Much of the cathedral was rebuilt during the late 13th and 14th centuries, building materials being local stone from Beer and Purbeck limestone, and this provides perhaps England's finest example of Decorated Gothic architecture. Other notable aspects are the 14th century minstrels' gallery, the bishop's throne which dates from 1312 and is one of the finest examples of wood carving surviving from this period, the elaborate choir stalls with 13th century misericords and the 500 year old astronomical clock.

Falkland Palace (NTS), *Fife*   108 A2
☎ 0844 493 2186   www.nts.org.uk
Built in the 1500s, Falkland Palace formed the country residence of the Stewart Kings and Queens. Restored period rooms on view include the Chapel Royal, the King's Bedchamber and the Queen's Room. The fine gardens contain the original royal tennis court, built in 1539 and the oldest still in use in Britain today.

Farleigh Hungerford Castle, *Som.*   72 C2
☎ 01225 754026   www.english-heritage.org.uk
Extensive ruins of a 14th century castle built by Sir Thomas Hungerford. The chapel has undergone major conservation work and contains particularly fine wall paintings, stained glass and tombs of the Hungerford family.

Felbrigg Hall (NT), *Norf.*   92 C4
☎ 01263 837444   www.nationaltrust.org.uk
This magnificent 17th century house is set in an estate of over 1700 acres (690ha). The house contains superb 18th century furniture and paintings collected by William Windham II (who inherited the house in 1749) when on his Grand Tour. The parkland has lovely waymarked walks taking visitors past some very ancient trees. There is also a 500 acre (200ha) wood and a walled garden which includes decorative planting and a traditional kitchen garden.

Fenton House (NT), *Gt.Lon.*   83 F5
☎ 020 7435 3471   www.nationaltrust.org.uk
A late 17th century house containing collections of fine porcelain, early keyboard instruments and Georgian furniture. Outside is a walled garden with roses, orchard and a kitchen garden.

Finch Foundry (NT), *Devon*   70 C4
☎ 01837 840046   www.nationaltrust.org.uk
Opened in 1814, this water-powered forge produced hand tools for the agricultural and mining industries until 1960. Regular demonstrations show the three waterwheels driving the massive tilt hammers and grindstone.

Fishbourne Roman Palace, *W.Suss.*   74 C4
☎ 01243 785859   www.sussexpast.co.uk
Discovered in 1960, the remains of the north wing of this 1st century palace are enclosed by a modern building. The largest collection of in-situ Roman mosaics in Britain can be seen, along with remains of a bath suite, courtyards, corridors and hypocausts. A museum displays artefacts from excavations on and around the site and there is a Roman garden that has been replanted to its original plan.

Floors Castle, *Sc.Bord.*   109 D6
☎ 01573 223333   www.floorscastle.com
Thought to be Scotland's largest inhabited castle, this magnificent, castellated Georgian mansion was designed by William Adam although the more flamboyant turrets and cupolas were added in Victorian times. The public apartments display an outstanding collection of 17th and 18th century French furniture, together with magnificent Brussels tapestries, paintings by Matisse and Augustus John, and European and Chinese porcelain. The herbaceous borders in the walled garden are splendidly colourful in summer, while the extensive parkland which overlooks the River Tweed offers a range of woodland walks.

Forde Abbey, *Dorset*   72 A4
☎ 01460 220231   www.fordeabbey.co.uk
In a superb location on the banks of the River Axe, this former Cistercian monastery, founded in 1140, became a private home in 1649. The beautifully furnished rooms have splendid plaster ceilings, and a particular treasure is the set of Mortlake Tapestries of designs originally drawn for the Sistine Chapel. The 30 acre (12ha) gardens are considered amongst the best in England, with borders displaying vivid colour, an impressive rockery, wonderful bog garden with drifts of Asiatic primulas and a background of sweeping lawns and mature specimen trees.

Fort Brockhurst, *Hants.*   74 B4
☎ 023 9258 1059   www.english-heritage.org.uk
A 19th century fort, one of several in the area built for the protection of Portsmouth. It has remained essentially unaltered, particular features being the moated keep, parade ground and gun ramps. Opening is limited so it is advisable to telephone in advance.

Fort George, *High.*   113 E1
☎ 01667 462777   www.historic-scotland.gov.uk
A vast site of one of the most outstanding artillery fortifications in Europe, having been planned in 1747 as a base for George II's army and completed in 1769. It continues to serve as a barracks and remains virtually unaltered. There is much to see, including the Queen's Own Highlanders Regimental Museum.

Fountains Abbey & Studley Royal Water Garden (NT), *N.Yorks.*   **95 F3**

☎ 01765 608888   www.fountainsabbey.org.uk

This amazing 800 acres (325ha) World Heritage Site, situated in the valley of the River Skell, shelters the ruins of over 10 historic buildings. One of the ruins is the imposing remains of a 12th century Cistercian Abbey, with its 15th century tower rising 170ft (52m). The wonderful landscaped gardens contain an 18th century Water Garden, ornamental lakes with temples, statues and cascades, all of which can be enjoyed and admired. Additionally, hundreds of Red, Sika and Fallow deer roam in the medieval deer park.

Foxton Locks, *Leics.*   **90 B6**

☎ 0116 279 2657   www.foxtonlocks.com

Located on the Grand Union Canal, Foxton Locks were built to solve the problem of raising boats the 75ft (22.5m) between Market Harborough and the hill summit a few miles north. Ten locks were constructed between 1810 and 1814 to form the 'Foxton Staircase' and it takes 45 minutes and 25,000 gallons (113,650l) of water for one boat to negotiate all ten; the water passing into side ponds, where it is stored. At the start of the 20th century, in order to speed up the passage of boats in an attempt to compete with the railways, the famous 'Inclined Plane' was built. It consisted of two tanks, each filled with water, large enough to carry two narrow boats or a barge. A 25 horsepower engine enabled the tanks to travel up and down the slope in 12 minutes, also saving many thousands of gallons of water.

Foxton Locks

Framlingham Castle, *Suff.*   **85 E1**

☎ 01728 724189   www.english-heritage.org.uk

This 12th century castle, surrounded by grass-covered earthworks, has crenellated towers topped with Tudor chimneys linked by impressive 43ft (13m) high curtain walls. The wall walk along the top is open to visitors and commands excellent views. Within the walls, the visitor centre now occupies what was once a poor house dating from 1729. This is one of a number of uses the castle has been put to over the years; it has also served its time as a prison and a school.

Furness Abbey, *Cumb.*   **94 A3**

☎ 01229 823420   www.english-heritage.org.uk

The extensive red sandstone ruins of this medieval abbey are found in a peaceful setting in a wooded valley. Founded in 1123 by Stephen, later King of England, Furness became one of the richest Cistercian abbeys in England.

Fyvie Castle (NTS), *Aber.*   **115 D2**

☎ 01651 891266   www.nts.org.uk

Adorned with turrets, gables and towers, Fyvie is one of the finest examples of Scottish baronial architecture. The oldest part dates from the 13th century and there are ghosts and legends associated with the castle. The interior has some original 17th century plaster ceilings, an impressive decorated wheel staircase and collections of portraits, arms and armour, and 17th century tapestries. In the landscaped parkland visitors can enjoy a variety of scenic lochside walks. Traditional Scottish fruits and vegetables are grown in the old walled garden.

Geevor Tin Mine, *Cornw.*   **68 A5**

☎ 01736 788662   www.geevor.com

A working tin mine until 1990, this is one of the largest mining history sites in the country. The mine's surface buildings have been restored and visitors can look round the processing plants where the ore was crushed. A highlight is an underground tour of an adit, or horizontal passage, which gives the merest hint of the former working conditions.

Geevor Tin Mine   Photo © Pendeen Community Heritage

Georgian House (NTS), *Edin.*   **60 B1**

☎ 0131 226 3318   www.nts.org.uk

The north side of Charlotte Square has been referred to as Robert Adam's masterpiece and is perhaps the finest example of neo-classical architecture in the country. The Georgian House at number 7 has had three floors elegantly restored to reflect the way the house would have looked during its ownership by the Lamont Family who bought the house in 1796.

Gladstones Land (NTS), *Edin.*   **60 B2**

☎ 0131 226 5856   www.nts.org.uk

A superb example of a 17th century tenement house, this six-storey mansion has been wonderfully restored to indicate what life was like here in the 1600s. Particularly impressive are the decorated ceilings and wall friezes of the Painted Chamber.

Glamis Castle, *Angus*   **114 B6**

☎ 01307 840393   www.glamis-castle.co.uk

Originally a 14th century, three-storey keep, the present turreted castle was modified in the 17th century. One of the oldest parts is Duncan's Hall, legendary setting for Shakespeare's 'Macbeth'. Family home to the Earls of Strathmore, it was the late Queen Mother's childhood home and birthplace of Princess Margaret.

Glasgow School of Art, *Glas.*   **106 C4**

☎ 0141 353 4500   www.gsa.ac.uk

The work of Charles Rennie Mackintosh (1868 – 1928) has become synonymous with Glasgow. Mackintosh was a student at the Glasgow School of Art before winning a competition to design a new building to house the school. Built between 1897 and 1907, the building is today considered to be his finest example of work and is the earliest example of a complete art nouveau building in the country. The only way to see the interior of the building is on a student-led guided tour.

Glastonbury Abbey, *Som.*   **72 A3**

☎ 01458 832267   www.glastonburyabbey.com

Magnificent ruins of an historic abbey whose foundation by Saxon kings in the 7th century probably predates the town. The repeated target of Viking attacks in the 8th and 9th centuries, the abbey's fortunes were revitalised by St Dunstan's appointment as abbot in AD940, and the building was considerably enlarged. A devastating fire in 1184, and the subsequent need for rebuilding funds, led to the Arthurian legend when the monks fortuitously 'discovered' the bodies of Arthur and Guinevere buried in the graveyard. The abbey did not survive the Dissolution of the Monasteries, but the remains, together with an interpretation area, clearly indicate its wealth and importance in medieval times. The Glastonbury Thorn, legendary off-shoot of Joseph of Arimathea's staff, still grows in the grounds.

Glenluce Abbey (NTS), D. & G.   98 B3
☎ 01581 300541   www.historic-scotland.gov.uk
Founded in 1192, the Cistercian monks' diligence
in draining the surrounding marshes to create
productive land ensured the abbey's survival. The
chapter house, built around 1500, has endured
almost intact with unusual decorative carvings
and a ribbed vault ceiling providing splendid
acoustics. More prosaic, but equally interesting
are the well preserved clay drains and waterpipes
laid by the monks. A small museum displays
artefacts relating to the abbey, which was finally
abandoned in 1560.

Gloucester Cathedral, Glos.   81 E4
☎ 01452 528095   www.gloucestercathedral.org.uk
Christian worship has taken place on this site
since AD679 though the present building was
started in 1089 and consecrated in 1100. King
Henry III was crowned here, the only monarch to
have been crowned outside Westminster since the
Norman conquest. The 14th century fan vaulted
cloisters are amongst the earliest and finest in the
world. There are frequent exhibitions and guided
tours to the top of the tower (for which there is a
charge), reached by climbing 269 steps.

Gloucester Cathedral

Godolphin House, Cornw.   68 B5
☎ 01736 763194   www.godolphinhouse.com
Dating from around 1475, this delightful Tudor/
Stuart mansion was for generations home to the
Godolphin family whose fortune was founded on
tin. The house contains some fine 16th and 17th
century English oak furniture and paintings, and
there are interesting formal medieval gardens and
a wagon collection in the Elizabethan stables.

Goodrich Castle, Here.   81 D4
☎ 01600 890538   www.english-heritage.org.uk
Guarding an ancient crossing point of the River Wye,
this well-preserved 12th century ruin is constructed
out of the red sandstone on which it sits. Despite
seeing action during the Civil War, much of the
castle is complete, including the three-storey keep
as well as archways, pillars and passageways
giving a good idea of the castle as it was.

Great Coxwell Barn (NT), Oxon.   82 A5
☎ 01793 762209   www.nationaltrust.org.uk
A substantial medieval barn built in the 13th
century as part of a Cistercian cell under the control
of Beaulieu Abbey. It is constructed chiefly from
Cotswold stone, with the original doors still in place
on the east and west walls. Internally the roof is
supported by the original oak posts and trusses,
though most of the rafters have been replaced.

Great Dixter, E.Suss.   76 C4
☎ 01797 252878   www.greatdixter.co.uk
A beautiful Tudor house built circa 1460 and
restored in 1910 by Edwin Lutyens. The 5 acre
(2ha) garden, contains clipped topiary, wild
meadow flowers, mixed borders including the
famous 'long border' which is some 200ft (60m)
long, ponds, walls, stone steps and paths.

Greenwich, Gt.Lon.   84 A6
☎ 0870 608 2000   www.greenwichwhs.org.uk
Situated on the River Thames and a designated
World Heritage Site, Greenwich is of international
significance. It has a long and interesting history
with strong royal and maritime links. Greenwich
Park, which affords superb views, is the oldest
royal park in London. The 17th century Royal
Naval College, designed by Sir Christopher Wren, is
built on the site of the Royal Palace of Greenwich.
The National Maritime Museum, which includes
the Palladian style Queen's House designed by
Inigo Jones, can also be visited. The Old Royal
Observatory, built by Wren in 1675, is the home
of Greenwich Mean Time and the world's Prime
Meridian – Longitude 0°, where the eastern and
western hemispheres meet. The brass meridian
line can be seen set into the ground, and you can
stand with a foot in each hemisphere. The building
contains a collection of time keeping, astronomical
and navigational objects. Also of interest are the
19th century Ranger's House and St Alfege Church.

Grey's Court (NT), Oxon.   83 D5
☎ 01494 755564   www.nationaltrust.org.uk
An unusual 14th century house, rebuilt in the
16th century and subsequently modified but still
retaining one of the original towers. A distinctive
feature is the Tudor wheelhouse where donkeys
turned the wheel which brought water up from a
200ft (61m) well. The 8 acre (3ha) gardens are a
particularly attractive aspect, set among the ruins
of the 14th century building. Telephone in
advance to check for opening times.

Grime's Graves, Norf.   92 A6
☎ 01842 810656   www.english-heritage.org.uk
These fascinating Neolithic flint mines date from
4000 to 5000 years ago. Visitors can descend
30ft (10m) by ladder into one of the shafts and
see the radiating galleries where ancient man
worked the high quality flint with antler picks.

Grimsthorpe Castle, Lincs.   90 C4
☎ 01778 591205   www.grimsthorpe.co.uk
Dating from the 13th century, this castle with its
impressive baroque frontage has an interesting
collection of tapestries, paintings and fine furniture,
including thrones from the House of Lords.
Surrounded by 3000 acres (1213ha) of parkland,
there is a family cycle trail, a Woodland Adventure
Playground, a tour with the Park Ranger, a shop
and a café.

H.M.S. Belfast, Gt.Lon.   63 B4
☎ 020 7940 6300   hmsbelfast.iwm.org.uk
Launched in 1938, this was the Royal Navy's
largest cruiser of World War II. It participated in the
sinking of the German battle cruiser Scharnhorst
in 1943 and remained in Navy service until 1965.
Most of the ship can be visited, including the
engine room, boiler room and the bridge.

H.M.S. Victory, Ports.   74 B4
☎ 023 9286 1533   www.hms-victory.com
Now lying in dry dock, the Victory is the oldest
commissioned warship in the world and the
flagship of the Second Sea Lord, though she is of
course best known as Lord Nelson's flagship at
the Battle of Trafalgar in 1805. Commissioned in
1778, her excellent sailing qualities caused
several admirals to choose her as their flagship,
and although her active career ended in 1812 it
was agreed that she should be preserved as a
memorial to Nelson and this distinguished period
of the Royal Navy's history. Tours are not
available from July to the end of school summer
holidays due to pressure of numbers, but guides
are on hand to answer visitors' questions.

H.M.S. Warrior, Ports.   74 B4
☎ 023 9283 9766   www.hmswarrior.org
Launched in 1860, HMS Warrior was the world's
first iron-hulled, armoured battleship and was
then considered the most formidable ever seen.
Visitors are able to explore the four large decks
which illustrate life in the Victorian navy.

Haddo House (NTS) & Country Park, Aber. 115 D2
☎ 01651 851440   www.haddo.co.uk
Haddo House is an elegant Georgian mansion
designed by William Adam in 1732 for the 2nd
Earl of Aberdeen, while much of the splendid
interior decoration is Adam Revival style dating
from the 1880s. Haddo has a beautiful library and
contains some fine furniture and an extensive art
collection. The formal garden includes terracing
with rose beds.

Haddon Hall, *Derbys.* 89 E2

☎ 01629 812855 www.haddonhall.co.uk

Parts of the hall date back to 1170, when it was held by the illegitimate son of William the Conqueror. However, it was not until 200 years later that the building was completed. Remarkably well preserved, it has featured in many period dramas and films.

Haddon Hall

Hadrian's Wall, *Northumb.* 102 C3

☎ 01434 322002 www.hadrians-wall.org;
www.english-heritage.org.uk

The wall is a well preserved and impressive Roman frontier fortification, built between AD122-128 on the orders of Emperor Hadrian at the height of the Roman Empire. It extends 73 miles (118km) from Bowness-on-Solway to Wallsend. No doubt intended as a symbol of Roman power, it was used to control trade and the movement of people in the region. It is now a designated World Heritage Site. The original height of the wall was around 15ft (5m) and was bounded on the north by a defensive ditch and on the south by a ditch between turf ramparts. It included turret watch towers, milecastles and forts. The wall is all the more dramatic for much of it being built on ridges and crags and set amidst beautiful countryside. Numerous car parks on the B6318 give walkers access to the paths alongside the wall. At the east end of the wall is Segedunum, the remains of a fort once holding a garrison of 600 soldiers, and now an award-winning museum. It includes a reconstructed section of wall and Roman baths, while nearby is 88yds (80m) of original wall.

Hadrian's Wall

Hagley Hall, *Worcs.* 89 D6

☎ 01562 882408

The home of Lord and Lady Cobham was originally built between 1756 and 1760 by the 1st Lord of Lyttelton. In 1925 a fire destroyed parts of the house, including the library and some of the extensive art collection, though it was subsequently restored to its former glory. The Hall is surrounded by a 350 acre (135ha) deer park.

Hailes Abbey (NT), *Glos.* 81 F3

☎ 01242 602398 www.nationaltrust.org.uk

This Cistercian abbey was founded in 1246 and in 1270 was gifted a phial containing what was said to be the blood of Christ. After the 1539

Dissolution, parts of the site survived as a mansion house but fell into disuse in the 18th century. Little is left of the buildings apart from the remains of the cloister arches.

Ham House (NT), *Gt.Lon.* 83 F6

☎ 020 8940 1950 www.nationaltrust.org.uk

An outstanding 17th century house, built in 1610 and enlarged in the 1670s, containing an impressive collection of paintings, furniture and textiles. The formal 17th century gardens have been restored to their original form.

Hammerwood Park, *E.Suss.* 76 A4

☎ 01342 850594 www.hammerwoodpark.com

This neo-classical house was built in 1792, by Benjamin Latrobe who was later responsible for the Capitol, and the porticos of the White House in Washington D.C. It was converted into flats after World War II and owned by the pop group Led Zeppelin in the 1970s. It gradually fell into disrepair until rescued in 1982 by the present owners who give guided tours and tell of the continuing process of restoration.

Hampton Court Palace and Garden, *Gt.Lon.* 83 F6

☎ 0870 751 5175 www.hrp.org.uk

Located on the banks of the River Thames, this impressive building, covering approximately 6 acres (2.5ha), was originally built by Cardinal Thomas Wolsey, and dates from the early 16th century. He presented it to Henry VIII in 1528 to try and regain favour after he failed to annul the king's marriage to Catherine of Aragon. After becoming a royal palace, it was rebuilt and extended a number of times. Henry was responsible for the construction of the magnificent hammerbeamed hall and the vast kitchens. In the 1690s William and Mary commissioned Sir Christopher Wren to rebuild the palace, but due to a lack of time and money much of the Tudor palace survived. The two differing architectural styles can be seen clearly today.

Visitors can enjoy the magnificent state apartments which contain furniture, tapestries and paintings from the Royal Collection. Other attractions include a rare 'real tennis' court on which Henry VIII once played. The grounds include 60 acres (25ha) of beautiful gardens. There is a 1 mile (1.6km) long canal, extensive radiating avenues of limes and clipped yews, an orangery, and the famous maze.

Hanbury Hall (NT), *Worcs.* 81 F1

☎ 01527 821214 www.nationaltrust.org.uk

A William and Mary style country house built in 1701 which features splendid painted ceilings and an impressive staircase. There is a collection of porcelain on display as well as exhibitions on the family and local history. The grounds include a 20 acre (8ha) garden which is surrounded by parkland covering 400 acres (160ha). Amongst the many interesting features are an orangery, mushroom house, ice house and an 18th century bowling green.

Hardwick Hall (NT), *Derbys.* 89 F2

☎ 01246 850430 www.nationaltrust.org.uk

Designed by Robert Smythson for the wealthy Bess of Hardwick, no expense was spared to build this magnificent example of Elizabethan grandeur. Imposing symmetrical towers and acres of glittering glass windows give a stunning first impression. Hardwick Hall displays the National Trust's most important collection of textiles in the country, including the Gideon Tapestries, which hang in the Long Gallery and cover the 167ft (50m) long wall. Other items of interest include period furniture, portraits and armour.

Before living here, Bess lived in Hardwick 'Old' Hall (now managed by English Heritage), the remains of which can be seen on the hilltop next to the 'New' Hall. It was the wealth accumulated from her four husbands that enabled her to move ! Outside, a herb garden, orchard and formal flower beds are enclosed by courtyards, and surrounding this is a country park containing rare breeds of sheep and cattle. There is also a Stonemasons' centre, which can be visited.

Harewood House, *W.Yorks.* 96 A4
☎ 0113 218 1010   www.harewood.org
Renowned for its wonderful architecture and
interiors by Robert Adam, this exceptional stately
home belongs to the Earl of Harewood. Collections
include exquisite Chippendale furniture, fine
porcelain, and 18th century and Italian
renaissance works of art. There are also Royal
photographs and memorabilia, from the 1930s to
1960s, when HRH Princess Mary lived here.

The impressive grounds, landscaped by 'Capability'
Brown, include lakeside and woodland walks.
Alternatively, take a boat trip across the lake.

A visit to the Bird Garden is a must, with over 100
rare and exotic birds from around the world,
including threatened species from Africa, America
and Australia. There is also an excellent adventure
playground.

Harlech Castle, *Gwyn.* 86 C4
☎ 01766 780552   www.cadw.wales.gov.uk
This rugged castle was built on the rocks above
Cardigan Bay, once lapped by waves, but now
overlooking sand dunes where the sea has
retreated. Construction began during Edward I's
second campaign in Wales from 1283, and its
protected position, walls and artillery platforms
made the castle stoutly defensible. It was taken
by Owain Glyndwr in the siege of 1404, in the last
great uprising of the Welsh against the occupying
English, and was held by him for four years.

The castle is concentric, with strong outer walls.
The inner walls contained the main living quarters,
and the imposing twin-towered gatehouse, with
its residential apartments, is one of the main
features of the castle. The massive eastern façade,
the guardroom and the castle's wide round
towers, designed to intimidate attackers, are all
impressive. The entrance is at the position of a
second drawbridge which used to lower onto
towers, of which only the foundations remain. The
mighty structure commands superb views out to
sea and to the mountains of Snowdonia.

Harlech Castle   Photo © RAC

Harvard House, *Warks.* 82 A2
☎ 01789 204016   www.shakespeare.org.uk
This impressive timber-framed building was built
in 1596 by Thomas Rogers and has remained
unchanged since then. His grandson, John
Harvard, emigrated to America in 1647 and died
only a year later. It was a bequest in his will that
helped to establish Harvard University in
Cambridge, Massachusetts. The Museum of
British Pewter is housed within the building.

Harvington Hall, *Worcs.* 81 E1
☎ 01562 777846   www.harvingtonhall.com
The largest number of priest's holes in Britain are
to be found in this Elizabethan manor house
which was originally built in 1580 and is now
owned by the Roman Catholic Archdiocese of
Birmingham. Many of the original wall paintings
still adorn the walls, having been discovered
beneath a layer of whitewash in 1936. Large
numbers of birds are attracted by the moat and
the two lakes in the gardens which also include a
Georgian chapel and a malt house.

Hastings Castle (ruins), *E.Suss.* 76 C5
☎ 01424 781111   www.hastingscastle.co.uk
Originally built by William the Conqueror in 1066
as a wooden fort on an earth motte, it was rebuilt
in stone in 1070 as the first permanent Norman
castle in the country. It is now a ruin commanding
panoramic views of Hastings. Visitors to the castle
can see an audio visual show 'The 1066 Story'
about the Battle of Hastings and the history of
the castle.

Hatchlands (NT), *Surr.* 75 D2
☎ 01483 222482   www.nationaltrust.org.uk
An 18th century brick built mansion set in a 430
acre (174ha) park designed by Humphrey Repton.
The interior contains early examples of work by
Robert Adam as well as a fine collection of
keyboard instruments once owned, or played by
famous composers including J.C. Bach, Beethoven,
Chopin, Mozart and Purcell.

Hatfield House, *Herts.* 83 F4
☎ 01707 287010   www.hatfield-house.co.uk
This superb Jacobean house, set in 4000 acres
(1600ha) of parkland, was built in 1611 by Robert
Cecil, 1st Earl of Salisbury, who was Chief Minister
to James I. It has remained in the Cecil family ever
since. The luxurious interior exhibits superb
examples of Jacobean craftsmanship, such as the
magnificent carved oak staircase and long gallery.
There are also impressive paintings by Reynolds,
Hilliard and Mytens, an armoury and fine 16th,
17th and 18th century furniture and tapestries.

The house was built on the site of an earlier 15th
century palace which was home to Elizabeth I for
much of her childhood. Most of the old Tudor red
bricked palace was destroyed to build the new
house but one wing, including the great
banqueting hall, where Elizabeth held her first
Council of State on her accession in 1558, still
survives in the grounds of the current mansion.

The beautiful 42 acre (17ha) gardens situated
adjacent to the house were originally laid out by
John Tradescant the Elder, who was employed by
the 1st Earl. Tradescant was a great plant hunter
and he brought huge quantities of plants from
Europe. Over the years the layout of the gardens
has changed many times, most notably in the
18th century when the fashion for landscape
gardening resulted in much of the earlier
Jacobean formality being swept away. Today, the
gardens are totally organic and have been
restored to display much of their varied history,
with a knot garden, lime walk, privy garden with
yew hedges and a wilderness garden.

Haughmond Abbey, *Shrop.* 88 B5
☎ 01743 709661   www.english-heritage.org.uk
Once part of a thriving and prosperous
community, this ruined Augustinian Abbey is now
in the care of English Heritage. The medieval
beamed ceiling in the Chapter House is
impressive, as is its 12th century entrance. Work
on the surrounding fields has revealed that the
abbey ruins were incorporated into the grounds of
the now demolished 18th century Sundome
House.

Heaton Hall, *Gt.Man.* 95 D6
☎ 0161 773 1231   www.manchestergalleries.org.uk
Heaton Hall is a fine neoclassical country house
set in 650 acres (263ha) of public parkland. Many
of the building's original features have been
retained, such as the ornate scrolling plasterwork,
the classically inspired paintings and the unusual
Pompeiian Cupola room. The principal rooms in
the house have been restored and furnished to
reflect life here as it was in the late 18th and early
19th centuries.

Helmsley Castle (Ruins), *N.Yorks.* 96 B2
☎ 01439 770442   www.english-heritage.org.uk
The dramatic ruins of Helmsley Castle include the
12th century keep and Tudor mansion. Two deep
ditches cut down into the solid rock around the
castle form impressive earthworks.

Hereford Cathedral, *Here.* 81 D3

☎ 01432 374200   www.herefordcathedral.org

Standing on the banks of the River Wye, much of the original 12th century cathedral still survives today although extensive restoraton took place in the 18th and 19th centuries. It is probably most famous for the Chained Library and Mappa Mundi exhibitions housed in the New Library building. Mappa Mundi dates from around 1300 and is the most complete and largest medieval world map still in existence. Entry to the Cathedral is free but there is a charge for the exhibitions.

Hermitage Castle, *Sc.Bord.* 101 F2

☎ 01387 376222   www.historic-scotland.gov.uk

A vast, eerie ruin of a forbidding fortress in a bleak moorland setting, dating from the 14th and 15th centuries and consisting of four towers and connecting walls. The imposing medieval exterior is deceptive as certain features resulted from a Victorian restoration, and inside the structure is little more than a ruin.

Hever Castle, *Kent* 76 A3

☎ 01732 865224   www.hever-castle.co.uk

This romantic, double-moated, 13th century castle was the childhood home of Anne Boleyn, and later owned by Anne of Cleves. The castle contains prayer books inscribed and signed by Anne Boleyn. The spectacular gardens were constructed between 1904 and 1908. Features include a 35 acre (14ha) lake, Italian gardens with statuary and sculptures, a 360ft (110m) herbaceous border and herb garden.

Highclere Castle, *Hants.* 74 A2

☎ 01635 253210   www.highclerecastle.co.uk

This former Georgian mansion, set in magnificent parkland landscaped by Lancelot 'Capability' Brown, was extravagantly refurbished both internally and externally by Sir Charles Barry in the 1840s. The lavishly decorated rooms embrace a variety of styles including Gothic, Moorish and rococo, which somehow combine to form a splendid example of High Victorian architecture. The castle is the ancestral home of the Earls of Carnarvon, and there is an exhibition of Egyptian artefacts brought back by the 5th Earl following the Tutankhamen excavations in the 1920s.

Hill House (NTS), *Arg. & B.* 106 A3

☎ 01436 67900   www.nts.org.uk

Charles Rennie Mackintosh designed this house for the publisher Walter Blackie in 1904. A masterpiece of domestic architecture synthesizing traditional Scottish style with avant-garde innovation, this extraordinary building still looks modern today.

Hill of Tarvit Mansion House & Garden (NTS), *Fife* 108 B2

☎ 0844 493 2185   www.nts.org.uk

Sir Robert Lorimer designed this fine Edwardian house to provide a setting for his important collection of French, Chippendale style and vernacular furniture. Lorimer also designed the formal gardens.

Holker Hall, *Cumb.* 94 B3

☎ 015395 58328   www.holker-hall.co.uk

The Cavendish family stately home originally dates from the 17th century but has many later additions and alterations. The pink sandstone Victorian west wing, open to the public, was rebuilt in Elizabethan style after a fire in 1871. The interior is richly furnished and decorated with ornate plaster ceilings, linenfold panelling, silk wall hangings, marble fire surrounds and a carved oak staircase. Paintings grace the walls and there is a collection of Wedgwood Jasper Ware.

Holker Hall is surrounded by a deer park and 25 acres (10ha) of award-winning formal and woodland gardens, with ornamental ponds and fountains and also a wild flower meadow. Rhododendrons, magnolias and azaleas are spectacular in spring and there is a National Collection of Styracaceae. The Great Holker Lime, probably planted in the early 17th century, has an enormous fluted trunk measuring 26ft (8m) across.

The Lakeland Motor Museum, housed in the former stables, has an extensive collection of transport and motoring memorabilia, and includes a display illustrating the record-breaking speed exploits of the Campbell family. There is a full size replica of the Bluebird. A number of special events are held at Holker including an annual garden festival.

Holker Hall

Holkham Hall, *Norf.* 92 A3

☎ 01328 710227   www.holkham.co.uk

This impressive Palladian mansion was built on the site of an earlier manor house between 1734 and 1764 for the 1st Earl of Leicester, Thomas Coke, and is based on designs by William Kent. During his 'Grand Tour' of Europe the 1st Earl had amassed a vast collection of valuable art and artefacts and he wanted a suitably grand house in which to display them. The resulting mansion, built of sand-coloured local brick, with its pedimented portico, square corner towers and side wings, has been little altered over the years, but unfortunately the 1st Earl never saw the finished building as he died in 1759, five years before it was completed.

The interior of the house is superb, the pink marble and alabaster entrance hall, designed by the 1st Earl in collaboration with Lord Burlington, being particularly impressive. Stairs from the hall lead to the elaborate state rooms on the first floor with their superb collections of statuary, furniture, tapestries and splendid paintings by Gainsborough, Van Dyck, Rubens, Claude Lorraine and Poussin. The 3000 acre (120ha) landscaped grounds surrounding the house were set out by Lancelot 'Capability' Brown and include a mile-long lake and thousands of trees. There is no charge to enter the grounds and there are lovely walks around the lake and, in the summer, boat trips.

Holy Island, *Northumb.* 109 F5

☎ Priory: 01289 389200;   www.english-heritage.org.uk;
☎ Castle: 01289 389244;   www.nationaltrust.org.uk;
☎ Heritage Centre 01289 389044   www.lindisfarne.org.uk

Holy Island is accessible by a causeway passable at low tide and is set within the Lindisfarne National Nature Reserve. Founded in the 7th century by St Aiden, the monastery at Lindisfarne became an important centre of Christian learning and the beautiful illuminated Lindisfarne Gospels were written here. The ruined 12th century Benedictine priory has a rainbow arch still standing over the nave, and the museum contains notable Anglo Saxon carvings and illustrates how the monks lived.

With stones taken from the priory, the formidable looking Lindisfarne Castle was built in the 16th century to protect the island from the Scots. Converted into a private home in 1903 by architect Edwin Lutyens, the castle contains a fine collection of early 17th century oak furniture and has a small walled garden designed by Gertrude Jekyll. Also on the island is a Heritage Centre and St Aiden's Winery, where Lindisfarne Mead is made. Entry to the island is free but there are charges for the attractions.

Hopetoun House, *W.Loth.* — 107 E4

☎ 0131 331 2451 — www.hopetounhouse.com

Set in 100 acres (40ha) of magnificent parkland on the shores of the Firth of Forth, this house is one of Scotland's finest stately homes. It is the work of William Bruce, the architect who designed Holyroodhouse, and was later extended by William Adam. The magnificent state rooms feature the original 18th century furniture; remarkable paintings including works by Gainsborough, Raeburn and Canaletto; rococo ceilings; 17th century Aubusson tapestries; Meissen porcelain and some spectacular chandeliers in the Ballroom. The extensive parkland has woodland and riverside walks, a deer park and a walled garden.

Houghton Hall, *Norf.* — 92 A4

☎ 01485 528569 — www.houghtonhall.com

This superb Palladian house, surrounded by 350 acres (142ha) of parkland and gardens, was built between 1722 and 1735 for Britain's first Prime Minister, Sir Robert Walpole. Designed by James Gibbs, and later refined by Colen Campbell, the whole house was built to impress; the main block features magnificent corner towers topped by domes, and is connected to service blocks by curved colonnades.

The extravagant interiors were designed and furnished by William Kent and include the highly ornamented Stone Hall, which features a bust of Sir Robert and lavish ornamentation and sculptures by Rysbrack. The Great Staircase is made of carved mahogany and rises to the full height of the house. The rooms are a magnificent showcase for the impressive collection of pictures, sculptures, china, and tapestries. Visitors can also see the huge Model Soldier Collection, amassed during the lifetime of the 6th Marquess of Cholmondeley, the current owner's father.

The beautiful grounds include extensive parkland, home to a large herd of white fallow deer, and a 5 acre (2ha) walled garden which is divided into areas devoted to fruit and vegetables, a 400ft (120m) long herbaceous border, a formal rose garden with over 150 varieties, glass houses and a croquet lawn.

House of Dun (NTS), *Angus* — 114 C6

☎ 01674 810264 — www.nts.org.uk

Overlooking the Montrose Basin is this beautiful Georgian house, designed in 1730 by William Adam and containing superb contemporary plasterwork. Home during the 19th century to Lady Augusta Kennedy-Erskine, daughter of William IV, many of her belongings remain, as well as her wool work and embroidery.

House of the Binns (NTS), *W.Loth.* — 107 E4

☎ 0844 493 2127 — www.nts.org.uk

Built between 1612 and 1630 by Thomas Dalyell, the house reflects the change in style of Scottish homes during the 17th century, from fortified stronghold to spacious mansion. Outside there are woodland walks to a panoramic viewpoint over the Firth of Forth. The house is only open from June to September.

Houses of Parliament, *Gt.Lon.* — 63 B3

☎ 020 7219 4272 — www.parliament.uk

Also known as the Palace of Westminster and home to the main seat of Government. The original palace was built in the first half of the 11th century by Edward the Confessor and remained the main residence of the monarch until the first half of the 16th century when it moved to Whitehall. The Lords, however, continued to meet at Westminster. In 1834 the building was badly damaged by fire and only the crypt, Jewel Tower and Westminster Hall survived.

The hall, which is 240ft (73m) by 60ft (18m) has a magnificent hammerbeam oak roof. Most of the present building was constructed in Gothic Revival style between 1840 and 1888 by Charles Barry and Augustus Pugin and contains 1100 rooms, 100 staircases and over 2 miles (3km) of passages.

Situated on the River Thames, the building is an impressive sight with its two towers, one at each end. The Victoria Tower on the south west corner, on which the Union Jack flies when parliament is sitting, rises to a height of 336ft (102m) . St Stephens' clock tower to the north, is 316ft (96m) high and is famous the world over. It has four clock faces, each 23ft (7m) in diameter and contains the 13 ton bell, 'Big Ben', cast in 1858.

The Houses of Parliament are worth a visit, just to see the exterior, but visitors can also take a guided tour of the palace during the summer recess and see the impressive interiors.

Housesteads (Vercovicium), *Northumb.* — 102 B3

☎ 01434 344363 — www.english-heritage.org.uk; www.nationaltrust.org.uk

The best-preserved Roman fort in Britain, Housesteads was one of sixteen bases along Hadrian's Wall. Built around AD124 to house 800 infantry soldiers, it was in use until the end of the Roman occupation of Britain in the early 5th century. The fort contains the headquarters building, commander's house, barracks, hospital, latrines and granaries.

Huddersfield Narrow Canal & Standedge Experience, *W.Yorks.* — 95 E6

☎ 01484 844298 — www.standedge.co.uk

The Huddersfield Narrow Canal, which runs for 23 miles (40km), is split in two by Standedge Tunnel. At 3.25 miles (5km) long and 645ft (200m) high, it is Britain's highest, longest and deepest canal tunnel. The Standedge Visitor Centre, with its interactive exhibition and guided boat trip through part of the tunnel, provides a remarkable account of how it was engineered in the 18th century.

Hughenden Manor (NT), *Bucks.* — 83 D5

☎ 01494 755573 — www.nationaltrust.org.uk

The home of former prime minister, Benjamin Disraeli, from 1847–71, and extensively restyled during this period by the Victorian Gothic architect E.B. Lamb. The interior has been left much as Disraeli would remember it, with his books, furniture, pictures and other memorabilia of his life. The 5 acre (2ha) gardens were designed by Disraeli's wife, Mary Anne. There are colourful herbaceous borders and formal annual bedding, woodland walks and an orchard with old varieties of apples and pears. Limited opening so it is advisable to telephone in advance.

Huntingtower Castle, *P. & K.* — 107 E1

☎ 01738 627231 — www.historic-scotland.gov.uk

Known as Ruthven Castle until 1600, Huntingtower Castle is a 15th century castellated mansion. A 17th century range links its two fine and complete towers. A key feature is the outstanding painted ceiling. Noteworthy historic events include a visit by Mary, Queen of Scots, the capture of King James the VI, and the birth of the Jacobite commander, Lord George Murray.

Houses of Parliament — Photo © Visit London

ckworth (NT), *Suff.*   84 C1

☎ 01284 735270   www.nationaltrust.org.uk

This unusual house dates from 1795 and was built to display the collection of art accumulated by Frederick Hervey, Bishop of Derry. Many of the descendents of the 4th Earl were also great collectors and today the house has a superb array of paintings, including works by Gainsborough, Titian and Velázquez. The Hall is set in a 1800 acre (73ha) Lancelot 'Capability' Brown landscaped park which features some magnificent ancient specimen trees. There are lovely gardens laid out in formal Italianate style dating from the 19th century.

Ightham Mote (NT), *Kent*   76 B3

☎ 01732 810378   www.nationaltrust.org.uk

A very attractive moated manor house dating from 1330 surrounded by a lovely garden with lakes and woodland. The interior of the house has a rich history with the Great Hall dating from the 1340s, a 14th century crypt, a Tudor chapel and a Jacobean fireplace.

Imperial War Museum, *Gt.Lon.*   63 B3

☎ 020 7416 5320   www.iwm.org.uk

The museum has displays covering warfare from World War I to the present day and majors on Britain and the Commonwealth. Natural light from the domed atrium illuminates an impressive collection of tanks and weapons including a V2 rocket and also a Spitfire. Not only does it include conventional hardware of war but also interesting exhibits relating to war's impact on the population at large. For example there are displays on rationing, morale-boosting, censorship and there is also an exhibition on the Holocaust.

Imperial War Museum (Duxford), *Cambs.*   84 A2

☎ 01223 835000   duxford.iwm.org.uk

Built during World War I, the aerodrome at Duxford was one of the earliest RAF stations in the country and saw action during World War II. It is now home to one of the world's largest collections of preserved civil and military aircraft and is Europe's premier aviation museum. The 7 acres (2.8ha) of exhibition space include some two hundred planes. In the Land Warfare Hall is a huge collection of tanks, military vehicles and artillery. Other hangars contain naval helicopters and midget submarines, a Battle of Britain exhibition and a British aircraft collection.

Inveraray Castle, *Arg. & B.*   105 E1

☎ 01499 302203   www.inveraray-castle.com

The present building, in the style of a castle, was erected between 1745 and 1790, replacing a previous fortified keep. Explore the grand staterooms, and some of the former bedrooms, and view the famous collections of armour, French tapestries, paintings, and fine Scottish and European furniture.

Iona (NTS), *Arg. & B.*   110 B6

☎ 01681 700512   www.nts.org.uk

St Columba began to spread the gospel here in AD563, from where Christianity spread throughout Scotland and beyond. Explore the abbey, home to the Iona Community, with a beautiful interior and carvings, the 13th century priory, the oldest cemetery in Scotland, containing the graves of many kings and chiefs, the restored St Oran's Chapel, and the 10th century St Martin's Cross. There are also superb long sandy beaches, turquoise seas and unrivalled views.

St Martin's Cross, Iona Abbey

Photo © Argyll, the Isles, Loch Lomond & Trossachs Tourist Board

Ironbridge Gorge, *Tel. & W.*   88 B5

☎ 01952 884391   www.ironbridge.org.uk

The Iron Bridge, the first bridge in the world to be constructed completely out of iron, is the focal point of the 'Valley of Invention' which was at the centre of the industrial revolution in Britain. Now a World Heritage Site, ten museums tell the story of the industrial revolution and the part this area played in it. The Blists Hill Victorian Town is an open-air re-creation of a late 19th century working community where even old money can be bought at the bank and used in the local shops and pubs. The Museum of the Gorge looks at the effects of the revolution on the beautiful gorge itself, and the Broseley Pipeworks, which closed in 1957, is presented as if it were still a working factory. There is also a Museum of Iron, China Museum and Tile Museum, as well as the Bridge and Tollhouse where there is an exhibition and souvenir shop. A passport ticket can be bought to give access to all ten museums and, as they cover an area of around 6 square miles (15 sq km), a shuttle bus runs between them at weekends and on bank holidays.

Ironbridge Gorge   Photo © West Midlands Tourist Board

Jarlshof Prehistoric & Norse Settlement, *Shet.*   123 E6

☎ 01950 460112   www.historic-scotland.gov.uk

A complex of ancient settlements within 3 acres (1.2ha) can be found on this extraordinarily important site. The oldest is a Bronze Age village of oval stone huts. Above this is an Iron Age broch and wheelhouses, and even higher still is an entire Viking settlement. A house, built around 1600, sits on the crest of the mount. Displays in the visitor centre explain Iron Age life and the history of the site.

Jedburgh Abbey, *Sc.Bord.*   102 A1

☎ 01835 863925   www.historic-scotland.gov.uk

Dominating the skyline in Jedburgh's centre, this red sandstone abbey was founded by David I in the 12th century, probably on the site of a 9th century church. The remarkably complete abbey church is mostly Romanesque and early Gothic in design, with a fine rose window and richly carved Norman doorway. Cloister remnants have been uncovered and artefacts found are on display at the visitor centre, together with an excellent exhibition on life in the monastery.

Jorvik, *York*   66 B2

☎ 01904 543403   www.jorvik-viking-centre.co.uk

Viking history is re-created using the well-preserved remains discovered on the site on which the museum now stands. Journey back over 1000 years to AD975 and experience the Viking way of life through the reconstructed streets, complete with sights, sounds and smells. Visitors travel in 'time-capsule' viewing cars to be taken past and through two storey dwellings and over backyards and rooftops. From the archaeological finds, the houses and shops are laid out exactly as they were, and even the faces of the people on exhibition have been reconstructed from actual Viking skulls. Special exhibitions throughout the year feature hands-on activities, artefacts and new academic research based around themes such as seafaring, craft skills, bones and warfare.

Jurassic Coast, *Dorset*   **72 A5**
www.jurassiccoast.com
This stretch of East Devon and Dorset coastline between Exmouth in the west and Studland in the east has been designated a World Heritage Site. Its outstanding geological and palaeontological locations, coupled with stunning and varied coastal scenery, make a visit almost compulsory to appreciate this fine example of the natural landscape.

Kedleston Hall (NT), *Derby*   **89 E3**
☎ 01332 842191   www.nationaltrust.org.uk
A mansion in the neoclassical style with a remarkable array of Robert Adam interiors. The state rooms still have their original furniture, and an amazing display of Indian artefacts (collected by Lord Curzon, Viceroy of India in the early 1900s) can be seen in the Eastern Museum. The mansion is surrounded by parkland, which includes a restored 18th century garden.

Kellie Castle (NTS), *Fife*   **108 C2**
☎ 01333 720271   www.nts.org.uk
The oldest part of Kellie Castle dates from 1360, but most of the present building was completed around 1606. It was sympathetically restored by the Lorimer family, who lived here in the 1870s. Inside, there are splendid painted ceilings and panelling, as well as excellent furniture designed by Sir Robert Lorimer. The extensive grounds include a lovely organic Victorian walled garden.

Kelso Abbey, *Sc.Bord.*   **109 D6**
☎ 0131 668 8800   www.historic-scotland.gov.uk
The largest of the Border abbeys founded by David I in 1128, Kelso was a fine example of Romanesque architecture. Little now remains of this once wealthy and powerful establishment; English raids in the first half of the 16th century focused on the abbey and destruction was completed in 1545 when 100 defenders were slaughtered. All that remains is part of the north west transept, tower and a fragment of the nave.

Kenilworth Castle, *Warks.*   **82 A1**
☎ 01926 852078   www.english-heritage.org.uk
An impressive 11th century ruined castle which has been radically altered and extended since then. John Dudley acquired the castle in the 16th century but was executed for his part in the plot to place Lady Jane Grey on the throne. His son, Robert Dudley, created formal gardens where he entertained Queen Elizabeth I on several occasions. Now in the care of English Heritage, some of the 12th century buildings in the inner courtyard survive, as does the Tudor gatehouse.

Kensington Palace, *Gt.Lon.*   **83 F6**
☎ 0870 751 5170   www.hrp.org.uk
Built by Sir Christopher Wren and bought by William III in 1689. Queen Victoria was born here in 1819 and on her 70th birthday the State Apartments were opened to the public. It was home to Diana, Princess of Wales, and is currently the residence of several members of the Royal Family. The Royal Ceremonial Dress Collection, dating from the 18th century, is on display, including some of Diana's dresses.

Kentwell Hall, *Suff.*   **84 C2**
☎ 01787 310207   www.kentwellhall.co.uk
This beautiful red brick moated Tudor mansion, dating from the mid 16th century, is approached by a three quarter mile long lime-tree avenue. The interior of the house was remodelled in 1825 and contains a large collection of 16th century artefacts. On selected weekends visitors can enjoy re-creations of everyday Tudor life. In the courtyard there is a superb brickwork maze in the shape of a Tudor rose, and the grounds contain clipped yews, a fine walled garden with original 17th century layout and a rare breeds animal farm.

Kenwood House, *Gt.Lon.*   **83 F5**
☎ 020 8348 1286   www.english-heritage.org.uk
This impressive neoclassical mansion, adjacent to Hampstead Heath, was remodelled by Robert Adam between 1764 and 1773. The house contains an outstanding collection of paintings with works by Turner, Gainsborough, Rembrandt, Vermeer, Van Dyck and Reynolds.

Kidwelly Castle , *Carmar.*   **79 D4**
☎ 01554 890104   www.cadw.wales.gov.uk
The substantial and well preserved remains of Kidwelly Castle, south of Carmarthen, are set within the site of an earlier earth and timber ringwork. The massive, concentric castle was started in the mid 13th century and developed impressively over three centuries, eventually becoming a judicial court. The entrance is guarded by a large gatehouse and visitors can climb the round towers, walk on the extensive walls and explore the dungeons.

Kilchurn Castle, *Arg. & B.*   **106 A1**
☎ 0131 668 8800   www.historic-scotland.gov.uk
A substantial ruin based on a square tower built by Colin Campbell of Glenorchy, circa 1550. It was much enlarged in 1693 by Ian, Earl of Breadalbane, whose arms are over the gateway with those of his wife. The castle incorporates the first purpose built barracks in Scotland and commands spectacular views down Loch Awe. There are boat trips from Lochawe to the castle during the summer months.

Kildalton Church & Crosses, *Arg. & B.*   **104 B4**
☎ 0131 668 8800   www.historic-scotland.gov.uk
The Old Church at Kildalton is the site of the finest intact High Cross in Scotland. Carved in the late 8th century, the Celtic cross stands 9ft (2.7m) high.

Killerton (NT), *Devon*   **71 E3**
☎ 01392 881345   www.nationaltrust.org.uk
A hillside garden of around 20 acres (8ha) landscaped by John Veitch. The garden is particularly lovely in spring, although attractive throughout the year. The 18th century house contains period furniture and is home to a significant costume collection which changes annually.

Killiecrankie 1689, *P. & K.*   **113 F5**
☎ 01796 473233   www.nts.org.uk
Just north of Pitlochry is the site of the battle of Killiecrankie in 1689, won by the Highland Jacobites under Bonnie Dundee. On the edge of the wooded gorge is the Pass of Killiecrankie Visitor Centre, which relates the fierce encounter. From here, a path leads to 'Soldiers Leap', where a fleeing government soldier made a spectacular jump over the River Garry during the battle.

Kilmartin House Museum, *Arg. & B.*   **105 D2**
☎ 01546 510278   www.kilmartin.org
Within a six-mile radius of Kilmartin Valley, over 350 ancient monuments can be found, including 150 that are prehistoric. This award winning archaeological museum examines the relationship between Scotland's richest prehistoric landscape and its people. Artefacts from ancient monuments, reconstructions and interactive audiovisual displays make a fascinating exhibition.

Kingston Lacy (NT), *Dorset*   **73 D4**
☎ 01202 883402   www.nationaltrust.org.uk
Designed in the 17th century for the Bankes family following the slighting of Corfe Castle, and later restyled by Sir Charles Barry, this mansion is home to a wealth of treasures. These include paintings by Titian, Rubens and Raphael, an impressive marble staircase from Italy and a striking Spanish room decorated in gilded leather. The formal garden is surrounded by 250 acres (100ha) of wooded parkland with waymarked walks, or there are longer walks along ancient trackways that can be taken through the 8795 acre (3520ha) estate.

Kirkstall Abbey, *W.Yorks.*   **95 F5**
☎ 0113 230 5492   www.kirkstall.org.uk/abbey
Situated on the River Aire in attractive parkland, Kirkstall Abbey is one of the UK's best preserved Cistercian monasteries. The Abbey was built between 1152 and 1182 and much of it has survived up to eaves level including the church, part of the 16th century tower, the transept, cloisters and the Chapter House.

Knebworth House, *Herts.* 83 F3
☎ 01438 812661 www.knebworthhouse.com
Home to the Lytton family since 1490, the
original red brick Tudor manor house underwent
extensive remodelling in the 19th century. This
resulted in the rather eccentric Gothic appearance
we see today with its extravagant façade of turrets,
domes and gargoyles. The house is situated
within 250 acre (101ha) grounds which include a
deer park and lovely woodland areas. Features of
the garden include an attractive formal rose
garden, twin pleached lime avenues, herbaceous
borders and a maze. Other attractions include a
giant children's adventure playground, a three-
quarter mile (1.2km) miniature railway and a
dinosaur trail with 72 life-size fibreglass dinosaurs.

Knebworth House   Photo © Knebworth House

Knightshayes Court (NT), *Devon* 71 E3
☎ 01884 254665 www.nationaltrust.org.uk
Designed by William Burges, this elaborate
Victorian Gothic house features ornate interior
decoration including painted ceilings and a
minstrels' gallery. The 50 acre (20ha) gardens,
amongst the finest in the county, are of interest
throughout the year and contain both formal and
informal plantings.

Knole (NT), *Kent* 76 B3
☎ 01732 462100 www.nationaltrust.org.uk
This enormous Tudor mansion, made of Kentish
ragstone and set in a 1000 acre (405ha) deer park
with 26 acre (10.5ha) landscaped grounds, was
built in the mid 15th century for the Archbishop
of Canterbury, Thomas Bourchier. It later passed
to Henry VIII and then in 1603 it was gifted by
Elizabeth I to her cousin Thomas Sackville, 1st Earl
of Dorset. Extensive alterations and additions
were made by the 1st Earl up to 1608 which
transformed the house dramatically, particularly
the interior. Today the house is notable for its 365
rooms – one for each day of the year, 52
staircases – one for each week of the year, and its
7 courtyards – one for each day of the week.

Lacock Abbey (NT), *Wilts.* 81 F6
☎ 01249 730459 www.nationaltrust.org.uk
Founded in 1232, but converted to a country house
around 1540 following the Dissolution of the
Monasteries. The cloisters, chapter house, sacristy
and monastic rooms have been preserved, while
an octagonal tower was built in the Tudor period,
and further work in the 18th century included a
fine Gothic entrance hall. The grounds have lovely
displays of spring flowers, a Victorian woodland
garden and restored botanic garden. A converted
16th century barn houses the Fox Talbot Museum
of Photography, which commemorates the work
of the pioneering photographer who lived here.

Lamphey Palace, *Pembs.* 78 B4
☎ 01646 672224
Just east of Pembroke, the ruins of this medieval
bishop's palace remain an impressive sight,
surrounded by fishponds, orchards and parkland.
Of particular note are the shell of the Great Hall
and the chapel.

Lanhydrock (NT), *Cornw.* 69 D3
☎ 01208 265950 www.nationaltrust.org.uk
This imposing residence originally dates from the
17th century but was largely rebuilt following a
devastating fire in 1881. Fifty rooms are open to
the public, including state rooms and nurseries,
sculleries and kitchens, containing state-of-the-
art Victorian furniture and equipment. However,
the centrepiece is the impressive 96ft (30m) Long
Gallery, chief relic of the 17th century building,
with its splendid plasterwork ceiling depicting
scenes from the Old Testament. The 900 acre
(364ha) estate, extending down to the banks of
the River Fowey, includes both formal and
woodland areas as well as parkland, and contains
some exceptional specimen trees from a collection
started in the early 17th century. Magnificent
spring displays of magnolias, camellias and
rhododendrons give way in summer to colourful
herbaceous borders and annual bedding in the
formal garden.

Launceston Castle, *Cornw.* 70 B4
☎ 01566 772365 www.english-heritage.org.uk
Located in a commanding position above the
town where it formerly controlled the main route
into Cornwall, this is now a medieval castle ruin
built on the motte of the original Norman
stronghold.

Laxey Wheel, *I.o.M.* 98 C6
☎ 01624 648000 www.gov.im
The Laxey Wheel, also known as 'Lady Isabella'
after the wife of the former Lieutenant Governor
of the Isle of Man, has a diameter of 22m (72ft)
and is the largest working waterwheel in the
world. It was built in 1854 to pump water from
the nearby mines through which there are short
tours available. There is little cover so a dry day is
the best time to visit.

Laxey Wheel, Isle of Man

Layer Marney Tower, *Essex* 85 D4
☎ 01206 330784 www.layermarneytower.co.uk
This 16th century Tudor gatehouse is the tallest
in Britain at some 80ft (24m) tall. It was originally
planned as a large palace by Henry, 1st Lord
Marney, Henry VIII's keeper of the Privy Seal, but
he died in 1523, followed two years later by his
son, leaving no male heirs and an unfinished
building. The gatehouse has superb Italianate
terracotta decoration and fine brickwork, and is
set in formal gardens. There are exhibitions within
the tower including a model of the palace as it
may have looked had it been completed. Other
attractions include a rare breeds farm and a
medieval barn.

Leeds Castle & Gardens, *Kent* 76 C3
☎ 01622 765400 www.leeds-castle.com
Set on two islands in the middle of a large
artificial lake, this beautiful castle was
constructed in the 12th century as an
impregnable stronghold, the barbican being built
during the reign of Edward I. Six of the medieval
queens of England have occupied the castle
including Eleanor and Margaret, the wives of
Edward I. Converted into a royal palace by Henry
VIII, it has been restored and now contains a
magnificent collection of medieval furnishings,
French and English furniture and fabrics,
tapestries and paintings by Degas, Pissarro, and
Vuillard. Inside are also the Queen's Gallery,
Banqueting Hall and Chapel. There are 500 acres
(202ha) of parkland and gardens to explore,
within which are an aviary, a maze and a grotto.

Leighton Hall, Lancs. 94 B3
☎ 01524 734474 www.leightonhall.co.uk
This neogothic mansion is home to the furniture-making Gillow family, and is set in 1550 acres (627ha) of landscaped parkland. The hall has early and rare examples of Gillow furniture and fine paintings. There is a 19th century walled garden, and a small collection of birds of prey which fly daily.

Lennoxlove, E.Loth. 108 C4
☎ 01620 823720 www.lennoxlove.org
Lennoxlove House is the seat of the Duke of Hamilton and there are fine collections of furniture and family portraits belonging to the Hamilton family. The earliest part of the house, the rectangular keep, was built well before 1400 and there have been extensions and additions during every century since. The various owners of the house have associations with the Stewarts and there are a number of mementoes belonging to Mary, Queen of Scots, including her death mask.

Letocetum Roman Baths & Museum (NT), Staffs. 89 E5
☎ 0121 625 6820 www.nationaltrust.org.uk
The remains of a Roman bathhouse and an inn have been excavated at this site which was an overnight halt on Watling Street, the main road from London to North Wales. A museum exhibits many of the artefacts that have been discovered here and gives the historical background to the site.

Levens Hall, Cumb. 94 B2
☎ 015395 60321 www.levenshall.co.uk
An imposing grey stone Elizabethan mansion built round a large square medieval pele tower which has been lived in by the Bagot family for centuries and is still a family home. The house has fine ceiling plasterwork, oak panelling, carved oak chimney pieces, embossed leather wall coverings and notably contains a collection of Jacobean furniture and some early English patchwork.

It is for the yew topiary gardens, however, that Levens is world-renowned. The gardens were designed around 1694 by a Frenchman, Guillaume Beaumont, who had previously laid out the gardens at Hampton Court. Beaumont's original design at Levens remains unchanged today. A huge number and variety of shapes have been clipped out of the common and golden yew and there are also impressive box and beech hedges. Each year it takes from August to December for all the hedges to be clipped.

Lewes Castle, E.Suss. 76 A5
☎ 01273 486290 www.sussexpast.co.uk
This ruined castle dates from around 1069 and is unusual in having two mottes. The shell keep dates from the early 12th century and two semi-octagonal towers were built in the 13th century along with a range of buildings inside the shell wall. The impressive barbican, one of the best preserved castle barbicans in England, was added in the 14th century.

Lichfield Cathedral, Staffs. 89 E5
☎ 01543 306240 www.lichfield-cathedral.org
Situated in a peaceful close surrounded by half-timbered buildings, this Gothic cathedral dates from the 14th century. With three spires, known as the 'Ladies of the Vale', it is unique amongst medieval cathedrals. The Lichfield Gospels, an 8th century manuscript, is on display in the Chapter House, which dates from 1249 and is one of the most beautiful parts of the cathedral.

Lincoln Castle, Lincs. 90 C2
☎ 01522 511068 www.lincolnshire.gov.uk
Built in 1068, this impressive and massive early Norman castle on its hilltop houses one of the four surviving copies of the Magna Carta, sealed by King John in 1215. There are still many original features to see, and a walk along the walls outside provides superb views across the surrounding countryside.

Lincoln Cathedral, Lincs. 90 C2
☎ 01522 561600 www.lincolncathedral.com
Sharing the central hill with Lincoln Castle, this magnificent cathedral is one of the finest medieval buildings in Europe. Originally built in 1072 from local limestone, it was consecrated in 1092 and has been a place of worship ever since. It was damaged by fire in 1141 and an earthquake in 1185 caused considerable collapse. Rebuilt by the Bishop of Lincoln (St Hugh), he incorporated huge flying buttresses on the outside so that fewer supporting structures were needed on the inside. This allowed large windows to be installed and gave the inside an open and airy feel. In 1237 the central tower collapsed, which was not replaced for several years. By 1549 there were three towers, each with a spire; the central one blew down and the others were eventually removed, being considered unsafe !

Lincoln Cathedral Photo © Helen Brown

Linlithgow Palace, W.Loth. 107 E4
☎ 01506 842896 www.historic-scotland.gov.uk
The ruin of a great 15th century Palace on the edge of Linlithgow Loch which is associated with many of Scotland's best known historical figures; James V and Mary, Queen of Scots, were both born here. The palace was damaged by fire in 1746 and it has been a roofless ruin ever since.

Little Moreton Hall (NT), Ches. 88 C3
☎ 01260 272018 www.nationaltrust.org.uk
Arguably Britain's finest timber-framed manor house, which has an exterior virtually unchanged since it was built in 1580. The interior is unfurnished but the wainscotted long gallery, cobbled courtyard and 17th century knot garden are well worth a look.

Liverpool, Mersey. 88 A1
Originally a fishing village on the River Mersey estuary, Liverpool experienced rapid expansion during the 18th century due to the transatlantic trade in sugar, spices and tobacco as well as the slave trade. It became one of the world's major trading centres. The city was designated a World Heritage Site in 2004 in recognition of its role in the development of modern dock technology, transport systems and port management.

Liverpool Cathedral, Mersey. 88 A1
☎ 0151 709 6271 www.liverpoolcathedral.org.uk
Nothing about this cathedral has been done on a small scale. It is the largest Anglican cathedral in Europe and the fifth largest cathedral in the world. It has the largest working organ with over 9700 pipes, the highest and heaviest church bells, and the highest Gothic arches ever built. This neogothic structure looks much older than it really is – it was only completed in 1978. It is well worth a climb up the tower, as there are panoramic views over Liverpool and towards the Welsh Hills. Part of the way up the tower is the Elizabeth Hoare Embroidery Gallery where there is a sumptuous display of Victorian and Edwardian ecclesiastical embroidery.

Llansteffan Castle (ruins), Carmar. 79 D4
☎ 01267 241756 www.cadw.wales.gov.uk
The castle ruins sit on a steep ridge overlooking Carmarthen Bay and are witness to its expansion since its Norman origins. There is a Tudor Gatehouse and two baileys, Upper and Lower, which are surrounded by thick curtain walls.

Llanthony Priory (ruins), *Mon.* 80 B3
☎ 029 2082 6185 cadw.wales.gov.uk
Hidden in a remote valley in the Black Mountains, the substantial ruins of this ancient Cistercian priory form a striking picture against the green surrounding hillsides. The priory was built in the 12th century and includes examples of both Gothic and Norman architecture.

Llechwedd Slate Caverns, *Gwyn.* 87 D3
☎ 01766 830306 www.llechwedd-slate-caverns.co.uk
Tours of the massive slate caverns in Blaenau Ffestiniog include underground rides, sound and light shows, and a hard hat walk bringing to life the days of the Victorian miners. The Deep Mine tour descends steeply by railway car and the Miners' Tramway focuses on the historical details of the industry.

London's Transport Museum, *Gt.Lon.* 63 A3
☎ 020 7379 6344 www.ltmuseum.co.uk
Telling the story of the world's largest urban passenger transport system, the museum contains gleamingly preserved survivors from the first cabs to trolleybuses and modern day tube trains. There are lots of hands-on exhibits where visitors can try out the controls.

Longleat House, *Wilts.* 72 C2
☎ 01985 844400 www.longleat.co.uk
A magnificent Elizabethan mansion set in 900 acres (360ha) of rolling park landscaped by Lancelot 'Capability' Brown. The house, built for Sir John Thynne, and still belonging to his descendants, was completed in 1580. Inside, it has been sumptuously decorated with gilded, painted Italianate ceilings designed by John Dibblee Crace in the 1870s and 1880s. Furniture ranges from 16th century English pieces to splendid French work of the 17th and 18th centuries, together with some unusual Italian examples. The grounds, bordered by woodland, include formal gardens, plantings of rhododendrons and a handsome lake.

Loseley House, *Surr.* 75 D2
☎ 01483 304440 www.loseleypark.com
Beautiful Elizabethan mansion set in the 1400 acre (566ha) Loseley Park. The house, dating from 1562, was built with stone from the ruins of Waverley Abbey and contains many fine works of art and panelling from Henry VIII's Nonsuch Palace. The estate comprises a formal 2.5 acre (1ha) walled garden (which is subdivided into five themed components), managed woodland and agricultural land. The well known Loseley ice cream and other dairy products are produced from the estate's herd of Jersey cows.

Ludlow Castle, *Shrop.* 81 D1
☎ 01584 873355 www.ludlowcastle.com
Built in the late 11th century to repel Welsh marauders, the castle has much that is original, including the keep, chapel and some of the doorways. It became a royal palace under Edward IV, and home of the Council of the Marches, responsible for the government of Wales and the borders. There are many exhibitions, displays and events throughout the year.

Lullingstone Castle, *Kent* 84 B6
☎ 01322 862114 www.lullingstonecastle.co.uk
Situated in the lovely Darenth valley, this historic family mansion, first built in the late 15th century, was extensively altered during the reign of Queen Anne who was a frequent visitor to Lullingstone. The Tudor gatehouse was one of the earliest in England to be built entirely of bricks. There are fine state rooms, the impressive Great Hall, the grand staircase and library.

Lullingstone Roman Villa, *Kent* 84 B6
☎ 01322 863467 www.english-heritage.org.uk
Discovered in 1939, the site has been preserved within a modern building. The villa is thought to have been built during the 1st and 2nd centuries, although much of what can be seen today dates from the 4th century and includes well preserved floor mosaics, frescoes and a bathing complex.

Lyme Park (NT), *Ches.* 89 D1
☎ 01663 762023 www.nationaltrust.org.uk
This country estate covers nearly 1400 acres (567ha) of wild moorland and parkland which are home to red and fallow deer. The property at its centre combines Elizabethan, Georgian and Regency architecture, together with an Italianate interior. The state rooms have Mortlake tapestries, Grinling Gibbons wood carvings and a fine collection of English clocks. Back outside, the hall is surrounded by 17 acres (7ha) of Victorian gardens boasting a flowering sunken garden, Jekyll-style herbaceous borders and a reflection lake.

Lynton & Lynmouth Cliff Railway, *Devon* 71 D1
☎ 01598 753486 www.cliffrailwaylynton.co.uk
Funded by Sir George Newnes (the wealthy London publisher of 'Tit Bits' and 'The Strand') and completed in 1890, the cliff railway is a magnificent example of Victorian engineering and ingenuity. At the time, it greatly enhanced the tourist potential of this picturesque area, by giving visitors easy access from Lynmouth, where the boats docked, to Lynton, at the top of the 500ft (152m) cliff.

Lynton & Lynmouth Cliff Railway Photo © Lynton & Lynmouth Cliff Railway

Lytes Cary Manor (NT), *Som.* 72 B3
☎ 01458 224471 www.nationaltrust.org.uk
Delightful manor house, with 14th century chapel, dating mainly from the 15th century when the Great Hall was built, but extended in the 16th century. The house was restored in the 20th century and furnished in period style, while the garden was also replanted in a series of 'rooms' with topiary and colourful, well-stocked herbaceous borders.

Lyveden New Bield (NT), *Northants.* 90 C6
☎ 01832 205358 www.nationaltrust.org.uk
Designed in the shape of a cross, Sir Thomas Tresham built (but did not complete) this Elizabethan 'Lodge' to show his religious convictions. It has remained almost unchanged since 1605. The layout of the water garden is also original, containing terraces and fascinating spiral mounds.

Maes Howe, *Ork.* 122 A3
☎ 01856 761606 www.historic-scotland.gov.uk
This chambered cairn is the finest megalithic (Neolithic) tomb in the British Isles. It consists of a large mound 115ft (35m) in diameter covering a stone-built passage and a large burial chamber with cells in the walls. Vikings and Norse crusaders carved the runic inscriptions in the walls.

Maiden Castle, *Dorset* 72 B5
☎ 01305 267992 www.english-heritage.org.uk
The name deriving from the Celtic 'Mai Dun', or Great Hill, this is one of the largest Iron Age hillforts in Europe, first developed in Stone Age times around 3000BC. Bronze Age burials have been discovered in one area, but the site was increased to its current size of 47 acres (19ha) in the Iron Age, around 450 – 300BC. Around AD43 the fort was taken by the Romans. The foundations of a Roman temple built in the 4th century can still be seen.

Manderston, *Sc.Bord.* — 109 D5
☎ 01361 882636 www.manderston.co.uk
Manderston could well be described as a
celebration of opulence; a relatively modest 18th
century house transformed by architect James
Kinross into an extravagant, neoclassical
Edwardian mansion. Luxurious rooms boast
intricate plasterwork, silk and velvet wall hangings,
panelling and fine furniture. Marble abounds, from
inlaid floors to the magnificent, probably unique
staircase with its silver-plated balustrade. For
contrast, the 'below stairs' element is also on view,
together with a large collection of Blue John pieces
and a biscuit tin museum. Similarly, no expense
was spared on the 56 acre (22ha) grounds. There
are four splendid formal Edwardian terraces
overlooking a lake and informal woodland
gardens, while the walled gardens combine
colourful plantings with fountains and statuary.

Manorbier Castle, *Pembs.* — 78 B5
☎ 01834 871394 www.manorbiercastle.co.uk
Accessed by a delightful narrow lane, Manorbier
Castle overlooks a sandy bay in south
Pembrokeshire. Once a Norman stronghold,
today's structure dates from the 12th century and
is in remarkably good condition. The castle has
many interesting features, including a baronial
hall, stout gatehouse, state apartments, gardens
and a chapel. The family of the current owners
have lived here for over 300 years and it was the
birthplace, in 1146, of Giraldus Cambrensis who
wrote extensively of his travels around Wales.

Mapledurham House & Mill, *Oxon.* — 82 C6
☎ 0118 972 3350 www.mapledurham.co.uk
An attractive H-shaped red brick house built in the
late 16th century and set in pleasant parkland on
the banks of the River Thames. Within the house
are fine plasterwork ceilings and an impressive
oak staircase, while a private family chapel designed
in 'Strawberry Hill' Gothic with original elaborate
plasterwork was added in 1797. There are literary
connections with Alexander Pope, John Galsworthy
and Kenneth Grahame. Opening mainly restricted
to weekends in the summer season.

Mary Rose, *Ports.* — 74 B4
☎ 023 9272 9766 www.maryrose.org
A favourite ship of Henry VIII, the Mary Rose sank
in 1545; the king was watching from Southsea
Castle as he took part in a skirmish with the
French. She was not seen again above water until
1982 and is now on display in the Ship Hall. Built
around 1510, the Mary Rose was quite innovative
for her time in that she could fire a broadside
using heavy cannon. Prior to this, ships engaged
at close quarters for hand-to-hand fighting. A
short walk away, the Mary Rose Museum displays
over 1200 artefacts retrieved from the wreck and
surrounding sea bed. In addition there is
information on how the wreck was raised.

Meigle Sculptured Stones, *P. & K.* — 114 A6
☎ 01828 640612 www.historic-scotland.gov.uk
This is one of the most notable collections of Dark
Age sculpture in Western Europe. There are 26
carved stones, the largest over 8ft (2m) tall.

Melford Hall (NT), *Suff.* — 84 C2
☎ 01787 376395 www.nationaltrust.org.uk
Queen Elizabeth I was entertained in this red brick
Tudor mansion in 1578. The exterior has changed
little since then and is notable for its six octagonal
towers with pepper-pot roofs and tall chimneys.
The interior features a panelled banqueting hall,
Regency library, an 18th century drawing room
and a display of watercolours by Beatrix Potter.
Outside is an attractive garden with lawns and
specimen trees.

Mellerstain, *Sc.Bord.* — 108 C6
☎ 01573 410225 www.mellerstain.com
A superb Georgian mansion representing some of
the best architectural work of William Adam, who
began the building in 1725, and his son, Robert,
who completed it some 50 years later, giving a
wonderful opportunity to compare their styles.
The Robert Adam interior decoration is an
outstanding feature of Mellerstain, the exquisite
ceilings preserved in the original colours being
particularly remarkable. Interior decoration is
matched by the furnishings; pieces by
Chippendale, Hepplewhite and Sheraton, and
paintings by Van Dyck, Gainsborough and
Aikman. The gardens are formal, comprising
Italianate terraces with magnificent views of the
Cheviot Hills whilst the grounds, designed by
William Adam in the style of Lancelot 'Capability'
Brown, make a splendid backdrop to the house.

Melrose Abbey, *Sc.Bord.* — 108 C6
☎ 01896 822562 www.historic-scotland.gov.uk
A Cistercian abbey founded in 1136 by David I,
noted for its elegant and elaborate masonry.
Largely demolished by the English in 1385, it was
rebuilt in the Gothic style but was largely
destroyed in 1545 and is now a ruin. It is
considered the most beautiful of the great Border
abbeys, delicately carved stonework giving an
intimation of its former splendour. The outer shell
of the abbey church is still extant, with its
magnificent east window. An embalmed heart,
thought to be that of Robert the Bruce, was found
here. On his express wish it was taken for burial in
the Holy Land, but the courier was killed in Spain
and the heart returned to Scotland.

Merchant Adventurers Hall, *York* — 66 B2
☎ 01904 654818 www.theyorkcompany.co.uk
Built in the mid 14th century, this Guildhall is
York's largest timber-framed building and is
believed to be one of the finest medieval halls in
Europe. In addition to the Great Hall, where
merchants conducted their business, there is the
Undercroft, or hospital, and the Chapel. On
display are fine collections of furniture, portraits,
silver and jewellery, together with information
about the lives of the merchants during medieval
times.

Merseyside Maritime Museum, *Mersey.* — 88 A1
☎ 0151 478 4499 www.merseysidemaritimemuseum.org.uk
This huge museum in Liverpool's Albert Dock is
the second largest of its kind in the country and
tells the story of one of the world's greatest ports.
There are a number of fascinating exhibitions
including the International Slavery Museum that
explores the worldwide slave trade and another,
the Emigrant Gallery, that allows the visitor to
share in the experiences of those who left
Liverpool for the New World. There are numerous
objects associated with nautical archaeology,
maritime paintings, ships' models, and galleries
about the Titanic and the Lusitania.

Michelham Priory, *E.Suss.* — 76 B5
☎ 01323 844224 www.sussexpast.co.uk
Sitting on an island surrounded by the longest
water-filled medieval moat in England, the
building dates from 1229. Originally an
Augustinian Priory until the Dissolution in 1537,
it then became a country house. Exhibits include
furniture, tapestries and artefacts. The gardens
are in a variety of historic and contemporary
styles and include a physic garden, cloister garden
and orchard. There is also a working water mill.

Middleton Railway, *W.Yorks.* — 96 A5
☎ 0113 271 0320 www.middletonrailway.org.uk
Of great historical importance, this is the oldest
railway in the world, having been established by
an Act of Parliament in 1758. It was also the first
to commercially succeed with steam locomotives
in 1812, as well as being the first standard gauge
railway to be operated by volunteers in 1960.
View the collection of industrial steam and diesel
engines or travel on the railway for a family day
out at Middleton Park.

Mount Grace Priory (NT), *N.Yorks.* — 96 A2
☎ 01609 883494 www.nationaltrust.org.uk
Built in the late 14th century, the Priory is better
preserved than any of the other ten Carthusian
monasteries in England. The Carthusian monks
lived a hermit's life in small two-storey cells with
a garden. One of these has been reconstructed to
replicate how the monks lived and worked.

Mount Stuart, *Arg. & B.*   106 A5
☎ 01700 503877   www.mountstuart.com
A spectacular Victorian Gothic house, Mount
Stuart is the ancestral home of the Marquess of
Bute. Its splendid interiors and architecture
include a mix of astrological designs, stained glass
and marble. In the 300 acres (121ha) of grounds
and gardens there is a mature Victorian pinetum,
arboretum and exotic gardens.

Mountfitchet Castle, *Essex*   84 B3
☎ 01279 813237   www.mountfitchetcastle.com
A Norman castle destroyed in 1215 with only
fragments of masonry remaining. In the early
1980s an earth and timber castle was constructed
along with a village of thatched buildings, including
a smithy, a brew house and a dovecote, where
visitors can learn about life in Norman England.

Mousa Broch, *Shet.*   123 E5
☎ 01856 841815   www.historic-scotland.gov.uk
This is the finest surviving Iron Age broch tower,
standing over 40ft (12m) high. The stairs can be
climbed to the parapet.

Muncaster Castle, *Cumb.*   94 A2
☎ 01229 717614   www.muncaster.co.uk
Situated in a remote part of Cumbria, Muncaster
is a 19th century castle incorporating parts of
earlier buildings including the medieval pele
tower. It has been in the same family since the
13th century and is said to be haunted. The
elegant rooms, including the Great Hall and
Octagonal Library, display a great number of
treasures collected over the centuries. There are
77 acres (31ha) of gardens and woodland to
explore with walks overlooking Eskdale. In late
spring there are carpets of bluebells and many
species of rhododendrons in flower. An Owl Centre
in the grounds has owls, buzzards, kestrels and
red kites, and is the headquarters of the World
Owl Trust. The centre has flying displays and video
footage from cameras placed in nesting boxes.

Museum of East Anglian Life, *Suff.*   85 D2
☎ 01449 612229   www.eastanglianlife.org.uk
This 70 acre (28ha) open-air museum has a
variety of historic buildings including the 13th
century Abbot's Hall tithe barn. Many of the other
buildings have been moved from their original
settings and reconstructed on the site, such as the
attractive working Alton Water Mill, Edgar's
Farmhouse and Eastridge Windpump. There are
also various rare breed farm animals to see
including Suffolk Punch horses, Suffolk sheep and
Red Poll Cattle, as well as working steam engines.

Museum of London, *Gt.Lon.*   63 A3
☎ 0870 444 3852   www.museumoflondon.org.uk
Over 2000 years of London's history are on
display, divided into seven permanent and well
laid out galleries. These range from the Iron Age
'London before London', through Roman, Tudor
and Stuart times, to 'World City' (1789 to 1914)
when London became the world's first metropolis.
Exhibits include over 1.1 million objects and there
are attractive reconstructions of streets and
interiors as well as an exhibition about the Great
Fire of London in 1666. The River Thames is
shown to have a key role in the development and
life of the city through the ages.

Museum of Scotland, *Edin.*   60 B2
☎ 0131 247 4422   www.nms.ac.uk
Scotland's national museum is housed in a
striking, modern sandstone building completed in
1998. The museum traces the history and
achievements of Scotland and its people, from the
country's geological beginnings right up to the
present day. The lower floors cover the period up
to about 1700 with displays of rocks and fossils,
Roman, Pictish and Gaelic artefacts. Two floors
are devoted to Industry and Empire and tell of
how the Scots pioneered many aspects of heavy
engineering. The top floor covers the 20th century
and is based around items that Scottish people
thought best represented their country, which has
resulted in displays on Irn-Bru and football strips,
amongst others.

Museum of Scottish Lead Mining, *D. & G.*   100 C1
☎ 01659 74387   www.leadminingmuseum.co.uk
Set in Wanlockhead, Scotland's highest village in
the dramatic Lowther Hills, the museum traces
300 years of local lead mining history. A walk-
through exhibition in the excellent visitor centre
explains mining and extraction processes, and
there is a good display of local minerals, including
galena, chalcopyrite and sphalerite. A village trail
includes a guided tour round Lochgell Lead Mine,
together with restored miners' cottages.

National Army Museum, *Gt.Lon.*   83 F6
☎ 020 7730 0717   www.national-army-museum.ac.uk
Tells the story of the British Army over the last
500 years, from Agincourt to the present day. It
chronicles all the major British campaigns and has
a large 400 sq ft (37 sq m) model of the battle of
Waterloo, containing over 70,000 model soldiers.
Other exhibits include the skeleton of Napoleon's
horse, a reproduction of a World War I trench and
a lamp used by Florence Nightingale.

National Maritime Museum, *Gt.Lon.*   84 A6
☎ 020 8858 4422   www.nmm.ac.uk
Housed in architecturally important buildings
including The Queen's House by Inigo Jones, the
museum tells the story of Britain and the sea; its
navy, merchants and explorers. A nautical
enthusiast's paradise, there are some 20 galleries
with exhibits including models of ships, clocks and
watches, contemporary and historic paintings,
carved figureheads, weapons and fine silver
collections.

**National Maritime Museum Cornwall,
*Cornw.***   68 C5
☎ 01326 313388   www.nmmc.co.uk
In a striking building which dominates the
quayside, this museum is devoted to the sea,
boats and their importance in people's lives, with
particular emphasis on Cornwall.

National Portrait Gallery, *Gt.Lon.*   63 B3
☎ 020 7306 0055   www.npg.org.uk
Founded in 1856 by historian Philip Stanhope as
a gallery of original portraits to commemorate
British history. Today, visitors can see over 1000
works which are arranged chronologically within
the gallery, from medieval times to the present
day. The focus of the collection is the subjects of
the paintings rather than the painters themselves.
The full portrait collection, the largest in the
world, contains over 10,000 pictures in a variety
of media: oils, watercolours, sculptures,
caricatures, miniatures, photographs and also
silhouettes. Paintings of kings, queens, politicians,
musicians, artists and poets, ranging from the
likes of Shakespeare to Madonna are on display.
In addition to the permanent galleries there is a
varied programme of temporary exhibitions
throughout the year.

National Railway Museum   Photo © Sylvia Gray

National Railway Museum, *York*   66 B1
☎ 0870 421 4001   www.nrm.org.uk
Over 200 years of railway history is celebrated in
style, providing a terrific family day out – for free.
Complete with sounds and smells, the atmosphere
of steam and rail travel is wonderfully re-created.
A splendid collection of locomotives can be found

on display in the Great Hall, recounting the story of the railway from Rocket to Eurostar. Inspect the Mallard, the world's fastest steam train, explore Queen Victoria's luxurious royal carriage and examine the Japanese Bullet Train, in conjunction with a short video presentation. There are millions of railway artefacts, too, including models, silver and crockery, nameplates, clocks and watches, tickets, photographs, workshop tools, posters, engineering drawings, and even a lock of Robert Stephenson's hair.

The Working Railway demonstrates how signals work, the technology behind them and their development over time. Children will enjoy the Interactive Learning Centre where hands-on exhibits explain the workings of trains and the railway. Engineers and craftspeople can be watched in the Works Wing while they carry out conservation work, and children can also build their own model train here. Rides on the miniature railway are available most weekends and school holidays, and on the steam train during school holidays.

National Roman Legion Museum, *Newport*   80 C5
☎ 01633 423134   www.nmgw.ac.uk
North of Newport stand the substantial remains of a Roman fortress, including the baths, barrack blocks, fortress wall and 5000-seater amphitheatre, together with an imaginative Roman legionary museum. This is the site of the significant 50 acre (20ha) Roman fortress of Isca, encompassing a complete town dating from AD75, with much still on view. The museum shows how the Romans lived and fought, with interactive displays and special events suitable for all ages, sufficient for several hours' visit.

National Slate Museum, *Gwyn.*   86 C3
☎ 01286 870630   nmgw.ac.uk
The vast, old Dinorwig slate quarry in the Padarn Country Park near Llanberis has been transformed into an imaginative museum of the bygone industry. Exhibitions, demonstrations, multimedia presentations, restored buildings, children's activities and tours bring to life the work of the quarrymen. The museum offers a fascinating, free day out for the whole family.

National Waterways Museum, *Glos.*   81 E4
☎ 01452 318200   www.nwm.org.uk
200 years of Britain's waterway heritage is exhibited over 3 floors of this historic listed warehouse built in 1873. There are many interesting displays. The entrance to the museum is through a replica lock chamber complete with dripping water.

Neidpath Castle, *Sc.Bord.*   108 A6
☎ 01721 720333
A rare example of a 14th century castle converted to a 17th century tower house, in a spectacular setting above the River Tweed. Massive walls, some 12ft (3.5m) thick in places, withstood Civil War bombardment longer than any other castle in the area, while inside is a pit prison cut out of the rock. The Great Hall hosts an exhibition of beautiful batik wall hangings depicting the life of Mary, Queen of Scots.

New Lanark World Heritage Site, *S.Lan.*   107 D5
☎ 01555 661345   www.newlanark.org
New Lanark is a superb example of a restored industrial village with plenty to keep a family busy for most of the day. Founded in 1785 by David Dale and Richard Arkwright as a centre for cotton spinning, the elegant sandstone buildings sit alongside the River Clyde in a remarkable rural setting. Dale's son-in-law, Robert Owen, took over the management of the site in 1798 and his belief in looking out for the welfare of his workers led to him setting up a cooperative store, a nursery to allow mothers with young children to work, adult education facilities, decent housing and a social centre for the community of 2500 people. Owen's 'social experiment' was viewed with scorn by all of his competitors but his beliefs soon proved fruitful and the business was greatly improved. The Institute for the Formation of Character now

houses the award winning visitor centre and the Millennium Experience, an innovative ride which explains Owen's aspirations and ideas for a better future. Visitors can also look around the village store, Owen's house and mill workers' cottages. A passport ticket gives access to all of these attractions.

New Lanark World Heritage Site   Photo © Gtr. Glasgow & the Clyde Valley Tourist Board

Newark Park (NT), *Glos.*   81 E5
☎ 01453 842644   www.nationaltrust.org.uk
A Tudor hunting lodge originally built in around 1550 which was converted into a castellated house by James Wyatt at the end of the 18th century. Limited opening from April to October but also open on weekends in February for an impressive display of snowdrops.

Newstead Abbey, *Notts.*   90 A3
☎ 01623 793557   www.newsteadabbey.org.uk
A 'must see' for Byron devotees, Newstead houses mementoes of one of England's most notorious poets. Originally built as an Augustinian priory, it was converted into a country house by the Byron family in the mid 1500s. Although much of the Abbey is now a ruin, there are beautifully furnished period rooms – although look out for the 'White Lady' ghost ! The walled garden, lake and exquisite Japanese gardens are set within the 300 acre (121.5ha) estate.

Nine Ladies Stone Circle (NT), *Derbys.*   89 E2
☎ 01629 816200   www.english-heritage.org.uk
On Stanton Moor, a circle of nine evenly spaced stones stand in a 33ft (10m) diameter circle in a large, open woodland glade. The tallest stone stands at 2.3ft (0.7m) and there is one outlier, the King Stone. An atmospheric reminder of the mysterious past.

Norwich Cathedral, *Norf.*   92 C5
☎ 01603 218300   www.cathedral.org.uk
Founded in the 11th century, with many later changes and additions, the present cathedral has a tall elegant spire, and, at 315ft (96m), it is second only in height to Salisbury. The 180ft (55m) square monastic cloisters, which feature intricate fan vaulting, date from the 14th and 15th centuries and are the largest in England. The cathedral is also notable for the large number of attractive, brightly painted, roof bosses in the nave and cloisters.

No. 1 Royal Crescent, *B. & N.E.Som.*   81 E6
☎ 01225 428126   www.bath-preservation-trust.org.uk
The first to be built in Royal Crescent in 1768, this Palladian town house has been meticulously restored complete with authentic furnishings and pictures.

Oakham Castle, *Rut.*   90 B5
☎ 01572 758440   www.rutnet.co.uk
The superb Great Hall remains from the original 12th century castle. It contains fine sculptures and an amazing collection of horseshoes, mounted on the walls, the oldest of which probably dates from 1470. The custom was that every visiting peer of the realm had to give a horseshoe to the Lord of the Manor on his or her first visit. HRH The Princess Royal gave one of the latest in 1999.

Orford Castle, *Suff.* 85 F2
☎ 01394 450472 www.english-heritage.org.uk
This unusual 90ft (27m) high multi-sided keep was built in the mid to late 12th century by Henry II and was once part of a larger castle. Spiral stairs lead to a maze of rooms. A climb to the top is rewarded by impressive views over the surrounding countryside.

Ormesby Hall (NT), *R. & C.* 103 F6
☎ 01642 324188 www.nationaltrust.org.uk
Set in an attractive garden, this 18th century Palladian mansion has some notable interior plasterwork and carved wood decoration. There is an impressive stable block still in use and a restored Victorian laundry and kitchen with scullery and game larder. Also of interest is a model railway exhibition.

Osborne House, *I.o.W.* 74 B5
☎ 01983 200022 www.english-heritage.org.uk
This was the rural retreat for Queen Victoria and her family, away from the pressures of ceremonial life. The house was designed by Prince Albert with technical input from Thomas Cubitt. The Prince was an admirer of Italian art and architecture and his design was based on the style of an Italian villa, complete with towers and terraces. As a widow, Victoria was a frequent visitor until her death in 1901, and many of the apartments have been preserved with little change since then, in keeping with her wishes.
  The interior design of Osborne House is equally lavish. The Grand Corridor is lined by marble sculptures, and there are portraits and frescoes which underline the family's links with Europe and the Empire. Particularly sumptuous is the Durbar Room, built in the early 1890s to celebrate the Queen's role as Empress of India. Within the grounds, 'Swiss Cottage', the royal equivalent of a Wendy House, was built with Prince Albert's intention of providing his children with the basics of housekeeping and cookery. There is also the ultimate boys' toy, Victoria Fort, which the royal princes helped to construct. The pleasant gardens were laid out by Prince Albert in Italianate terraces, with beautiful views across the Solent, and there is a restored walled garden.

Osterley Park & House (NT), *Gt.Lon.* 83 F6
☎ 020 8232 5050 www.nationaltrust.org.uk
Set in extensive parkland, the original Tudor mansion was transformed in the 18th century into a neoclassical villa by Robert Adam. Considered by many to be some of his finest work, it features superb plasterwork, carpets and furniture.

Oxburgh Hall (NT), *Norf.* 92 A5
☎ 01366 328258 www.nationaltrust.org.uk
This magnificent red brick moated manor house was built by the Bedingfeld family and dates from 1482. It has an unusual appearance with its ornate stepped gables and tall, twisted chimney stacks. Although remodelled extensively during the mid 19th century, the Gatehouse, with its octagonal turrets rising to 80ft (24m), remains relatively unaltered. Within the hall can be seen finely carved oak furniture, some original Victorian wallpapers and fine textiles, including needlework by Mary, Queen of Scots and Bess of Hardwick. Outside there are walled and kitchen gardens and a Victorian French parterre.

Oystermouth Castle (ruins), *Swan.* 79 E5
☎ 01792 368732 www.cadw.wales.gov.uk
Although ruined, Oystermouth Castle, on its mound at the west of Swansea Bay, is well preserved. Of note are its late 13th century decorated windows, gatehouse, chapel and Great Hall.

Packwood House (NT), *Warks.* 82 A1
☎ 01564 783294 www.nationaltrust.org.uk
This 16th century house was extensively restored between the two World Wars by Graham Baron Ash and donated to the National Trust in 1941. It played host to Henry Ireton, Cromwell's general, before the Battle of Edghill in 1642, and also to Charles II after his defeat at Worcester in 1651. There is a large number of sundials and clocks adorning the walls while the impressive gardens include yew trees with a theme of the 'Sermon on the Mount' and a great deal of attractive brickwork.

Palace of Holyroodhouse, *Edin.* 60 B3
☎ 0131 556 5100 www.royal.gov.uk
Largely a 17th century building, the north-west tower was built in 1501 for James IV. Holyroodhouse is the Queen's official residence in Scotland and it is used for state ceremonies. The Great Gallery occupies the whole of the first floor of the north wing, and in it hang 89 portraits of real and legendary kings of Scotland. The state apartments reflect the changing tastes of successive monarchs and are renowned for their fine stucco ceilings. The Queen's Gallery, for which there is a separate charge, hosts a programme of changing exhibitions from the Royal Collection, focusing primarily on works from the Royal Library at Windsor Castle.

Paxton House, *Sc.Bord.* 109 E5
☎ 01289 386291 www.paxtonhouse.com
Superb 18th century Palladian mansion, designed by John and James Adam and further embellished by brother Robert, providing an interesting contrast in styles. As well as the notable interior decoration, this is essential viewing for furniture enthusiasts, with one of the greatest Chippendale collections in Scotland and fine Regency furniture by William Trotter of Edinburgh. The large art gallery, an out-station for the National Galleries for Scotland, has a programme of temporary exhibitions. The 80 acres (32ha) of parkland surrounding the house offer walks along the banks of the River Tweed and an adventure playground.

Peel Castle & Round Tower, *I.o.M.* 98 B6
☎ 01624 648000 www.gov.im
Peel Castle occupies St Patrick's Isle and includes ruins of a religious settlement from the 11th century St Patrick's Church and Round Tower. The curtain walls and gatehouse were added in the 13th century and are in a better state of preservation. An electronic guide leads the visitor through the site and a visit to the 'House of Manannan' Heritage Centre in Peel gives a useful introduction to the site and the area in general.

Pembroke Castle, *Pembs.* 78 B4
☎ 01646 681510 www.pembroke-castle.co.uk
Its defensive situation above the river in Pembroke enhances the grandeur of this largely intact castle. The birthplace of Henry VII, the first Tudor king, it has a remarkable history dating back 800

Osborne House

years. The stronghold survived ferocious attacks during the Civil War, but still much remains, including the enormous 80ft (24m) high round keep, thick ramparts, a gatehouse, barbican, Great Hall and dungeon tower.

Pencarrow, Cornw. 69 D3
☎ 01208 841369   www.pencarrow.co.uk
A grand, family-owned Georgian mansion with splendid collections of furniture, porcelain and pictures. The 50 acre (20ha) grounds comprise fine formal and woodland gardens with waymarked walks and over 700 varieties of rhododendron giving a spectacular display in spring. The woodland contains a large number of Monkey Puzzle trees – the name is said to have originated here after a guest scraped his hand on one and commented: 'It would puzzle a monkey.'

Pendennis Castle, Cornw. 68 C5
☎ 01326 316594   www.english-heritage.org.uk
This formed part of the coastal defences set up by Henry VIII in response to the threat of war from France and Spain following his divorce from Catherine of Aragon. Occupying a superb site on a headland overlooking the entrance to Carrick Roads, the castle consists of a round tower and gate surrounded by a lower curtain wall. A further outer defence was added by Elizabeth I, but the castle was only attacked during the Civil War when it was besieged by Parliamentarians for five months.

Penhow Castle, Newport 80 C5
☎ 01633 400800   www.castlewales.com
This is reputedly Wales' oldest lived-in castle, spanning 860 years. Once the home of medieval knights, it is now the ancestral home of the Seymour family. The entrance fee includes a choice of themed audio tours, such as musical, domestic history, cooks, young adventurer or, in the evening, a candlelight tour.

Penmon Priory (ruins), I.o.A. 86 C1
☎ 01248 713177   www.castlewales.com
The ruins of the 12th century priory lie at the eastern edge of Anglesey, alongside the old St Seiriol's Well, church and ancient dovecot. The rocky coastline provides views of the Puffin Island seabird colonies.

Penrhyn Castle (NT), Gwyn. 86 C2
☎ 01248 371337   www.nationaltrust.org.uk
This imposing 19th century castle outside Bangor was built in Norman style and contains remarkably luxurious furnishings, artworks and decor. The kitchen and service rooms have been restored to their 1894 state, ready prepared for a banquet for the Prince of Wales. Outbuildings house a railway museum and a doll museum. The 45 acres (18ha) of grounds include a walled garden, special plant collections and parkland overlooking the Menai Strait.

Penshurst Place, Kent 76 B3
☎ 01892 870307   www.penshurstplace.com
Built of local sandstone, this impressive castellated manor house dates from the 14th century and has been occupied by the Sidney family since 1552. The house is notable for its outstanding medieval Barons Hall built in 1341 with its 60ft (18m) high chestnut-beamed roof. The State Rooms contain a collection of paintings from the 15th to 17th centuries, furniture, tapestries and armour. The vast 10 acre (4ha) walled garden created between 1570 and 1666 is formed into a series of garden rooms divided by 1 mile of yew hedging.

Peterborough Cathedral, Peter. 91 D6
☎ 01733 343342   www.peterborough-cathedral.org.uk
This magnificent Norman cathedral dates from 1118 and has a dramatic 13th century west front with three enormous arches. The interior is equally impressive with a rare 13th century painted wooden nave ceiling and exquisite fan vaulting in the retro-choir dating from about 1500. The cathedral is the burial place of Henry VIII's first wife, Catherine of Aragon.

Petworth House (NT), W.Suss. 75 D3
☎ 01798 343929   www.nationaltrust.org.uk
Situated on the edge of a 700 acre (283ha) landscaped deer park and adjacent to the town of Petworth, this magnificent 17th century mansion was built around an older manor house owned by the Earls of Northumberland. The park, landscaped in the mid 18th century, is considered to be one of Lancelot 'Capability' Brown's finest and is home to Europe's largest herd of fallow deer.

The house contains the National Trust's largest and finest collection of pictures, the foundations of which were laid by Charles Seymour, 6th Duke of Somerset, when he acquired the house in 1690 on his marriage to the Earl of Northumberland's daughter. On the Duke's death the house passed by marriage to the Wyndham family. Charles Wyndham, the 2nd Earl of Egremont, added to the existing collection of Italian, French and Dutch Old Masters and acquired ancient sculpture from Rome and Greece. The 3rd Earl of Egremont continued the tradition. He collected contemporary British paintings. Interestingly, he was a patron of Turner, providing a studio for him at Petworth. Many of Turner's paintings can be seen in the house. The 3rd Earl also acquired work from Gainsborough and Reynolds.

Petworth House (NT)   Photo © The National Trust

Pevensey Castle, E.Suss. 76 B5
☎ 01323 762604   www.english-heritage.org.uk
Dating from Roman times, and occupied by the Normans in 1066, the castle's location as a possible invasion point led to several sieges during its history. It eventually became uninhabited by the 16th century and fell into ruin. A gun emplacement was built there at the time of the Spanish Armada and the castle was again used during World War II. Pillboxes from that time can still be seen. There are towers, battlements and dungeons to explore.

Peveril Castle, Derbys. 89 E1
☎ 01433 620613   www.english-heritage.org.uk
Built in the 11th century to guard the King's Manor, this castle, on its high vantage point, offers superb views across the Peak District of Derbyshire.

Plas Newydd (NT), Anglesey, I.o.A. 86 C2
☎ 01248 715272   www.nationaltrust.org.uk
Splendidly set on the Anglesey coast of the Menai Strait, this 18th century stately mansion, enjoying spectacular views to Snowdonia, was the former home of the Marquess of Anglesey. The house combines classical and Gothic architecture and featured inside are paintings by Rex Whistler, including his largest work. The cavalry museum in the servants' quarters commemorates the Battle of Waterloo and displays various campaign relics.

Expansive gardens offer informal walks among fine collections of flowering trees and shrubs, with many exotic plants thriving in the mild climate. In addition to the spring garden, there is a summer terrace, Australasian arboretum, a formal Italianate garden, a woodland area and an adventure play trail. The rhododendron garden, situated some way from the house, is only open from April to early June during flowering time.

Polesden Lacey (NT), *Surr.*   75 E2
☎ 01372 452048   www.nationaltrust.org.uk
Attractive Regency house in a beautiful setting on
the North Downs. It was the home for many years
of society hostess, Mrs Ronald Greville, who was a
friend of Edward VII. It contains sumptuous
interiors and is especially renowned for its
paintings. The future George VI and Queen
Elizabeth spent part of their honeymoon here in
1923. The gardens have lovely views and extend
to 30 acres (12ha), including lawns, walled garden
and herbaceous borders.

Pollok House (NTS), *Glas.*   106 C4
☎ 0141 616 6410   www.nts.org.uk
The Pollok Estate has been the home of the
Maxwell family since the 13th century and the
current house, an impressive Edwardian country
mansion, was built in 1740. Sir William Stirling
Maxwell (1818 – 1878) was an authority on the
art and history of Spain and his collection of
works by Goya and El Greco is superb. There is
also a fine collection of the work of English poet
and artist William Blake, as well as silverware and
furnishings from the Edwardian period.

Portchester Castle, *Hants.*   74 B4
☎ 023 9237 8291   www.english-heritage.org.uk
One of England's oldest fortifications, Portchester
was originally built in the 3rd century AD by the
Romans as part of a chain of fortresses known as
the Saxon Shore forts, built in response to Saxon
raids. The massive walls, 20ft (6m) high and 10ft
(3m) thick, are amongst the finest surviving
examples of this period in northern Europe.
Subsequently occupied almost continuously until
the 19th century, the site was initially a walled
settlement with an impressive Norman keep, part
of which still stands, then respectively a castle,
royal palace, military hospital and a gaol for
French prisoners during the Napoleonic Wars.

Portland Castle, *Dorset*   72 B6
☎ 01305 820539   www.english-heritage.org.uk
A well preserved example of Henry VIII's coastal
fortresses overlooking Portland Harbour. Although
not seeing action until the 17th century, when it
was seized by both Parliamentarians and
Royalists, the castle has always had a significant
role in coastal defence, being a seaplane station in
World War I and heavily involved in D-Day
preparations in World War II.

Portsmouth Cathedral, *Ports.*   74 B5
☎ 023 9282 3300   www.portsmouthcathedral.org.uk
Formerly the parish church of Portsmouth,
cathedral status was granted in 1927 when the
diocese of Portsmouth was created. The original
building dates from the 12th century, and the
transept and sanctuary still remain, combined
with a 17th century nave and tower, rebuilt
following Civil War damage. A cupola was added
in 1703 and the modern nave and aisles in the
mid 20th century.

Portsmouth Historic Dockyard, *Ports.*   74 B4
☎ 023 9272 9766   www.flagship.org.uk
The development of the dockyard at Portsmouth
was initiated by Richard I in the 1190s and
evolved over succeeding centuries. It became the
construction centre for Henry VIII's fleet and
received Royal Dockyard status in 1670 when
Charles II founded the Royal Navy. By 1800 the
navy had nearly 700 ships and the dockyard was
considered the largest industrial complex in the
world. Apart from a blip at the end of the
Napoleonic Wars, expansion was almost
continuous throughout the 19th century. In the
20th century the dockyard was vital to Britain's
successes in both World Wars, but since then has
been in decline due to defence cuts and
streamlining of the armed services.
    The historic Georgian part of the dockyard is
now open to the public and this provides a unique
opportunity to experience 500 years of the Royal
Navy's history from the remains of the 16th
century ship Mary Rose to Action Stations, which
uses interactive technology to illustrate the role of
the modern navy. In between, a visit to HMS

Victory reveals the privations suffered by sailors in
Nelson's fleet, the scrupulously restored HMS
Warrior displays a state of the art mid-19th
century warship, the Royal Naval Museum gives a
detailed history of the service from the 18th century
onwards, while Warships by Water harbour tours
give a glimpse of the modern operational fleet.

Powderham Castle, *Devon*   71 E4
☎ 01626 890243   www.powderham.co.uk
Home to the Courtenay family since 1390, the
castle lies in a beautiful setting in a 4000 acre
(1600ha) estate on the River Exe estuary. The
state rooms are richly decorated and furnished
and the marble hall is also of interest, containing
a 13ft (4.5m) long case clock. The grounds provide
a variety of activities, including woodland walks,
working blacksmith and wheelwright and
children's secret garden.

Powis Castle & Garden (NT), *Powys*   87 F5
☎ 01938 551944   www.nationaltrust.org.uk
This medieval castle was built on a prominent rock
by Welsh princes, and over the course of later
centuries was endowed with fine collections of
artwork and furniture by the Herbert and Clive
families. The castle overlooks 55 acres (22ha) of
world-famous terraced gardens designed in Italian
and French styles with sumptuous plantings,
statues, an orangery and an aviary. Rare and
tender plants are sheltered by large yew hedging;
the terrace walls and herbaceous beds exude
colour, and containers display imaginative
arrangements of plantings. In the lower gardens
can be found pyramidal apple trees, a vine tunnel
and roses. An informal area of woodland was laid
out in the 18th century on the ridge opposite the
formal gardens and specimen trees are planted on
the grassland slopes.

Powis Castle & Garden (NT)   Photo © National Trust

Preston Mill & Phantassie Dovecot (NTS), *E.Loth.*   108 C4
☎ 01620 860426   www.nts.org.uk
A picturesque 18th century grain mill that was
used commercially up until 1959. Today the mill
no longer produces grain but visitors can see and
hear the machinery and water wheel in action.
There is an exhibition on milling and the history of
the history of Preston Mill. It is a short scenic walk
to the Phantassie Dovecot which once held 500
birds.

Quarry Bank Mill & Styal Estate (NT), *Ches.*   88 C1
☎ 01625 527468   www.quarrybankmill.org.uk
Situated in 384 acres (155ha) of the beautiful
countryside of Styal Country Estate, this museum
is a fantastic place to learn about the social and
industrial history of this country. Quarry Bank Mill
is a fully preserved and working example of a
Georgian cotton mill powered by the largest
working water wheel in Europe. Cotton is still spun
and woven here and is available for sale in the
shop. Inside the mill there are hands-on displays,
demonstrations from hand spinning to large-scale
factory weaving, and an 1840s steam-powered
beam engine which is worked daily. The
Apprentice House was built in 1790 to house
pauper children who worked at the mill. The
conditions in which these children lived and
worked is now brought to life with the aid of
enthusiastic guides in period costume who engage
visitors in conversation and discussion. Visitors are

encouraged to ask questions, test the straw filled beds, touch all the objects in the house and pump water from the well in the yard. Styal village was a tiny hamlet before the mill arrived but by 1840 it was a thriving village with most of its inhabitants working at the mill. The estate land around the village and mill has some wonderful riverside and woodland walks.

Raby Castle, *Dur.*   103 D5
☎ 01833 660202   www.rabycastle.com
An impressive medieval castle set in a 200 acre (80ha) deer park, Raby was built by the Nevills' and has been home to Lord Barnard's family for over 350 years. The interior chambers provide many historical insights and range from the Barons' Hall, where 700 knights gathered to plot the 'Rising of the North', to the medieval kitchen which was used until 1954. Many of the rooms date from the 18th and 19th centuries and contain works of art and fine furniture. Visitors can also enjoy the grounds which include a large walled garden, rose garden and old yew hedges.

Raglan Castle , *Mon.*   80 C4
☎ 01291 690228   cadw.wales.gov.uk
Situated in central Monmouthshire, Raglan Castle is a fine example of a medieval fortress palace. Building commenced in 1435 and it developed more as a luxurious Tudor residence than a military base, although it was subjected to siege during the Civil War and greatly damaged by Cromwell's troops. Raglan was further ransacked after the Restoration and by the 19th century had become very much a ruin. The oldest remaining structure is known as the Yellow Tower of Gwent, named after the colour of the stone from which it was built. The tower was surrounded by more walls and a moat. Later additions included the Pitched Stone Court, the Great Gatehouse and Fountain Court, the rather grand living quarters. The Great Hall is positioned between two courtyards and dates mainly from Elizabethan times.

Ragley Hall, *Worcs.*   81 F2
☎ 01789 762090   www.ragleyhall.com
The family home of the Marquess and Marchioness of Hertford, this magnificent Palladian house was built in 1680 and stands in grounds of over 400 acres (160ha) designed by 'Capability' Brown. The Great Hall has superb baroque plasterwork by James Gibbs and included in the fine art collection is the mural 'The Temptation' by Graham Rust. The grounds include woodland walks, a maze, adventure playground and rose garden.

Rhuddlan Castle & Twt Hill , *Denb.*   87 E2
☎ 01745 590777   cadw.wales.gov.uk
Just south of Rhyl stand the stone remains of Edward I's 13th century stronghold. Today the most prominent structures are the gatehouse, walls and towers, as well as the decorative fireplaces of the drawing room. The grounds contain formal gardens, woodlands and ponds. Limited opening in summer only.

Ribchester Roman Fort & Museum, *Lancs.*   94 C5
☎ 01254 878261   www.ribchestermuseum.org
This museum is built on the site of a Roman fort occupied from AD78 and is dedicated to the history of Bremetenacum Veteranorum, the roman name for Ribchester. There are some interactive exhibits, Roman replicas like the Ribchester Parade Helmet, and collections of weaponry, jewellery, coins and pottery. The external remains of the Roman granary can also be seen by visitors.

Richborough Castle, *Kent*   77 F2
☎ 01304 612013   www.english-heritage.org.uk
Now a ruin, this fort is thought to date from the Roman invasion in AD43 and, with Watling Street starting at its east gate, became their main entry point into Britain en route to London. Today, flint walls rising to 25ft (7.5m) high can be seen and the foundations of a triumphal arch that was originally over 80ft (24m) high. There is a museum containing artefacts found on site and an exhibition on Roman life.

Richmond Castle, *N.Yorks.*   95 F1
☎ 01748 822493   www.english-heritage.org.uk
High on the cliffs above the River Swale stands the imposing Richmond Castle. Built by William the Conqueror to control the north, some of its original 11th century walls remain. The rectangular keep, rising 100ft (30m) with walls 11ft thick (3.5m), was built in the 12th century and remains almost intact. There is also an exhibition centre displaying some of the artefacts excavated from the site, where the castle's history can be explored.

Ridgeway, The *Wilts.*   82 B5
☎ 01865 810224   www.nationaltrail.co.uk/Ridgeway
This ancient trackway, formerly used by drovers, traders and occasionally invaders, has been in use for at least 5000 years. There is much evidence of prehistoric occupation in the surrounding area in the form of burial mounds and hill forts, and there is a particularly memorable stretch taking in Wayland's Smithy, Uffington Castle and the adjacent White Horse. The track runs from Overton Hill near Avebury along the north edge of the Marlborough and Berkshire Downs, crosses the Thames at Goring and continues along the west edge of the Chiltern Hills to Ivinghoe Beacon.

Rievaulx Abbey, *N.Yorks.*   96 B2
☎ 01439 798228   www.english-heritage.org.uk
Set amongst the wooded hills of Rye Dale are the majestic ruins of this once powerful Cistercian monastery. Founded in 1132, this impressive abbey was built unconventionally, being hampered by the terrain, with its central aisle laid north to south, rather than the usual east to west direction. The nave dates from 1135, whilst the towering presbytery, which is virtually intact, was rebuilt in the 13th century. Several outbuildings can also be identified, some standing to a good height. The monks' refectory is clearly evident with its wonderful arched lancet windows, along with the spectacular remains of the 13th century choir.

Rievaulx Abbey   Photo © Yorkshire Tourist Board

Ring of Brodgar, *Ork.*   122 A3
☎ 01855 841815   www.historic-scotland.gov.uk
The Ring of Brodgar (also known as the Ring of Brogar) is a magnificent circle of upright stones, dating back to the Neolithic period. A ditch encloses the stones and is spanned by entrance causeways.

Ripley Castle, *N.Yorks.*   95 F3
☎ 01423 770152   www.ripleycastle.co.uk
Home to the Ingilby family since the early 1300s, discover 700 years of political, military, religious and social history. Most of the current building dates from the 16th century, including the three-storey, fortified tower complete with a priest's secret hiding hole. On display are fine paintings, furniture, books and china, and the tower houses a collection of Royalist armour. The delightful gardens include a walled garden, which contains the National Hyacinth Collection, the kitchen garden, with rare vegetables, and the hot houses are filled with tropical plants. There is also a deer park and lakeside walks.

Rockbourne Roman Villa, *Hants.*   73 E4
☎ 01725 518541   www.hants.gov.uk/museum/rockbourne
Discovered in 1942 by a farmer digging out a ferret, this extensive villa was occupied from the 2nd century AD until the end of Roman rule in Britain in the 5th century AD. Although much of the area has been excavated, part has been backfilled for protection since the site is not under cover. However, the outlines are marked out, and mosaic floors and underfloor heating systems can be viewed.

Roman Baths & Pump Room, *B. & N.E.Som.* 54 B2
☎ 01225 477785   www.romanbaths.co.uk

One of the outstanding Roman sites in Britain, founded in the first century for pilgrims visiting the sacred hot springs of the temple to Sulis Minerva. After the Romans left, the site fell into disrepair although the town continued to grow, but by the early 17th century the springs were again attracting interest. A visit in 1702 by Queen Anne further encouraged this interest and by 1720 the town was becoming a highly fashionable spa. Further development in the 19th century led to the uncovering and preservation of the Roman site. As far back as 10,000 years ago the hot springs had generated human attention as a source of healing. The magnificent Roman complex used lead pipes to conduct the water to a series of bathing rooms which have now been excavated and can be visited, together with the temple remains, hypocausts and cold plunges, aided by an audio guide. The elegant Pump Room (free entry) was the headquarters of fashionable 18th century society and the visitor can emulate this by taking the waters, or less adventurously, morning coffee or afternoon tea.

Rosslyn Chapel, *Midloth.* 108 A4
☎ 0131 440 2159   www.rosslynchapel.org.uk

A mysterious 15th century chapel that is thought to be just part of a much larger once-planned collegiate church whose foundations have been excavated. The carvings on the exterior and inside are outstanding; there are botanically accurate plants and leaves as well as biblical, pagan and masonic symbology.

Rousham House, *Oxon.* 82 B3
☎ 01869 347110   www.rousham.org

An unspoilt 17th century house, later extended and remodelled by William Kent in the style of a Gothic Tudor mansion. However, the original staircase and some 17th century panelling still remain, together with Kent's painted parlour containing some of his furniture and painted ceiling.

The landscape garden at Rousham, started by the royal gardener Charles Bridgeman, was further developed and elaborated on by Kent. It remains almost as he left it, with many 18th century water features and temples still in existence. There is also an attractive walled garden with colourful herbaceous border, parterre and pigeon house. The house opens two days a week in summer, but the garden is open all year. No children under 15.

Royal Academy of Arts, *Gt.Lon.* 62 B2
☎ 020 7300 8000   www.royalacademy.org.uk

Founded in 1768, the Royal Academy holds major temporary public exhibitions throughout the year. Sir Joshua Reynolds – who was the first president – Gainsborough, Turner and Constable all studied and have exhibited here. Located in Burlington House, a superb early 18th century mansion, one of the few surviving in the West End, the academy is probably most famous for its inspirational annual Summer Exhibition, which displays thousands of works by living artists for view and sale. In addition to the wide range of temporary exhibitions, a suite of rooms, restored to their former 18th century grandeur, houses highlights from the permanent collection. Entry to this is free. The full collection comprises mainly British art from the last 200 years and includes at least one work by all past and present members of the academy.

Royal Air Force Museum, *Gt.Lon.* 83 F5
☎ 020 8205 2266   www.rafmuseum.org.uk

Located on the former airfield at RAF Hendon, and opened in 1972, the museum, housed in five huge buildings, contains a collection of over 100 full-sized aircraft, along with artefacts and other memorabilia. 'Milestones of Flight' covers the history of flight, from the earliest attempts to modern day supersonic jet fighters. For younger visitors the Aeronauts Gallery has plenty of interactive exhibits where they can test their piloting skills.

Royal Botanic Gardens, Kew, *Gt.Lon.* 83 F6
☎ 020 8332 5655   www.rbgkew.org.uk

This superb 300 acre (121.5ha) botanic garden was founded by Princess Augusta (mother of George III) in 1759, and in July 2003 it was afforded World Heritage Site status. Kew's reputation as the foremost botanical institution in the world was originally developed by its first two directors, Sir William Hooker (appointed in 1841) and his son Sir Joseph (who succeeded his father in 1865).

The gardens have one of the largest and most diverse collections of plant species in the world; over 60,000 species of plant are displayed in both formal and informal settings, and in the many greenhouses, which themselves cover an area of 4 acres (1.5ha). Within the grounds are the Queen's Garden, which has been laid out in 17th century style, the grass garden and the herbaceous garden. The lake, aquatic garden and ten-storey pagoda were designed by Sir William Chambers in 1760. Major features are the magnificent curved glass Palm House (built in 1848) and the Temperate House (completed in 1868), designed by Decimus Burton and Richard Turner. In more recent years the Princess of Wales Conservatory was constructed and has a variety of climatic areas, from the humid tropics through to desert conditions.

Royal Pavilion, *B. & H.* 56 C2
☎ 01273 290900   www.royalpavilion.org.uk

With its 'Hindu Style' domes and minarets, this Regency Palace is one of the most distinctive and unusual buildings in Britain. Originally a farmhouse, it was transformed for the notoriously profligate Prince Regent (later George IV). In 1787 Henry Holland was commissioned to enlarge the property; further alterations and additions were made by John Nash between 1815 and 1822 . The result was the extravagant Indian and Chinese influenced palace that we see today. The Pavilion has undergone a substantial programme to restore it to its former glory, and stands in restored Regency gardens which have been replanted to Nash's original 1820s design.

The lavish interior features impressive and unusual rooms; notably the Entrance Hall with its Chinese motif wall decorations and the 162ft (49m) Long Gallery. also with a distinctly Chinese décor. The Banqueting Room is stunning with a 45ft (14m) high painted ceiling, with the huge one ton crystal chandelier suspended from a carved dragon. In 1820, the King's Apartments were finally finished, coinciding with George IV's accession and today contain much of the original furniture.

Royal Pavilion

S.S. Great Britain, *Bristol* 81 D6
☎ 0117 926 0680   www.ssgreatbritain.org

Built in Bristol by Isambard Kingdom Brunel in 1843, this is the world's first (and only surviving) ocean-going, iron hulled steam ship driven by a screw propellor. Designed as a passenger vessel for the North Atlantic crossing, she subsequently carried 15,000 migrants to Australia, 40,000 troops to the Crimea and coal to California, but ended up abandoned in the Falkland Islands. In 1970 she was returned to Bristol, to the same dry dock where she was built.

St Albans Cathedral, *Herts.*   **83 F4**
☎ 01727 860780   www.stalbanscathedral.org.uk
The cathedral, which dates from the 11th century, has had numerous additions over the years including the opening of a new Chapter House in 1982. It has a long low appearance, extending 550 ft (168m) east to west with a squat sturdy looking tower. The Norman part of the building was begun in 1077 using Roman bricks and tiles salvaged from the ruins of the nearby Roman town of Verulamium. These can be seen today in the walls of the tower. The cathedral is well known as a site of national pilgrimage as it contains the shrine of St Alban, the first Christian martyr, who was executed on this site in AD209. Also to be seen are medieval wall paintings and decorated ceilings.

St Andrews Cathedral, *Fife*   **108 C2**
☎ 01334 472563   www.historic-scotland.gov.uk
The remains of one of the largest cathedrals in Scotland and the associated domestic ranges of the priory. The museum houses an outstanding collection of early Christian and medieval monuments, and other objets trouvés. St Rules Tower, in the precinct, is part of the first church of the Augustinian canons at St Andrews, built early in the 12th century. A climb up 150 steps is rewarded with fabulous views at the top.

St David's Cathedral & Bishop's Palace, *Pembs.*   **78 A3**
☎ 01437 720517   stdavidscathedral.org.uk
Situated in the heart of the charming, small city of St David's, the Cathedral has been a dominant presence since the 12th century. It was built in Norman transitional style and has undergone many transformations under successive bishops. The nearby ruins of the Bishop's Palace date from the 14th century. Many notable features adorn the cathedral, and the surrounding gardens are an additional attraction.

St Fagans: National History Museum, *Cardiff*   **80 B6**
☎ 029 2057 3500   www.nmgw.ac.uk
A fascinating open-air museum covering 100 acres (40ha) near Cardiff illustrates the rich heritage of Wales, showing lifestyles, buildings and traditions through five hundred years of folk history. Original buildings have been transported here from many parts of Wales and painstakingly reconstructed, including craftsmen's workshops, a school, cottages, shops, a mill, farmhouse and a chapel. The museum is situated in the grounds of the impressive St Fagans castle which is also open, as are the surrounding gardens. Purpose-built, large indoor galleries house exhibits of costume, daily life and farming implements. Traditional festivals, music and dance events are staged regularly throughout the year.

St George's Guildhall (NT), *Norf.*   **91 F4**
☎ 01553 765565   www.nationaltrust.org.uk
Constructed between 1410 and 1420, this is the largest surviving English medieval guildhall. The impressive Great Hall, situated on the upper floor, with its impressive open timber roof, is 101ft by 29ft (30m x 8m). Other 15th century features which survive intact are the five large buttresses supporting the north wall.

St Giles Cathedral, *Edin.*   **60 B2**
☎ 0131 225 9442   www.stgiles.net
Not strictly a cathedral, as it was only the seat of a bishop on two brief occasions in the 17th century, but the historical title seems to have stuck. The basic structure of the church is late 15th century, although parts of the early 12th century Norman chapel still remain. The cathedral is renowned for its Victorian and 20th century stained glass, Reiger organ and beautiful Thistle Chapel.

St Kilda, *W.Isles*   **124 B2**
☎ 01463 232 034   www.kilda.org.uk
Owned by the National Trust for Scotland and designated a World Heritage Site, St Kilda is a collection of four small islands, Hirta, Soay, Boreray and Dun, 64 km (40 miles) west of the Outer Hebrides. The rugged cliffs and sea stacks are the most important breeding site for seabirds in north-west Europe. The final 36 inhabitants were evacuated to the mainland in 1930.

St Magnus Cathedral, *Ork.*   **122 B3**
☎ 01856 874894
The cathedral was founded by Jarl Rognvald and dedicated to his uncle, St Magnus. The remains of both men are in the massive east choir piers. The original building dates from 1137 – 1200, but sporadic additional work went on until the late 14th century. A charge applies to tour the tower and upper areas, and should be booked in advance.

St Margaret's Church, *Gt.Lon.*   **63 B3**
☎ 020 7654 4847   www.westminster-abbey.org/stmargarets
Located between Westminster Abbey and the Houses of Parliament, and commonly called 'the parish church of the House of Commons' even though it is not officially a parish church. The portcullis symbol of the House of Commons can be seen throughout the church and there has been a place reserved for the Speaker of the Commons since 1681. The church was designated in 1987 as a World Heritage Site along with Westminster Palace and the Houses of Parliament.

St Martin-in-the-Fields Church, *Gt.Lon.*   **63 B3**
☎ 020 7766 1100   www.stmartin-in-the-fields.org
Overlooking Trafalgar Square, this church was designed by James Gibbs and was consecrated in 1726. With its attractive spire and portico, its design has been much copied throughout the world, especially in the United States. Among the notable events to have taken place on this site are the christening of Charles II in 1630 and the burials of Nell Gwynne, William Hogarth, Sir Joshua Reynolds and Thomas Chippendale.

St Martin-in-the-Fields   Photo © London
Church   Tourist Board

St Mawes Castle, *Cornw.*   **68 C5**
☎ 01326 270526   www.english-heritage.org.uk
Located on a headland on the east side of the Carrick Roads, this castle was built to defend against a possible French and Spanish invasion following Henry VIII's divorce from Catherine of Aragon and is an excellent example of Tudor military architecture. Captured by Parliamentarians in 1646, with far less trouble than its neighbour Pendennis, it was not re-fortified until the early 20th century, when it formed part of the coastal defences for World Wars I and II.

St Michael's Mount (NT), *Cornw.*   **68 B5**
☎ 01736 710507   www.stmichaelsmount.co.uk
Dramatic granite island accessible on foot via a causeway at low tide and by ferry at other times. Although generally accepted as a place of spiritual significance, the original settlement on the island may have been a late Iron Age port. The 5th century saw the start of the mount's importance as a place of pilgrimage, when legend has it that a group of fishermen had a vision of St Michael. A Benedictine monastery was founded on the summit in 1135, and following the Dissolution of the Monasteries by Henry VIII the ruins of the building were incorporated into a castle.

St Paul's Cathedral, *Gt.Lon.* 63 A3
☎ 020 7236 4128   www.stpauls.co.uk

Designed by Sir Christopher Wren, the current St Paul's rises to a height of 365ft (111m) and is the fifth cathedral to stand on the site. It was built between 1675 and 1710, the previous cathedral having been destroyed the Great Fire of London. Its design was revolutionary and Wren encountered opposition from the Dean and Chapter who wanted a more traditional church. Fortunately, Wren's vision and determination won through, resulting in the masterpiece of design and engineering that we see today; the magnificent dome providing one of the best known London landmarks.

After St Peter's in Rome, St Paul's dome is the second largest in the world and has three viewing galleries. The Whispering Gallery runs around the interior and has unusual acoustics – a whisper against its walls is audible on the opposite side. Encircling the outside at 173ft (53.5m) is the Stone Gallery, and at 280ft (85.5m) is the Golden Gallery which runs around the highest point of the dome, from which the views across the city are superb. To reach her, visitors need to climb 530 steps.

The enormous scale and grandeur of the interior is breathtaking, with massive arches and lofty ceilings. The decoration is extravagant, richly gilded throughout and with brightly coloured mosaics in the Quire, which were originally planned by Wren, but not installed until 1891 – 1904. The interior also features carving by Grinling Gibbons, decorative metal work by Jean Tijou, sculpture by Henry Moore and the magnificent organ, which has been played by both Handel and Mendelssohn. Among the cathedral's 300 memorials is one to the Duke of Wellington whose body lies in the crypt, alongside the tombs of Admiral Nelson and Sir Christopher Wren.

St Paul's Cathedral

Salisbury Cathedral, *Wilts.* 73 E3
☎ 01722 555120   www.salisburycathedral.org.uk

At Salisbury, one of the world's most celebrated spires soars above an Early English masterpiece of a cathedral, the whole comprising a singularly beautiful medieval building which inspired the famous painting by John Constable. Raised between 1220 – 1258, and with the spire added between 1285 – 1315, this comparatively rapid construction led to a remarkable conformity of style, characterised by slender Purbeck marble pillars, narrow pointed arches and high vaulting.

The exceptional spire, at 404ft (123m) the tallest in Britain, rests on foundations only 6ft (2m) deep. Guided tours take visitors 332 steps up the tower to the base of the spire and give splendid views over the city. The cathedral is set in a delightful, large Close which itself contains some memorable buildings, many dating from the 18th century.

Saltaire, *W.Yorks.* 95 F5
☎ 01274 433 678   www.saltaire.yorks.com

A village located in the Heart of Brontë country and designated a World Heritage Site in 2001. Its layout is virtually unchanged since it was built in the 19th century by Sir Titus Salt as accommodation for the workers at his woollen mills. The buildings are now in everyday usage as shops, restaurants and pubs. The Salt Mill is now the 1853 Gallery exhibiting the work of local artist David Hockney.

Saltram House (NT), *Plym.* 70 C6
☎ 01752 333500   www.nationaltrust.org.uk

A former Tudor house redeveloped as a splendid Georgian mansion set in a landscaped park overlooking the Plym estuary. Many of the original contents remain and there are significant pieces by Chippendale and Wedgwood as well as several portraits by Sir Joshua Reynolds, who lived locally. There is also an interesting period kitchen, formal gardens and woodland walks.

Sandringham House   Photo © H.M. The Queen

Sandringham House, *Norf.* 91 F4
☎ 01553 612908   www.sandringhamestate.co.uk

The current house dates from 1870 and was built for the Prince of Wales (later Edward VII) in Neo-Elizabethan style from red brick with pale stone dressings. It has been passed down through the generations as a private royal residence and is used by the present Queen as her country retreat. The main ground floor rooms, which are still used regularly by the royal family, can be seen. Many objects collected by Queen Alexandra and Queen Mary are on show, and in the Ballroom there is an exhibition of the Duke of Edinburgh's collection of wildlife over the years. Outside in the coach and stable block there is a museum displaying many family possessions as well as some of the gifts given to the royal family over the years.

The house sits in beautiful 60 acre (24ha) gardens with lakes, glades and an abundance of trees. The acid soil allows the growth of stunning rhododendrons and azaleas, making it particularly attractive in the spring. There is also a 600 acre (243ha) country park, which is free, and which has some lovely woodland and heath areas with nature trails and a visitor centre.

Scarborough Castle, *N.Yorks.* 97 D2
☎ 01723 372451   www.english-heritage.org.uk

Towering above the town and harbour, Scarborough Castle stands on a headland 300ft (91m) above sea level. The castle was built in the 12th century and has endured numerous Civil War sieges and bombardment during World War I. The site also provides evidence of earlier Iron Age settlements and remains of a Roman signal station.

Science Museum, *Gt.Lon.* 83 F6
☎ 0870 870 4868   www.sciencemuseum.org.uk

Opened in 1857, on land purchased with the profits from the Great Exhibition of 1851, the museum comprises over 40 galleries spread over seven floors. The huge collection, with over 10,000 items on show, focuses on science and scientific advances over the last 300 years, not only from Britain but also from around the world. The exhibits range from steam power, where visitors can see Stephenson's Rocket, to space exploration with the surprisingly small Apollo 10 command module on display. There are a diverse range of galleries, with topics spanning computing, printing, nuclear power, flight, marine engineering and food, seen in a social as well as purely scientific light. The Wellcome Wing concentrates on contemporary science, medicine and technology and has an IMAX 3D cinema (for which there is a charge). Throughout the museum there are a vast number of interactive and hands-on displays, which really help to illustrate scientific principles, not only for the children, but for the adults too.

Scone Palace, *P. & K.* 108 A1

☎ 01738 552300   www.scone-palace.co.uk

A castellated palace, enlarged and embellished in 1803, incorporating the 16th century and earlier palaces. Notable for its grounds and pinetum, and its magnificent collection of porcelain, furniture, ivories, 18th century clocks and 16th century needlework. From the 9th century, Moot Hill at Scone was the site of the famous Coronation Stone of Scone (the Stone of Destiny), and crowning place of Scottish Kings. In 1296 the English seized the Stone and took it to Westminster Abbey. Returned to Scotland's Edinburgh Castle in 1997, a replica now stands on Moot Hill.

Scottish Maritime Museum, *N.Ayr.* 106 B6

☎ 01294 278283   www.scottishmaritimemuseum.org

An informative museum on the harbourside at Irvine, with sailing and working boats, lifeboats and a collection of documents, photographs and artefacts interpreting Scotland's maritime history.

Indoor exhibits are based in the huge Linthouse Engine Shop which was dismantled and relocated from the Linthouse Shipyard in Govan in 1992. Nearby is a restored tenement flat, typical home to a 1920s shipyard worker. The floating exhibits are moored by the quay.

Seaton Delaval Hall, *Northumb.* 103 E3

☎ 0191 237 1493   www.seatondelaval.org.uk

A splendid Palladian mansion designed by Sir John Vanbrugh in 1718, after he had already completed Blenheim Palace and Castle Howard. The central turreted block has a grand portico and is flanked by two substantial wings which creates a vast forecourt. A fine parterre, pond and fountain created in the 20th century complements the house and there are impressive stables in the east wing. Limited opening.

Segontium Roman Museum, *Gwyn.* 86 B2

☎ 01286 675625   www.segontium.org.uk

The museum depicts the significant Roman occupation of the area, dating back to AD77. Excavated finds from the nearby Roman fort are displayed, plus records of this remote Roman regiment.

Seton Collegiate Church, *E.Loth.* 108 B4

☎ 01875 813334   www.historic-scotland.org.uk

The chancel and apse of a lovely 15th century church with a transept and steeple added in 1513. Much of the church is in good condition and is full of interesting detail. The grounds of the church have the remains of a number of buildings thought to be priests' houses and there is a display of stonework from Seton Palace, destroyed in 1715.

Sewerby Hall & Gardens, *E.Riding* 97 E3

☎ 01262 673769   www.sewerby-hall.co.uk

Sewerby Hall is set in 50 acres (20ha) of parkland with fabulous coastal views over Bridlington Bay. This stylish Georgian house contains the East Yorkshire Museum featuring local history, archaeology, photography, and contemporary arts and crafts. One of the rooms is dedicated to the record-breaking aviator, Amy Johnson, displaying her souvenirs and mementoes. The gardens offer woodland walks, a delightful Old English Garden, pleasure gardens, children's zoo, adventure playground, 19th century Orangery, pitch and putt golf and putting green.

Shakespeare's Birthplace, *Warks.* 65 A2

☎ 01789 204016   www.shakespeare.org.uk

A half-timbered house bought by the Bard's father, John Shakespeare, in the mid 16th century, a few years before Shakespeare's birth in 1564, and which remained in the family until 1806. 16th and 17th century furniture adorn the interior and, of particular interest, are the signatures of famous visitors engraved into a window in the Birth Room. The visitor centre has a multitude of original exhibits and displays, and there is a lovely traditional English garden.

Shakespeare's Globe Theatre, *Gt.Lon.* 63

☎ 020 7902 1400   www.shakespeares-globe.org

The current Globe Theatre, officially opened in 1997, is a careful reconstruction of the original, which was built nearby in 1599, and for which Shakespeare wrote some of his greatest plays. The reconstruction was the dream of American actor-director Sam Wanamaker who, sadly, never lived to see its completion. In its construction, techniques and materials as close to the original as possible have been used. It is open to the elements in the centre and has a thatched roof; as a consequence, when it rains, the 'groundlings' (the audience standing in front of the stage) get wet, just as they did in Shakespeare's day. During performances, which take place between May and September, the whole atmosphere is designed to be just as it was 500 years ago; there is no hi-tech lighting or wizardry and the crowd is encouraged to participate by shouting, cheering and jeering.

In a space beneath the theatre is the UnderGlobe where there is an exhibition of Shakespeare's life and times, with displays on the original as well as the current Globe. The exhibition includes a range of live demonstrations and interactive displays. There are also interesting tours of the whole site when there are no plays in progress.

Sherborne Castle, *Dorset* 72 B4

☎ 01935 813182   www.sherbornecastle.com

A splendid Tudor mansion built by Sir Walter Raleigh in 1594 and subsequently extended in the 17th and 18th centuries by the Digby family who have owned it since 1617. The state rooms show a range of decorative styles from the 16th to 19th centuries and there are excellent collections of furniture and fine arts.

The grounds are considered to be amongst the finest to be created by Lancelot 'Capability' Brown, with a 50 acre (20ha) lake and magnificent specimen trees. The 20 acre (8ha) garden has delightful drifts of spring bulbs, colourful summer borders and striking autumn colour. Within the grounds are the remnants of a Norman castle destroyed in the Civil War.

Shibden Hall, *W.Yorks.* 95 F5

☎ 01422 352246   www.calderdale.gov.uk

Shibden Hall is an impressive, half-timbered manor house, dating back to 1420. Different rooms portray varying styles of architecture and furnishings associated with a particular era. Explore the 15th century kitchen, the 17th century dining room or the 16th century housebody. Its 17th century barn houses a folk museum with a notable collection of horse-drawn vehicles, while its reconstructed workshops display 19th century craft tools. The surrounding 90 acres (36ha) of parkland provide woodland walks, miniature railway, boating lake and play area.

Shugborough Estate (NT), *Staffs.* 89 D4

☎ 01889 881 388   www.shugborough.org.uk

This Georgian mansion is the ancestral home of Lord Lichfield and has exhibitions of period silver, furniture, paintings and china. Amongst the many events throughout the summer are craft, weaving and gardening weekends and also a fully working watermill where milling demonstrations take place and even the chance to wash and oil a pig! The 900 acres (360ha) of gardens and parkland include a yew tree which is thought to be the widest tree in the country.

Silbury Hill, *Wilts.* 81 F6

☎ 01672 539425   www.english-heritage.org.uk

Constructed around 2500BC, probably using some of the chalk rubble excavated from Avebury, this is thought to be the highest man-made mound in Europe at 130ft (40m). It is estimated that it would have taken 1000 men 10 years to build. No archaeological excavations have ever discovered anything of significance in the mound and its purpose has never been satisfactorily explained. Unfortunately, continuous wear and tear by people climbing the mound has meant that access is now prohibited.

Sizergh Castle & Gardens (NT), *Cumb.* 94 B2
☎ 015395 60951 www.nationaltrust.org.uk
Originally built in the 14th century by the Strickland family, who still live here, the massive fortified tower developed into a manor house with the addition of a Great Hall in the 15th century and two long wings during the Elizabethan period. There are some remarkable oak-panelled rooms, most notably the bedroom known as the Inlaid Chamber, and fine Elizabethan carved wooden chimneypieces. The house contents include period oak furniture, family portraits, china and Jacobite relics. Sizergh has an impressive limestone rock garden with a large collection of hardy ferns, a Dutch garden with flowering cherries and a rose garden underplanted with bulbs. Specimen trees and shrubs provide wonderful autumn colour. Extensive walks with views of the Lakeland fells and Morecambe Bay are to be enjoyed in the 1600 acre (638ha) estate.

Skara Brae, *Ork.* 122 A3
☎ 01856 841815 www.historic-scotland.gov.uk
This site contains the best preserved group of Stone Age houses in Western Europe. A storm in 1850 lifted the sand covering the area to reveal the remains of this former fishing village. Ten one-roomed houses can be found, joined by covered passages, and contain their original stone furniture, hearths and drains. They provide a remarkable illustration of life in Neolithic times. There is also a full-scale replica of a complete house.

Skipton Castle, *N.Yorks.* 95 E4
☎ 01756 792442 www.skiptoncastle.co.uk
A wonderfully preserved, fully roofed, medieval castle, having survived a three-year siege during the Civil War. Inspect the banqueting hall, the kitchen, bedchamber and privy, climb to the top of the Watch Tower and back down to the dungeons below. Furthermore, unwind in the Chapel Terrace overlooking the town and surrounding woodland, or in the cobbled Tudor courtyard complete with a yew tree planted in the 17th century.

Snowshill Manor (NT), *Glos.* 81 F3
☎ 01386 852410 www.nationaltrust.org.uk
In 1919 Charles Wade bought the ruined manor with its 14 acres (5.5ha) of land which he set about restoring using traditional skills. The renovated manor was used as a storage area for the enormous variety of artefacts collected from all over the world. Wade actually lived in the small cottage in the grounds. The tranquil organic gardens give lovely views across the surrounding Cotswold countryside.

Southend Pier, *S'end* 84 C5
☎ 01702 215620 www.southendpier.co.uk
The present iron pier first opened in 1889 and was extended to its current length in 1929. At 2360 yards (2158m) it is the longest pleasure pier in the world. A train service runs the length of the pier. At the shore end is a museum (admission charge) with exhibits giving an insight into the pier's history. At the pier head sea fishing is popular; there are also pleasure boat trips, a lifeboat station and information centre to visit.

Southsea Castle & Museum, *Hants.* 74 B5
☎ 023 9282 7261 www.southseacastle.co.uk
Built in 1544 as part of Henry VIII's coastal defences, and said to have been designed by the king himself. Its initial purpose was to protect the large fleet of warships based in Portsmouth Harbour, including the flagship Mary Rose which sank in front of the castle in 1545. The building remained an active military base until 1960. During the preceding 400 years it was captured by Parliamentarians in 1642, suffered major damage from an explosion in 1759, was renovated and enlarged in the early 19th century and used as a military prison in Victorian times.

Stafford Castle, *Staffs.* 89 D4
☎ 01785 257698
There is plenty to see and do at this 900 year old castle originally built by William the Conqueror but largely destroyed during the Civil War. The visitor centre has displays of finds made in archaeological excavations. Historical re-enactments and Shakespeare theatrical productions are a feature of the summer months, for which there is an admission charge. There is also a herb garden which was originally planted for medicinal purposes.

Standen (NT), *W.Suss.* 75 F3
☎ 01342 323029 www.nationaltrust.org.uk
Built between 1892 and 1894, the house was designed by Philip Webb, a lifelong friend and colleague of William Morris, and is a fine showpiece of the arts and crafts movement. It contains furniture, tapestries and paintings of the period, along with Morris textiles and wallpapers. There are lovely views from the beautiful 10 acre (4ha) hillside garden.

Stanford Hall, *Leics.* 82 C1
☎ 01788 860870 www.stanfordhall.co.uk
Lovely 17th century house in grounds alongside the River Avon. Beautifully furnished with a fine collection of Tudor and Stuart paintings and a magnificent library. The former stables house a motorcycle museum with racing and vintage machines, and there is a full scale replica of the early 'Hawk' flying machine. The grounds include a rose garden, nature trail and, of course, tearooms.

Stembridge Tower Mill (NT), *Som.* 72 A3
☎ 01935 823289 www.nationaltrust.org.uk
Located in a prominent position overlooking the Somerset Levels, this is the last remaining thatched windmill in England. It was built in 1822 and remained in operation until 1910.

Stirling Castle, *Stir.* 107 D3
☎ 01786 450000 www.historic-scotland.gov.uk
Considered by many as Scotland's grandest castle, it is certainly one of the most important. Most of the building dates from the 15th and 16th centuries, when it became a popular Royal residence. The castle architecture is outstanding. The Great Hall and the Gatehouse, built by James IV, the magnificent Renaissance palace, built by James V, and the Chapel Royal, rebuilt by James VI, are amongst the key highlights. Mary, Queen of Scots was crowned here in 1543 and narrowly escaped death by fire in 1561. Stirling Castle is set high on a volcanic outcrop, and commands stunning views, including the battlefields of Stirling Bridge and Bannockburn, Ben Lomond and the Trossachs.

Stirling Castle Photo © Argyll, the Isles, Loch Lomond & Trossachs Tourist Board

Stoke Bruerne Waterways Museum, *Northants.* 83 D2
☎ 01604 862229 www.thewaterwaystrust.org.uk
A former cornmill in the lovely village of Stoke Bruerne was chosen to house this fascinating museum, which recalls 200 years of the inland waterways. The busy Grand Union Canal is immediately outside, with boat trips available along it. Refreshments can be found in the village.

Stoke sub Hamdon Priory (NT), *Som.* 72 A4
☎ 01935 823289 www.nationaltrust.org.uk
A group of buildings, the remains of a chantry built for a provost and four chaplains in the 14th century by the Beauchamp family. The complex consists of a Great Hall, the only part open to the public, private rooms and a range of outbuildings.

Stonehenge   Photo © RAC

Stokesay Castle, *Shrop.*   **88 A6**
☎ 01588 672544   www.english-heritage.org.uk
This 13th century fortified manor house, now in
the care of English Heritage, is one of England's
finest and is set in beautiful countryside amongst
the Shropshire Hills, not far from the Welsh border.
Many parts of the castle are original, including the
Great Hall in which the roof timbers are soot
blackened from the open hearth. The solar chamber
has a magnificent Jacobean fireplace and the
delightful 17th century gatehouse is probably
more ornamental than strategic.

Stonehenge, *Wilts.*   **73 E2**
☎ 0870 333 1181   www.stonehenge.co.uk
An awe-inspiring prehistoric monument
constructed in stages between about 5000 and
3000 years ago, now designated a World Heritage
Site. The original purpose is uncertain, but
suggestions include an astronomical observatory,
temple or other sacred site. Stonehenge was
originally a simple bank and ditch excavated by
tools made of antler, wood and bone. Some
centuries later an inner stone circle was added,
though not completed, using bluestones from the
Prescelly Mountains in Pembrokeshire. The final,
and major building phase around 1500BC brought
massive sarsen stones of up to 50 tons (56 tonnes)
from the Marlborough Downs 20 miles (32km)
away. These were erected and capped by stone
lintels to make a continuous outer ring. The central
axis aligns with the point of sunrise on Midsummer
Day, giving credence, without supporting evidence,
to the idea of Stonehenge as an astronomical
calendar. Visitors cannot walk among the stones,
but the site is very atmospheric and views of the
stones, particularly near dawn or dusk, are
breathtaking.

Stones of Stenness, *Ork.*   **122 A3**
☎ 01856 850716   www.orkneyjar.com
A World Heritage Site dating from around
3100BC, the stones stand 6m (19ft) high and 44
metres (144ft) in diameter and are visible for
miles around. They were damaged in 1814 when
a farmer decided to try to remove them in order to
make ploughing easier. Fortunately he was
stopped by the native Orcadians but not before
two stones had been damaged.

Stonor Park, *Oxon.*   **83 D5**
☎ 01491 638587
The red brick Tudor façade disguises a building
dating originally from the 12th century and
extended in the 14th century, set in a lovely
wooded valley on the slopes of the Chilterns. The
attractive hillside gardens have displays of
daffodils, narcissi, irises and roses, and there are
good views over the surrounding deer park.

Stourhead (NT), *Wilts.*   **72 C3**
☎ 01747 841152   www.nationaltrust.org.uk
Unlike most estates, where the house takes pride
of place, here the 2600 acres (1052ha) of grounds
are by far the superior draw, providing an
exceptional example of the English landscape
garden. The house, built in 1721 by Colen Campbell
for the banker Henry Hoare, is an elegant example
of Palladian architecture and contains some good
early Chippendale furniture and choice paintings.
Henry Hoare's son, also Henry, designed the
garden after returning from a Grand Tour in 1741.
The centrepiece, a magnificent lake, was formed
by damming the River Stour. King Alfred's Tower,
the 150ft (46m) red brick folly at the far end of
the estate, provides magnificent views across the
grounds and surrounding countryside (open
summer afternoons only).

Stowe School, *Bucks.*   **82 C3**
☎ Garden: 01280 822850;   www.nationaltrust.org.uk;
☎ House: 01280 818166   www.stowe.co.uk
One of the finest Georgian landscape gardens (NT)
in the country, covering 350 acres (140ha) of
parkland, valleys, views, lakes and rivers. There
are over 30 temples dotted around the grounds,
designed by well-known architects of the day
such as William Kent and Sir John Vanbrugh, and
many of these have been restored. The Temple
family, who owned Stowe at this time, were
fortunate to have the successive services of three
of the great landscape gardeners of the time,
Charles Bridgeman, William Kent and Lancelot
'Capability' Brown. The magnificent house at the
centre of the park is now a public school, with
access limited mainly to school holidays, but the
park is open on a more regular basis.

Strata Florida Abbey, *Cere.*   **79 F1**
☎ 01974 831261   cadw.wales.gov.uk
Cistercian monks built the abbey in the 12th
century on the banks of the river Teifi in mid
Wales, but only the ruined church and cloister
survive from this once-important centre of
learning.

Sudbury Hall, *Derbys.*   **89 E4**
☎ 01283 585337   www.nationaltrust.org.uk
Richly decorated late 17th century house with a
very elaborate Great Staircase. Interesting
mythological decorative paintings, Grinling Gibbons
woodcarvings and magnificent plasterwork.

Sudeley Castle, *Glos.*   **81 F3**
☎ 01242 602308   www.sudeleycastle.co.uk
Once owned by Ethelred the Unready, and more
famously home to Katherine Parr, the sixth wife of
Henry VIII, Sudeley was a victim of Cromwell's
destruction and lay derelict for over 200 years
until an ambitious restoration project was started
in 1837. Ten distinct gardens covering 14 acres
(5.5ha) surround the castle and feature a ruined
15th century Tithe Barn. The tomb of Katherine
Parr lies in the 15th century St Mary's Church.

Sulgrave Manor, *Northants.*   **82 C2**
☎ 01295 760205   www.sulgravemanor.org.uk
Beautiful Tudor House where George Washington's
ancestors lived. Guided tours around the furnished
rooms, gardens and George Washington Exhibition.

Summerlee Heritage Park, *N.Lan.*   **107 D4**
☎ 01236 431261   www.northlan.gov.uk
Summerlee Heritage Park preserves and interprets
the history of the steel and engineering industries
that were once dominant in the surrounding area.
Spread over 25 acres (10ha), there is plenty to see
including a reconstructed Miners Row where the
living conditions of the miners from the 1840s to
the 1960s can be experienced, and a re-created
mine where their working conditions can be
examined. There is a large scale model of the
Ironworks as it was in 1880, lots of working
machinery and visitors can, for a small charge,
ride Scotland's only electric tramway.

Sweetheart Abbey, *D. & G.*   **101 D3**
☎ 01387 850397   www.historic-scotland.gov.uk
Splendid late 13th/early 14th century ruin founded
by Devorgilla, Lady of Galloway, in memory of her
husband John Balliol, and named because she
was buried with her husband's embalmed heart
which she carried with her in a casket after his
death. The 30 acre (12ha) site is dominated by
the shell of the abbey church with its substantial
central tower and lofty arched nave, but the most
interesting feature is the great precinct wall.

Syon House, Gt.Lon. 83 F6

☎ 020 8560 0882 www.syonpark.co.uk

This 16th century house, standing in 40 acre (16ha) grounds landscaped by Lancelot 'Capability' Brown, has been home to the Dukes of Northumberland since 1594. Catherine Howard, Henry VIII's fifth wife, was imprisoned here before her execution in 1542 and Lady Jane Grey began her 9-day reign here after Edward VI's death. Robert Adam made many alterations from 1762 – 1769, creating imaginative and elegant interiors – the variety of each room is exceptional.

Tabley House, Ches. 88 C2

☎ 01565 750151 www.tableyhouse.co.uk

This is the only 18th century Palladian house in the north-west. The son of the original owner was the first patron of British art and built up quite a collection of paintings, including works by Turner and Reynolds, many of which are still on display in the locations they were originally intended for. The house is also home to a collection of fine furniture, including pieces by Gillow and Chippendale.

Tamworth Castle, Staffs. 89 E5

☎ 01827 709629 www.tamworthcastle.freeserve.co.uk

A Norman motte and bailey castle dating from the 11th century, with numerous additions since then including the medieval Banqueting Hall. 15 rooms are open to the public with displays from throughout the castle's history. There are many events including ghost vigils and tours in search of the many ghosts allegedly seen in the castle. There are also frequent Shakespearian plays. Beneath the castle are the pleasure grounds with floral terraces, play areas, tennis courts, crazy golf and a café.

Tantallon Castle, E.Loth. 108 C3

☎ 01620 892272 www.historic-scotland.org.uk

This formidable castle has a majestic setting on cliffs overlooking the Firth of Forth and Bass Rock. A stronghold of the Douglas family, it was built at the end of the 14th century but after a number of sieges it was finally destroyed by Cromwell in 1651. The massive 50ft (15m) high curtain wall is all that remains intact.

Tate Britain, Gt.Lon. 63 B3

☎ 020 7887 8888 www.tate.org.uk/britain

Overlooking the River Thames, the gallery dates from 1897 and was built on the site of the Millbank Penitentiary, a former prison, to house the collection of 19th century art given to the nation by the sugar magnate, Sir Henry Tate. The permanent collection has grown enormously over the years, and today the gallery holds the largest collection of British art in the world, with works dating from 1500 to the present day. Visitors can see work by artists such as Gainsborough, Stubbs, Blake, Constable, Bacon, Hirst, Hockney and Hepworth. The adjoining Clore Gallery houses the Turner bequest, comprising thousands of paintings and studies, left to the nation by Turner on condition that they remained together.

Tattershall Castle (NT), Lincs. 91 D3

☎ 01526 342543 www.nationaltrust.org.uk

Imposing and impressive 15th century tower, one of the first to be built of red brick. Fortified and moated, it was restored in the early 1900s and has four storeys of huge rooms with massive Gothic fireplaces, stained glass windows and brick vaulting.

Tatton Park (NT), Ches. 88 C1

☎ 01625 534400 www.tattonpark.org.uk

This is one of the most complete historic estates open to visitors, and there is plenty here to occupy a whole day. There are two historic houses, 1000 acres (400ha) of parkland containing some magnificent gardens, and a working farm. The opulent mansion was built at the end of the 18th century and gives a wonderful glimpse into how the original owners, the Egerton family, lived. The second house is the Tudor Old Hall – downstairs paints a realistic picture of medieval life, whilst upstairs the rooms are styled as they would have been in the early 1600s. The final room of the tour

is a re-creation of an estate worker's cottage from 1958. The gardens, perhaps the best feature of the estate, are extensive and incorporate many different styles. There is a walled garden, a beech maze, a fernery, an Italianate garden and one of the finest examples of a Japanese garden in Europe. Home Farm is always popular with children, especially when the piglets are just being born, and the adjacent fields have sheep, cattle and chickens. The farm works as it did during the 1930s, with vintage farm implements and rare breeds of animal.

Tatton Park (NT) Photo © Joe Wainwright, Cheshire County Council

Temple Newsam, W.Yorks. 96 A5

☎ 0113 264 5535 www.leeds.gov.uk/templenewsam

Displayed within their original room settings in this wonderful Tudor-Jacobean mansion are extensive collections of fine paintings, furniture, silver, porcelain and Leeds pottery. Amongst the furniture collection are some excellent Chippendale masterpieces. The surrounding parkland, and gardens designed by Lancelot 'Capability' Brown, extend 2 sq miles (518ha) and incorporate a woodland garden, an Italian garden and a walled garden. Additionally, there is a Rare Breeds Centre, with over 400 animals.

Thirlestane Castle, Sc.Bord. 108 C5

☎ 01578 722430 www.thirlestanecastle.co.uk

Originally a 14th century fortress converted to a home by William Maitland, Secretary of State to Mary, Queen of Scots. Further restyling in the 17th century by Sir William Bruce created state rooms with arguably some of the finest plasterwork ceilings in Britain. Paintings include works by Gainsborough, Romney and Hopper, whilst the nursery wing contains a large collection of historic toys. The Border Country Life Museum is located here and there are woodland walks and an adventure playground in the grounds.

Threave Castle, D. & G. 100 C3

☎ 07711 223101 www.historic-scotland.gov.uk

Set on an island in the River Dee, access is by ferry following a 0.5 mile (1km) walk across fields. Though probably settled here as far back as AD500, the present structure, a massive 5-storey keep, was built by Archibald the Grim in the 1370s. The castle had a turbulent history as home of the 'Black' Douglas clan, and was extended in the 15th century with substantial artillery fortification during a significant disagreement with James II. Besieged by the Covenanters, it was slighted and abandoned in 1640, but briefly used to house Napoleonic prisoners of war.

Tilbury Fort, Thur. 84 B6

☎ 01375 858489 www.english-heritage.org.uk

Situated in a strategic position on the north bank of the River Thames, this late 17th century fort was designed to withstand heavy artillery fire; low lying, with double moats and brick-fronted earth embankments. There are exhibitions showing how the fort protected London from seaborne attack. Nearby, Elizabeth I gave a speech rallying her forces on the eve of their battle against the Spanish Armada.

Tintagel Castle, Cornw. 69 D2

☎ 01840 770328 www.english-heritage.org.uk

A dramatic clifftop location gives this extensive, ruined medieval castle spectacular views along the north Cornish coast. Situated on a promontory approached via a narrow neck of land, such an excellent defensive site is likely to have been in use from much earlier times, and Iron Age, Celtic and Roman occupations have been suggested. This lengthy history of occupancy, coupled with the windswept, romantic atmosphere, has helped enhance the idea of Tintagel as the legendary castle of King Arthur.

Tintern Abbey (Ruin), Mon.   81 D5
☎ 01291 689251   www.tintern.org.uk
Once a favoured site for artists and poets including William Wordsworth, the graceful ruins of the 13th century Cistercian Abbey overlook the beautiful Wye valley north of Chepstow. Much of the Abbey is preserved and it offers a fascinating glimpse into the life and times of the medieval monks.

Tonbridge Castle (Ruins), Kent   76 B3
☎ 01732 770929   www.tonbridgecastle.org
Remains of a Norman motte and bailey castle set in 14 acres (5.5ha) of grounds. Within the impressive 13th century gatehouse visitors can experience castle life through interactive displays and an audio-tour.

Torre Abbey, Torbay   71 E5
☎ 01803 293593   www.torre-abbey.org.uk
Founded in 1196, but partly destroyed during the Dissolution of the Monasteries in 1539, only fragments of the original buildings remain, including the medieval barn and gatehouse. It was converted to a country house and then substantially remodelled in the 19th century and now belongs to the local council, serving in part as a museum and art gallery. There are collections of silver, glass, maritime paintings, pre-Raphaelite and 20th century art and a room devoted to Agatha Christie memorabilia. Access is free to the grounds which include palm and cactus houses.

Tower of London, Gt.Lon.   63 B4
☎ 0870 756 6060   hrp.org.uk/tower
Dating back to the 11th century, the Tower has been part of London's history for over 900 years. During this time it has had many roles, serving as a royal palace, an arsenal, royal mint, jewel house, royal menagerie (the ravens are now the only survivors) and, most notoriously, as a jail and place of execution. There are many different things for the visitor to see, either independently, or with the help of the distinctively dressed Yeoman warders (Beefeaters), who are happy to combine their traditional ceremonial role with that of tourist guide.
 The oldest part is the massive rectangular 90ft (27.5m) high White Tower. Originally built as a fortress and residence providing accommodation for the king, today visitors can see a wide range of arms and armour. The Bloody Tower is associated with the deaths of the two princes in 1483. Sir Walter Raleigh was also imprisoned here for 13 years. The scaffold site on Tower Green is where seven famous prisoners were executed including Anne Boleyn, Catherine Howard and Lady Jane Grey, their bodies being buried in the adjacent Chapel of St Peter ad Vincula. Prisoners often entered the Tower from the Thames through Traitor's Gate. Be sure not to miss the Crown Jewels, a glittering and well laid out array which mainly date from the Restoration in 1660, when Charles II ascended the throne. Also worth a visit is the Medieval Palace which comprises a series of rooms shown as they may have looked during the reign of Edward I.

Traquair House, Sc.Bord.   108 B6
☎ 01896 830323   www.traquair.co.uk
Dating from the 12th century, and originally a royal hunting lodge, this is considered the oldest continuously inhabited house in Scotland. Presenting a striking, whitewashed façade, internally many original features remain, including vaulted cellars, a medieval staircase and priest's hole. Furniture, fittings and memorabilia bear a fascinating testimony to the vagaries of Scottish political and domestic life over the centuries. There is also an 18th century working brewery with tastings in summer, maze, trails and adventure playground.

Tredegar House, Newport   80 B5
☎ 01633 815880   www.newport.gov.uk
For more than five centuries this imposing mansion near Newport was home to the powerful Morgan family. Some 30 rooms are open to the public and the interior is furnished sumptuously with original pieces. Costumed guides lead tours describing life 'upstairs' and 'below stairs'. Outside are 90 acres (37ha) of landscaped gardens and parkland with lakes, carriage rides and craft workshops.

Trerice (NT), Cornw.   68 C4
☎ 01637 875404   www.nationaltrust.org.uk
An attractive Elizabethan manor house considered to be something of an architectural gem with its detailed plaster ceilings, splendid fireplaces and distinctive gabling following the Dutch style. Furnishings include a range of oak and walnut furniture, unusual clocks, embroideries and paintings. The pleasant grounds are planted with an eye for colour and foliage, and the former stables house a small museum tracing the development and history of the lawnmower.

Tretower Castle & Court , Powys   80 B3
☎ 01874 730279   cadw.wales.gov.uk
The stone keep of this castle in the Brecon Beacons was built as a fortification in the 13th century. The nearby Court was added in the following century to serve as a comfortable residence. Various stages in the development of both buildings can be seen, including the detailed craftsmanship of the Court. The recreated 15th century garden is at its best in early summer.

Truro Cathedral, Cornw.   68 C4
☎ 01872 276782   www.trurocathedral.org.uk
The first cathedral in Britain to be consecrated since the Reformation, this beautiful neo-Gothic building was designed by John Loughborough Pearson and completed in 1910. It was built on the site of St Mary's Parish Church (consecrated in 1259), and part of the old building was incorporated into the new cathedral which has a commanding central location in the city. The Victorian stained glass windows are considered amongst the finest in the world, and other notable features include the Father Willis organ and an excellent collection of Victorian embroidery.

Tutbury Castle, Staffs.   89 E4
☎ 01283 812129   www.tutburycastle.com
This 11th century castle has played host to many royal guests including giving safe harbour to Charles I and his nephew Prince Rupert during the Civil War. Because of this, Cromwell ordered the castle to be dismantled though it was rebuilt in 1662. Mary, Queen of Scots was imprisoned here and, of all the places she was imprisoned, it is said that she had a special loathing for Tutbury.

Tyntesfield (NT), N.Som.   81 D6
☎ 0870 458 4500   www.nationaltrust.org.uk
A splendid Victorian house built in the Gothic Revival style, with lots of towers and turrets. There is an extensive collection of Victorian decorative arts plus a range of domestic offices and a family chapel. The unspoilt 500 acre (200ha) estate comprises parkland, lovely formal gardens and a delightful kitchen garden. This is a recent acquisition by the National Trust, and is undergoing extensive renovation which may prevent access to certain rooms. It will be several years before the house is fully open. There is separate admission to the grounds and chapel.

Uffington Castle & White Horse (NT), Oxon. 82 A5
☎ 0870 333 1181   www.english-heritage.org.uk
Belying its name, Uffington Castle has no connection with medieval fortifications but is an imposing Iron Age hill fort covering 8 acres (3ha) close to the Ridgeway, an ancient track. The White Horse, cut into the chalk of the hillside to the east of the castle, is 374ft (114m) long and rather stylised in appearance. Tests indicate a Bronze Age origin, and the figure is thought to represent Epona, a horse goddess, though it will come as no surprise that many legends have developed around this feature.

Ugbrooke, *Devon*   **71 D5**
☎ 01626 852179   www.ugbrooke.co.uk
Home to the Clifford family for the past 300 years, this former Tudor mansion was substantially rebuilt by Robert Adam in 1750, the chapel and library wing being particularly characteristic of Adam's style. The house fell into some disrepair in the mid 20th century but has been handsomely and meticulously restored and contains fine displays of furniture, paintings, embroideries and a rare military collection. The parkland was landscaped by Lancelot 'Capability' Brown and contains many fine specimen trees, while the formal gardens include a box parterre, Spanish garden and lakeside walks.

Uppark (NT), *W.Suss.*   **74 C4**
☎ 01730 825857   www.nationaltrust.org.uk
A late 17th century house in an attractive setting high on the South Downs. The estate, extending to 50 acres (20ha), was designed by Humphrey Repton. The interior is Georgian and includes paintings, furniture, textiles and ceramics and an 18th century dolls' house with its original contents. The servants' quarters can also been seen.

Upton House (NT), *Warks.*   **82 B2**
☎ 01295 670266   www.nationaltrust.org.uk
This 17th century house has wonderful collections of 18th century furniture, tapestries, art and porcelain. The house was bought by Walter Samuel, the Chairman of Shell, in 1927. He carried out extensive modifications to both interior and exterior and gave the house and his collections to the National Trust in 1948. This included his splendid art collection of works by El Greco, Canaletto, Stubbs and Hogarth. There are 31 acres (12.5ha) of terraced garden containing herbaceous borders, fruit and vegetable gardens.

Urquhart Castle, *High.*   **113 D2**
☎ 01456 450551   www.historic-scotland.gov.uk
The ruins of one of the largest castles in Scotland are found on the shores of Loch Ness. First built in the 1230s on the site of a vitrified fort, the castle fell into decay after 1689 and was blown up in 1692 to prevent it being occupied by Jacobites. Many of the remains are 14th century and the Grant Tower is 16th century.

Verulamium Roman Town, *Herts.*   **83 F4**
☎ 01727 751810   www.stalbansmuseums.org.uk
At the height of the Roman occupation, Verulamium, now St Albans, was the third largest town in Britain. The museum includes recreated Roman rooms, hands-on displays and Roman mosaics and wall plasters. There are also sections of the boundary wall, hypocaust and the remains of a theatre built about AD140. This is the only known example in Britain of a Roman theatre with a stage, rather than an amphitheatre. The remains of some of the Roman buildings were used in the construction of St Albans Cathedral.

Victoria & Albert Museum, *Gt.Lon.*   **62 B1**
☎ 020 7942 2000   www.vam.ac.uk
Established in 1852 with profits from the Great Exhibition, and originally called the Museum of Manufactures, then the South Kensington Museum, it was finally renamed the V&A in 1899. This national museum of art and design has exhibits from all over the world, spanning over 2000 years. It is vast and labyrinthine, with four floors and over 145 galleries covering an area of 10 acres (4ha). The collection is immense and wide-ranging with over 4 million objects as diverse as the carved oak Great Bed of Ware, made in 1590, which measures 12ft (3.6m) square, and the tiny Indian miniature paintings. Other exhibits include Oriental ceramics, Chippendale and Art Nouveau furniture, Italian Renaissance sculpture, and a significant collection of paintings by John Constable. The museum also contains Indian film posters, photographs and around 500,000 watercolours, engravings and etchings. The British Galleries are a popular destination with exhibits dating from the 16th to 20th centuries, encompassing works by famous designers such as William Morris, Charles Rennie Mackintosh and Robert Adam. With 7 miles (11km)

of galleries to explore it is impossible to see everything in one visit. The V&A Museum of Childhood in Cromwell Road houses one of the largest and oldest collections of toys and children's items in the world.

Vindolanda (Chesterholm) Roman Fort, *Northumb.*   **102 B3**
☎ 01434 344277   www.vindolanda.com
The remains of a Roman fort (AD127) and surrounding civilian settlement about 2 miles south of Hadrian's Wall. There are ongoing excavations and archaeologists have revealed a succession of forts on the site. The well-preserved artefacts in the museum include armour, boots, shoes, jewellery and coins. Among the most significant finds have been letters and documents written in ink on wood; photographs of these tablets are on display. A section of Hadrian's Wall has been reconstructed in timber and stone to its original height and there are full-scale replicas of a Roman temple, shop, house and a Northumbrian croft.

Viroconium Roman Town, *Shrop.*   **88 B5**
☎ 01743 761330
With a population of over 6000, Viroconium (Wroxeter) was once the fourth largest city in Roman Britain. The remains are extensive and include city walls and the fully excavated public baths, beneath which there are timber buildings dating from the early part of the first century when a garrison was stationed here before it was moved to Chester and Viroconium became an important trading centre.

Vyne, The (NT), *Hants.*   **74 B2**
☎ 01256 883858   www.nationaltrust.org.uk
A splendid red brick Tudor mansion built for Henry VIII's Lord Chamberlain, Lord Sandys. Subsequent modifications in the 17th century include the first classical portico of its kind in the country, and there were some further 18th century alterations. Notable features include the Long Gallery, with its original linenfold panelling and rococo plaster ceiling, a sweeping Palladian staircase, and the Tudor chapel, with Renaissance stained glass and encaustic tiles. The garden has some good herbaceous border displays, and the estate consists of a further 500 acres (200ha) of park and woodland, providing attractive walks with views across the lake.

Waddesdon Manor (NT), *Bucks.*   **83 D4**
☎ 01296 653226   www.waddesdon.org.uk
The external appearance of this late Victorian building owes more to the style of a 16th century French chateau than a conventional English country house. It was built for Baron Ferdinand de Rothschild, its primary purpose being to display his splendid collection of French decorative arts. There are also paintings by Gainsborough, Reynolds, Romney, and Dutch and Flemish masters. The wine cellars contain a collection of over 15,000 bottles, some dating back to 1868. The late 19th century formal gardens surrounding the house are amongst the finest Victorian gardens in Britain, and include a magnificent, colourful parterre, carpet bedding, rose garden, specimen trees, fountains and an extensive collection of French, Dutch and Italian statuary. The centrepiece is the ornate, cast iron rococo aviary which has an interesting collection of exotic birds.

Wakefield Cathedral, *W.Yorks.*   **96 A5**
☎ 01924 373923   www.wakefield-cathedral.org.uk
First built in the 14th century and much restored in the 19th century, Wakefield Cathedral boasts the tallest spire in Yorkshire. Inside, it also features a 17th century font, 15th century masonry and carvings, and excellent Victorian stained-glass windows by Kempe.

Wallington (NT), *Northumb.*   **102 C2**
☎ 01670 773600   www.nationaltrust.org.uk
Built in 1688, Wallington was for generations home to the Blackett and Trevelyan families. The house contains fine rococo plasterwork and the central hall is decorated in Pre-Raphaelite style with pictures reflecting Northumbrian history.

There are paintings and porcelain as well as a collection of dolls' houses. The extensive grounds include a beautiful walled garden and Edwardian conservatory, woodland and a path along the banks of the River Wansbeck.

Walmer Castle & Garden, Kent   77 F3
☎ 01304 364288   www.english-heritage.org.uk
Tudor castle built 1539 to 1540 as a coastal artillery fortress for Henry VIII. In 1708 the castle became the residence of the Lords Warden of the Cinque Ports, some of the most famous encumbents being the Duke of Wellington, Sir Winston Churchill and the Queen Mother. Visitors can enjoy the attractive gardens and see the room where Wellington died.

Waltham Abbey, Essex   84 A4
☎ 01992 702200   www.walthamabbeychurch.co.uk
It is said that King Harold II left from here to face William of Normandy at the Battle of Hastings in 1066, his body being returned to the abbey for burial. Outside the present abbey church are two inscribed stones marking the spot where King Harold's body is believed to lie. Following the Dissolution, the abbey was partly demolished and the remains that can be seen today include a late 14th century gatehouse that was once part of the cloisters, and part of the Norman abbey nave which was incorporated into the present Waltham Abbey Church. Within the nave can be seen striking spiral and zig-zag patterned columns and a superb painted ceiling.

Warkworth Castle, Northumb.   103 D1
☎ 01665 711423   www.english-heritage.org.uk
Standing on a hill above the River Coquet, the well-preserved ruins dominate the town of Warkworth. The castle was once home to the powerful Percy family and was the setting for several scenes in Shakespeare's 'Henry IV'. Dating mainly from the 12th to the 14th centuries, the remains include a magnificent eight-towered keep, chapel, great hall and decorated lion tower. Special events for visitors are regularly staged here.

Warwick Castle

Warwick Castle, Warks.   82 A1
☎ 0870 442 2000   www.warwick-castle.co.uk
Set on the banks of the River Avon, this is one of the finest examples of 14th century fortifications in Britain. Real-life characters help to bring the castle to life and life-sized waxworks add detail to many of the displays, which include an accurate re-creation of the visit of the Prince of Wales, later to become Edward VII, in 1898. The macabre dungeon and torture chamber are reached down a narrow flight of stairs – the writings of a Royalist held during the Civil War can still be seen on the wall. The Great Hall is amongst the luxuriously decorated state rooms which has Oliver Cromwell's death mask on display and also paintings by masters such as Van Dyck and Rubens. The grounds were designed by Lancelot 'Capability' Brown and include walks along the Avon, an 18th century conservatory and Victorian Rose Garden. There is also a restored mill and engine house which was used to produce the electricity of the household at the turn of the 20th century. There are many events throughout the year including fireworks concerts, medieval festivals and birds of prey displays. A good day out for all the family though it is advisable to check prices before setting out.

Weald & Downland Open Air Museum, W.Suss.   74 C4
☎ 01243 811363   www.wealddown.co.uk
Almost 50 historic buildings dating from the 13th to the 19th century have been rebuilt on this attractive 50 acre (20ha) parkland site in the lovely South Downs countryside. The buildings were rescued from destruction and have been carefully dismantled and moved from their original locations to create this museum. The site illustrates traditional rural life in an inspiring way.

Wells Cathedral, Som.   72 B2
☎ 01749 674483   www.wellscathedral.org.uk
Dominating the centre of Wells, England's smallest city, this has been the site of a religious building since the 8th century. The present cathedral was founded in 1180, but was built in phases over the following 400 years, thus incorporating several different architectural styles. However, the original Saxon font was retained and is still used for baptisms.

The splendid west front, one of the most outstanding fasades in the country, was completed in 1250 and accommodates nearly 300 pieces of statuary. Within the magnificent Gothic interior are unusual scissor-shaped arches, constructed as additional support when the combined weight of tower and spire proved too much for the lower stage of the tower. The upper tower and spire were subsequently destroyed by fire and not rebuilt; the lower tower was rebuilt to a height of 182ft (55m), the highest in the county.

Other highlights include the 14th century clock, amongst the oldest in the world, mid 20th century colourful embroideries in the choir, medieval stained glass, and probably the longest medieval library building (168ft, 51m) in England, containing documents which date from the 10th century.

West Kennet Long Barrow, Wilts.   82 A6
☎ 0870 333 1181   www.english-heritage.org.uk
Possibly England's finest burial mound, this Neolithic chambered tomb was the site of around 50 burials. Measuring 343ft (105m) by 76ft (23m), the mound's entrance is protected by massive sarsen stones and it is possible to walk into the stone burial chamber a short way into the mound.

West Wycombe Park (NT), Bucks.   83 D5
☎ 01494 755571   www.west-wycombe-estate.co.uk
Extravagant 18th century Italianate mansion with the external appearance of a classical temple. Inspired by 'Grand Tours', there are splendid painted ceilings, and furniture, paintings and sculpture dating from the mid 18th century ownership of Sir Francis Dashwood, who founded the notorious Hell Fire Club. Club members were drawn from the upper echelons of society, and local mythology had them indulging in Satanic rites, though reality was probably wine, women and a spot of free thinking. Sir Francis also created the beautiful rococo landscape garden in the 300 acres (150ha) of parkland surrounding the house.

An unusual addition to the grounds are the Hell Fire Caves. Again the inspiration of Sir Francis, the existing caves were greatly extended in the 1750s by a remarkable feat of engineering. Although providing a suitably atmospheric meeting place for the Hell Fire Club, Sir Francis's motives were partly altruistic in that the work provided employment for local villagers following a series of failed harvests. The caves are privately owned and there is an additional entry fee.

Westbury White Horse, Wilts.   72 C2
☎ 01225 710535   www.wiltshirewhitehorses.org.uk
The chalk downs of central Wiltshire are ideal for these massive hill carvings which are not, as generally assumed, particularly ancient. The Westbury horse is considered the oldest in the county and is perhaps the best sited. It is thought to date from the late 17th century, replacing an earlier one, possibly of Saxon origin. Above the horse is a large Iron Age fort with excellent views

Westminster Abbey, *Gt.Lon.*   63 B3

☎ 020 7654 4900   www.westminster-abbey.org

Steeped in history, the abbey is the coronation church of all the crowned sovereigns since 1216. Very little of the original Norman structure remains; most of the magnificent Gothic building seen today was built by Henry III between 1245 and his death in 1272. After his death, progress was slow and the nave, which at 102ft (31m) is the highest in England, was not completed until 1517. The famous west towers, which rise to a height of 225ft (69m) were completed in 1745.

Both architecturally and historically, the abbey is an absolute feast with an impressive array of tombs and memorials to some of Britain's most important figures. Within the chapel of St Edward the Confessor is his great shrine along with the tombs of Henry III, Edward I, Edward III, Richard II and Henry V. Henry VII's Chapel is magnificent, with an intricately detailed fan vaulted ceiling. It is the final resting place of Henry VII, Mary I and Elizabeth I. Within the nave can be seen the tomb of the unknown warrior whose body was laid here as a memorial to the thousands who died in World

War I. The octagonal Chapter House, which between 1253 and 1547 was one of the regular meeting places of Parliament, still contains its original coloured tile floor and medieval wall paintings. Visitors can also see the Cloisters and the museum which is situated in the Norman undercroft.

Westminster Abbey   Photo © Richard Knight

Westminster Cathedral, *Gt.Lon.*   62 B2

☎ 020 7798 9055   www.westminstercathedral.org.uk

Completed in 1903, this is the principal Roman Catholic church in England. The neo-Byzantine style, with its distinctive red brickwork and horizontal white stone stripes, is eyecatching. The spacious interior has the broadest nave in England and is richly decorated with multicoloured mosaics and marble.

Weston Park, *Staffs.*   88 C5

☎ 01952 852100   www.weston-park.com

Mentioned in the 11th century Domesday Book, though the present house was built in 1671. There are nine elegant rooms, including a library with over 3000 books, and the magnificent dining room which has a large collection of art by Van Dyck. The expansive grounds, designed by Lancelot 'Capability' Brown, are formal around the house and include a restored terrace garden as well as parkland including lakes, pools and the deer park. There is plenty for children with a miniature railway, animal centre and adventure playground.

Wheal Martyn, *Cornw.*   69 D4

☎ 01726 850362   www.wheal-martyn.com

A fascinating look at the history of the china clay industry on a 26 acre (10ha) site dating from the 1870s and restored in the 1970s. Some areas of the site are still in active production and can be seen from a viewing platform. The visitor centre has displays and exhibits on both the raw materials and finished products of the industry and a trail takes the visitor round the old clay works.

Whitby Abbey, *N.Yorks.*   97 D1

☎ 01947 603568   www.english-heritage.org.uk

High on the cliff above the harbour stand the dramatic ruins of Whitby Abbey. Founded by Abbess St Hilda in AD657, the abbey was destroyed by the Vikings and rebuilt by the Normans in the 13th century. Amongst the ruins is the Benedictine Church, dating from the 13th and 14th centuries, complete with an impressive three-tiered choir

and north transept. The abbey's 2000 year history is interactively re-created with computer-generated images, audiovisual displays and activities in the visitor centre, housed in the remains of a 17th century house.

Whitby Abbey   Photo © Yorkshire Tourist Board

Whithorn Priory, *D. & G.*   98 C3

☎ 01988 500508   www.historic-scotland.gov.uk

St Ninian founded a church here around AD400, and this site is considered the cradle of Christianity in Scotland. The ruined priory, once the cathedral church of Galloway, was built in the 12th century as his tomb had become a place of pilgrimage. The ecclesiastical history of the site is complex, and finds from the ongoing archaeological work, including some fine Celtic crosses, are on display in the museum.

Wightwick Manor (NT), *W.Mid.*   88 C6

☎ 01902 761400   www.nationaltrust.org.uk

Built by the Mander family at the end of the 19th century to designs influenced by the Arts and Crafts movement, and decorated with original William Morris materials, Kempe glass and Pre-Raphaelite art. Descendants of the family still live in part of the manor. The 17 acre (7ha) garden is a delight with topiaries, terraces and ponds.

Wilton House, *Wilts.*   73 D3

☎ 01722 746729   www.wiltonhouse.co.uk

Following the Dissolution of the Monasteries, the Benedictine site and land at Wilton were granted by Henry VIII to William Herbert, who incorporated the abbey ruins into a Tudor mansion. After a fire in 1647, Inigo Jones and John Webb redesigned and rebuilt the house in the Palladian style. The chief features of this rebuilding are the state rooms, particularly the Single and Double Cube rooms, so-called because of their precise dimensions, and renowned for their outstanding painted ceilings and elaborate plasterwork. Elsewhere in the house there are paintings by Reynolds, Rembrandt, Brueghel, Rubens and Poussin, amongst others, making a collection which is considered one of the finest in Europe. The 21 acre (8.5ha) grounds, bounded by the Rivers Nadder and Wylye, contain both formal gardens and landscaped parkland. Fine specimen trees can be seen on the woodland walks and there are architectural features such as the well-known Palladian Bridge.

Winchester Cathedral, *Hants.*   74 A3

☎ 01962 857200   www.winchester-cathedral.org.uk

One of the great cathedrals of England, and perhaps one of the best examples of Gothic Perpendicular architecture to be found. The original minster was built by King Cenwalh of Wessex in AD643 and was the royal Saxon cathedral, burial place of kings. The foundations can still be seen adjacent to the West Door but this building was replaced by Bishop Walkelin, the first Norman bishop, who laid the foundations of the present cathedral in 1079, building materials including stone from the Isle of Wight and local timber. The cathedral was completed within 14 years, but over the following centuries underwent much modification, particularly between 1350 – 1450 when the original Romanesque nave was transformed to the English Gothic style, mainly due to the efforts of Bishop William of Wykeham. The nave measures 556ft (170m), making Winchester the longest medieval church in Europe. The whole building is an ecclesiastical and architectural treasure house.

Within the cathedral is a statue to William Walker, a deep sea diver who could be said to have single-handedly saved the cathedral from collapse at the beginning of the 20th century. He spent five years working underwater in complete darkness replacing the decaying timber of the ancient foundations.

Windermere Steamboat Museum, *Cumb.*   94 B2
☎ 015394 45565   www.steamboat.co.uk
A fascinating collection of historic steam and motor boats moored in a covered wet dock, with launch trips if the weather is fair. Among the vintage boats is the steam launch Dolly, reputedly the oldest mechanically powered boat in the world, built around 1850 and restored to her former glory after spending 67 years on the bed of Ullswater. Among other attractions at the museum are model boats and a model boats pond, 'Swallows and Amazons' exhibition, Beatrix Potter's rowing boat, and displays about how Windermere has been used for transport since Roman times.

Windsor Castle, *W. & M.*   83 E6
☎ 01753 831118   www.royal.gov.uk
Strategically placed above the River Thames and a day's march from London, William the Conqueror selected Windsor as the site for a fort to protect the western approach to the capital. Since then it has become the largest and oldest occupied castle in the world.

William's original building was a wooden motte and bailey fort constructed in 1079, Henry II replacing this with stone outer walls and a round tower in 1165. In the succeeding centuries monarchs have enlarged and modified the castle, militarily if necessary, or decoratively in more peaceful times, and the building today occupies a site of 12 acres (5ha). The magnificent State Rooms contain outstanding pictures from the Royal Collection including works by Holbein, Rembrandt and Canaletto, fine furniture, painted ceilings and carvings by Grinling Gibbons. These rooms are used for ceremonial and state occasions and may be closed when the Queen is in residence. In the winter months the richly decorated Semi State Rooms can also be viewed. The Drawings Gallery houses changing exhibitions of material drawn from the Royal Library and other treasures.

Within the precincts is St George's Chapel, built in the late 15th century and one of Britain's finest examples of Gothic architecture. It contains the tombs of 10 monarchs and the great battle sword of Edward III hangs on one of the walls. Outside the castle, one of the best known of British ceremonies, the Changing of the Guard, takes place throughout the year. It is advisable to telephone in advance to check days and times.

Woburn Abbey, *Beds.*   83 E3
☎ 01525 290333   www.woburnabbey.co.uk
Woburn has been home to the Earls and Dukes of Bedford for nearly 400 years. The current Palladian style mansion, built on the site of a 12th century Cistercian monastery, is set in a 3000 acre (1200ha) deer park. In the 17th century the 4th Earl built a new wing on the site of the old abbey church. This contains an intriguing grotto with elaborately carved stonework resembling stalactites and seaweed, as well as 18th century furniture carved in the shape of sea shells with dolphins supporting the seats and table tops. Within the house there are over 250 paintings dating from as early as the 16th century, including works by Van Dyck, Gainsborough, Reynolds and Velázquez. The Venetian Room has 21 views of Venice by Canaletto, commissioned by the 4th Duke during his Grand Tour. There is also some excellent 18th century furniture, silver pieces by renowned Huguenot silversmiths, and some superb porcelain, including the Sèvres dinner service presented to the 4th Duchess by Louis XV in 1763. The grounds were landscaped by Humphrey Repton at the beginning of the 19th century and are home to ten species of deer, including the rare Père David Chinese deer. There is a hornbeam maze, masses of rhododendrons and a lake. Within the estate is the famous Safari Park where visitors can enjoy seeing the animals wandering freely (additional charge).

Woodchester Mansion, *Glos.*   81 E4
☎ 01453 861541   www.woodchestermansion.org.uk
A highly unusual place to visit, the mansion was abandoned before completion in 1870 and is in virtually the same state now. Much of the impressive craftsmanship of the time can be seen, something that would not have been possible if the mansion had been finished. Endangered Lesser and Greater Horseshoe Bats live in the roof spaces which can be observed by closed circuit cameras. The mansion is open at weekends during the summer months.

Woolsthorpe Manor (NT), *Lincs.*   90 C4
☎ 01476 860338   www.nationaltrust.org.uk
Birthplace and home of Sir Isaac Newton, this small, 17th century manor house contains a 'Young Newton' exhibition and an early edition of his 'Principia' work. In the barn is a Science Discovery Centre and café, and a descendant of the apple tree, under which Newton is said to have discovered the principles of gravity, grows in the orchard.

Worcester Cathedral, *Worcs.*   81 E2
☎ 01905 28854   www.cofe-worcester.org.uk/cathedral
The Cathedral stands on the site of an ancient Saxon monastery which was largely destroyed in 1041. Rebuilding started in 1064 and, after a series of problems including a fire and collapse of the tower, was all but complete by the time of its dedication in 1218. Time took its toll on the Cathedral and it was not until the Victorians undertook a massive restoration programme that it took on the form that we see today. The richly decorated tombs of Prince Arthur and King John can be found near the High Altar.

Worcester Cathedral   Photo © West Midland Tourist Board

Yarmouth Castle, *I.o.W.*   74 A5
☎ 01983 760678   www.english-heritage.org.uk
Completed in 1547, this was the final castle to be built in Henry VIII's coastal defence system, following a French invasion of the Isle of Wight in 1545. It is of a fairly simple design, consisting of a basic square with no central tower. Bounded by the sea to the north and east, the south and west walls were protected by a moat, filled in at the end of the 17th century. Around 1600 a large gun battery was built in the north part of the courtyard, while domestic buildings filled the south side.

York Minster, *York*   66 B2
☎ 01904 557216   www.yorkminster.org
York Minster is a stunning medieval Gothic cathedral and the largest in northern Europe. Building began in the 13th century, but it took until the 15th century to be completed. The numerous, beautiful stained-glass windows are a key feature. Admire the Norman stained-glass windows in the nave, the Five Sisters Window in the north transept containing 100,000 pieces of glass, and the Great East Window with 27 panels. The Chapter House reveals fine carvings and the north transept is styled with polished stone columns.

Britain's heritage is not just represented in isolated sites. There is the architectural legacy of cities, towns and villages from Britain's agricultural, industrial and maritime history. There are old fishing villages and great seaports, the mining communities and mill towns of the industrial revolution and the rural villages and market towns from an economy once based mainly on farming.

Chester city centre

Photo © www.heritagecities.com

Below is a list of 50 recommended 'must-see' cities, towns and villages. It is not a complete list of recommendations, but a suggestion of places to see that represent the rich heritage of Britain's settlements.

Aberdeen	Cathedral city known as 'The Granite City' for the local stone used in many of its buildings. 115 E3
Alcester	Roman settlement on the River Arrow, now a market town with an almost intact medieval street pattern. 81 F2
Bath	Spa city with a wealth of Roman and Regency heritage. 81 E6
Berwick-upon-Tweed	Border town at the mouth of the River Tweed. 109 E5
Brighton	Seaside resort famed for its Regency architecture. 75 F4
Bristol	Port on the River Avon and Britain's second largest city in medieval times. 81 D6
Caernarfon	Medieval town and port on the Menai Strait. 86 B2
Cambridge	University city on the River Cam. 84 A2
Canterbury	Cathedral city with a rich ecclesiastical history. 77 E3
Cardiff	One of the world's busiest ports at the end of the 19th century and now the capital city of Wales. 80 B6
Carlisle	Cathedral city and former Roman stronghold towards the western end of Hadrian's Wall. 101 F4
Chester	County town and cathedral city on the River Dee, famed for its well-preserved medieval heritage. 88 A2
Chichester	Ancient cathedral city and site of a Roman town. 74 C4
Cirencester	Market town on the site of Roman town of Corinium which was second only to London in importance. 81 F4
Clovelly	Picturesque cobble-streeted fishing village on the North Devon coast. 70 B2
Colchester	The first Roman capital of Britain (Camulodunum) with many remains from this period. 85 D3
Conwy	One of Europe's best examples of a medieval walled town. 87 D2
Dartmouth	Small port and resort on the River Dart estuary. 71 D6
Dunster	A medieval town with an octagonal yarn-market that gained its prosperity from cloth-making. 71 E1
Durham	Cathedral city with a thousand year old history, dominated by a 900 year old Norman castle. 103 D4
Edinburgh	Capital of Scotland since the 15th century and home of the Scottish Parliament. 108 A4
Exeter	University and cathedral city on the River Exe. County capital of Devon. 71 E4
Glasgow	The largest city in Scotland and a port with a proud shipbuilding heritage. 106 C4
Glastonbury	Ancient centre of Christian culture and pilgrimage. 72 A3
Gloucester	2000 years of history, a world famous cathedral and historic docklands. 81 E4
Ironbridge	The birthplace of the Industrial Revolution and the site of the first bridge constructed of iron in the world. 88 B5
Lacock	Well preserved, mainly National Trust owned village on the banks of the Avon. 81 F6
Lincoln	On the site of the Roman town of Lindum with a 13th century cathedral. 90 C2
Liverpool	Originally a fishing village then a great seaport and still a centre of trade and tourism on the River Mersey. 88 A1
London	Capital of England and Europe's largest city, originally the Roman settlement of Londinium. 84 A5
Norwich	Textile exports made this the second richest city in medieval Britain with some remnants of the city walls. 92 C5
Nottingham	Originated in the 6th century and home to the oldest football club in the world, Notts County, formed in 1862. 90 A3
Oxford	World famous university city with distinctive 'dreaming spires' skyline. 82 C4
Peterborough	A city of considerable heritage despite being designated a New Town in 1967 and a centre for important archaeological digs. 91 D6
Portmeirion	20th century Italian-style village and the setting for the 1960s TV series 'The Prisoner'. 86 C4

Rochester	Ancient port, cathedral and commercial centre on the River Medway. 76 C2
Rye	Attractively preserved town from medieval, Tudor and Georgian times, formerly a port but now 3km (2 miles) from the sea. 77 D4
St Albans	Roman remains of the city of Verulamium, once an important trading centre. 83 F4
St Andrews	The 'Home of Golf' and Scotland's oldest university. 108 C2
St Davids	Britain's smallest city and a place of pilgrimage for over 1500 years. 78 A3
St Ives	Formerly a tin mining and fishing centre but now mainly a tourist centre. 68 B4
Salisbury	Market town at the confluence of the Rivers Avon and Nadder with the tallest cathedral spire in Britain. 73 E3
Stirling	Historic town on a rocky outcrop above the south bank of the River Forth. 107 D3
Stratford-upon-Avon	Shakespeare's birthplace with many attractive medieval buildings. 82 A2
Tenby	Seaside resort with remains of town walls and medieval castle. 78 C4
Wells	Cathedral city with a medieval city centre. 72 B2
Winchester	Ancient capital of Wessex and of Anglo-Saxon Britain. 74 A3
Windsor	Market town with royal residence at the castle and a guildhall designed by Sir Christopher Wren. 83 E6
Worcester	Sitting on the banks of the River Severn with city walls and timber buildings from the 15th - 17th century. 81 E2
York	City with Roman, Saxon and Viking heritage and the largest medieval cathedral in Europe. 96 B4

The three capital cities of London, Edinburgh and Cardiff have a rich heritage formed from the parts they have played in Britain's history.

Seven other British towns and cities – Bath, Brighton, Chester, Durham, Oxford, Stratford-upon-Avon and York have also been selected as examples of the great wealth of heritage that Britain has to offer. Further information is available at www.heritagecities.com

Brunswick Square, Brighton
Photo © www.heritagecities.com

Key to city & town centre plans

A36	Primary route dual / single carriageway		Restricted access street
A367	'A' road dual / single carriageway		Pedestrian street
B4632	'B' road dual / single carriageway		Path / Footbridge
	Other road dual / single carriageway	→	One way street
≢	Railway line / station		Tourist building
●	London Underground station		Higher Education building
P	Car park		Hospital
†	Ecclesiastical building		Other important building
ℹ ℹ	Tourist information centre (open all year / seasonally)	†	Cemetery
★	Place of heritage interest		Recreational area / Open space
★	World Heritage Site		

A World Heritage Site and the location of Britain's only natural hot springs was a site of veneration for local Celtic tribes even before the Romans arrived and built the amazing baths complex. However, following the Romans' departure, interest was lost in the springs and it was not until the early 18th century that it attained its position as the epitome of fashionable society. This was due largely to the efforts of Richard 'Beau' Nash, who transformed Bath from provincial town to unrivalled centre of fashion. He was assisted by Ralph Allen and both John Woods, father and son, who exploited the local stone and used it brilliantly in the construction of the unique buildings. The Woods are responsible for such masterpieces as the Circus, Royal Crescent and Assembly Rooms.

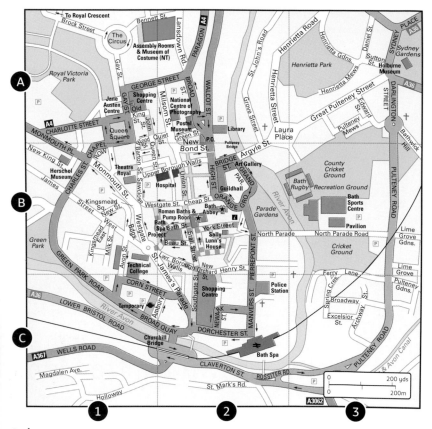

Index to street names

Pulteney Bridge   Photo © www.heritagecities.com

Sea bathing eventually superseded spas as the fashionable cure, but Bath was left with a splendid architectural heritage from which it still profits; 5000 of the buildings are now listed. The opening of Thermae Bath Spa in 2006 means visitors can once again bathe in the thermal spring water.

Pulteney Bridge is lined by shops on both sides and is still one of the distinctive images of Bath. It was completed in 1774 for William Pulteney, whose wife had inherited land on the east side of the Avon. In order to develop the land a bridge was required and his architect Robert Adam, inspired by the Ponte Vecchio in Florence, favoured a Palladian design despite protests from the city corporation. They considered it as being outdated, as this was at a time when buildings were being removed from bridges to ease access.

Bath was the home of Jane Austen, her parents and two sisters for five years until her father's death in 1805. Although she found it hard to

Roman Baths   Photo © www.heritagecities.com

settle and missed the countryside where she grew up, she set large parts of 'Northanger Abbey' and 'Persuasion' in Bath. She lived in Sydney Place, Green Park Buildings and Gay Street on which is also located the Jane Austen Centre which tells the story of her experiences in Bath and how it influenced her writing.

Prior Park, an 18th century mansion and garden, is located on a hillside to the south west of the city giving splendid panoramic views. It was created by local businessman Ralph Allen, with help from the poet Alexander Pope and Lancelot 'Capability' Brown. There is a particularly beautiful Palladian bridge, lakes and circular woodland walks giving further views. The house is now a school and not open to the public. There is no parking, but a frequent bus service runs from the city centre.

Elegant as Bath is, it was not designed for motor vehicles, and visitors are advised either to use public transport or to leave cars at one of the park and ride sites on the north, west or south sides of the city.

Circus & Royal Crescent   Photo © www.heritagecities.com

Between the South Downs and the south coast, Brighton is renowned for its Regency heritage as well as its current attraction as seaside resort, conference centre, specialist shopping area and venue for year-round cultural events. The town began as a fishing village known as Brighthelmstone. It became fashionable as a sea-bathing resort in the 18th century and in the 1780s it was patronised by the Prince Regent who built the Royal Pavilion as a summer palace in Oriental style. The Victorian Grade II listed pier is featured in Graham Greene's book 'Brighton Rock', Lewis Carroll took inspiration for the opening scenes of Alice's Adventures in Wonderland from Sussex Square Gardens and Charles Dickens wrote some of 'Dombey and Son' in the Bedford Hotel which was destroyed by fire in 1964.

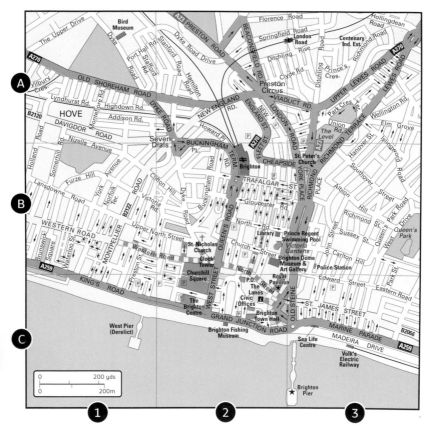

Index to street names

Cardiff has been the capital of Wales since 1955. The Romans founded a military fort and a small settlement on the site in AD55 and some of the original Roman walls can still be seen within the castle grounds, but Cardiff did not grow substantially until its prosperity as a great seaport in the 19th century. Since its establishment as the Welsh capital many governmental, administrative and media organisations have moved to the city. Recent attractions include the Millennium Stadium as an international sporting venue and the Cardiff Bay redevelopment of the docklands area. In the city centre the main site of historical interest is the castle. Work began on the castle keep in 1091 and features remain from that era together with medieval fortifications and the elaborate embellishments commissioned in Victorian times.

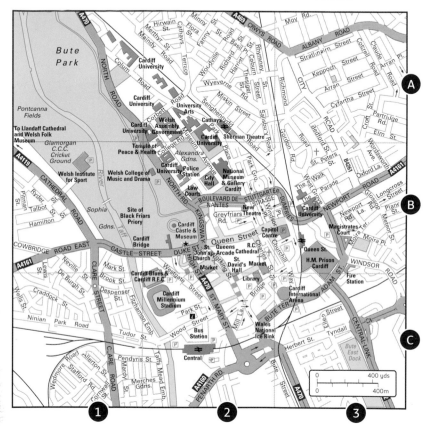

Index to street names

58 Chester

Chester is the most complete walled city in Britain. It grew up on the site of the Roman town of Deva and included the largest Roman amphitheatre in Britain where gladiators fought 2000 years ago. The well preserved medieval walls encircle the city and a walk along them is recommended as the best introduction to Chester. From the walls you can see Eastgate Clock which was built in 1897 to span the original entrance to the city. The castle, which is now the County Hall includes the 12th century Agricola Tower. Chester is famed for the striking black and white Tudor timber-framed buildings which include Chester Rows, two-tier galleried shops and Bishop Lloyd's House with its ornate 16th century carved façade. Towering above the city is Chester Cathedral.

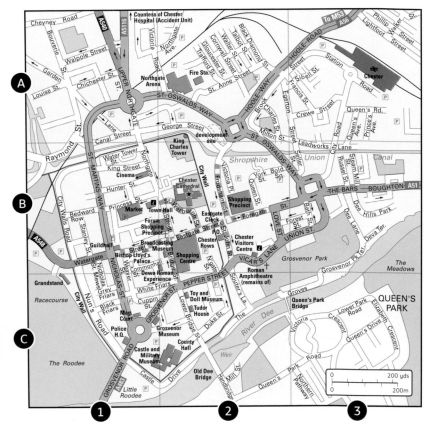

Index to street names

Durham

This cathedral city is sited on a rocky outcrop, protected on three sides by a narrow bend of the River Wear. The strategic value of the location was realised after the Norman conquest in 1066 after which Durham grew as a base from which to rule Northumbria and defend the region against the Scots. The castle was built in 1072 and work on the cathedral began in 1093. Today there is still a stunning view of Durham's dramatic skyline of castle and cathedral. There is also a reminder of the medieval town layout in the winding narrow streets of today's city centre. Just north of the centre, sitting on the banks of the River Wear is Crook Hall, a manor house dating back to at least the 13th century which is surrounded by four distinct cottage gardens as well as a maze, orchard and meadows.

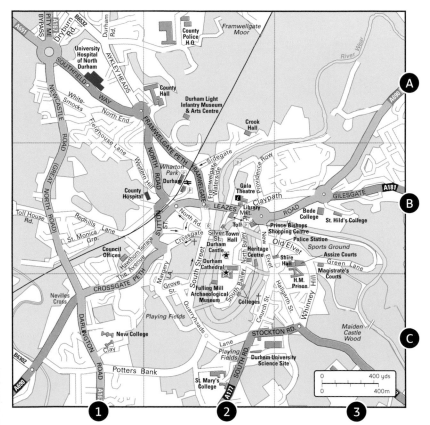

Index to street names

Durham Cathedral

The capital city of Scotland since the 15th century and designated a World Heritage Site in 1995 in recognition of the two distinct and contrasting characters of the medieval Old Town and the Georgian New Town.

Dominating the city is the castle which sits on the core of an extinct volcano at the western end of the Royal Mile. The 1 o'clock cannon which has fired every day since 1861 is linked with the Nelson Monument on Calton Hill which commemorates Admiral Lord Nelson's victory, and death, at the battle of Trafalgar, on 21 October 1805. In 1852, a large time ball was introduced and lowered at 1pm every day in order to let ships in Leith Harbour know the

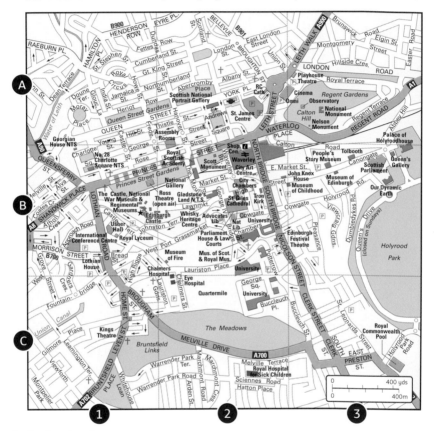

Index to street names

Edinburgh Castle

accurate time in order to reset the ships' clocks used for navigation. However, during foggy periods it was not able to be seen and the practice of firing a gun from the castle at 1pm was started in 1861 and continues to this day.

The National Gallery of Scotland

There are numerous museums, galleries and libraries including:

• The National Library of Scotland on George IV Bridge which was founded in 1682 and given National status in 1925. It houses over 8 million printed items and 120,000 volumes of manuscripts.

• The National Gallery of Scotland which is housed in a fine Greek Temple style building designed by William Henry Playfair and opened to the public in 1859. It houses Scotland's greatest collections of European paintings and sculpture from the Renaissance to Post-Impressionist periods.

• The Royal Scots Regimental Museum is housed in a 1900 Drill Hall in the grounds of Edinburgh Castle and contains paintings, artefacts, silver and medals illustrating the Regiment's illustrious history from its formation in 1633.

• Scottish National Portrait Gallery provides a unique visual history of Scotland, told through portraits of the figures who shaped it: royals and rebels, poets and philosophers, heroes and villains. The portraits are all of Scots although not all the artists are Scots – there are works by Rodin, Van Dyck and Gainsborough.

Royal Yacht Britannia

• Royal Yacht Britannia was launched in 1953 onto the Clyde and is now permanently moored in Leith Docks as a tourist attraction alongside the Ocean Terminal shopping centre. It served the Queen and royal family for state visits, diplomatic functions and royal holidays for 44 years.

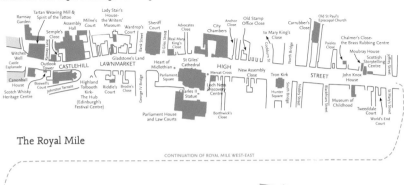

The Royal Mile

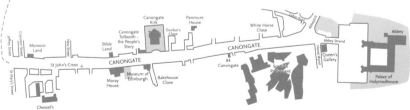

London is one of the world's greatest historical cities, capital city of England and modern business and financial centre. It is also home to the oldest parliamentary system in the world with many government offices housed in imposing buildings in Whitehall and Westminster. Just off Whitehall is Downing Street, the official residence of the British Prime Minister since 1732.

London has Roman origins dating back to the first century AD, when it grew as an administrative centre and port with the Thames being a major trading artery. Remains of the Roman walls are still visible today in the street called London Wall and near the Tower of London.

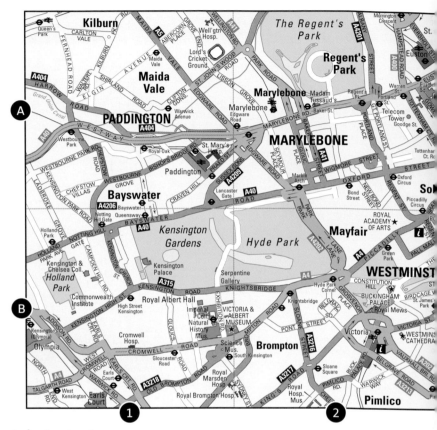

Index to street names

Over hundreds of years the city has been the principal residence of British monarchs and the Royal Family has left its mark on the capital city with many royal buildings and parks. London's museums and galleries contain some of the richest collections in the world and are full of surprising treasures. They range from the vast British museum to more recent and specialist additions, many of which incorporate interactive displays and exhibits.

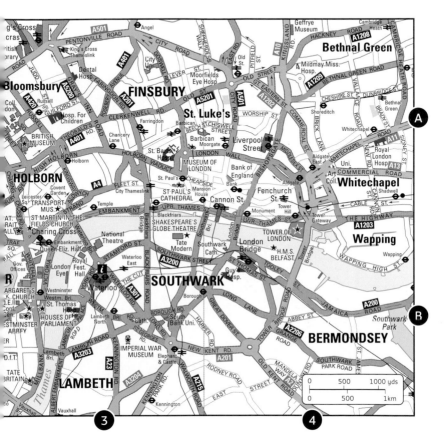

Yeoman Warder

Photo © London Tourist Board

Oxford developed in Saxon times around a nunnery founded by St Frideswide on the site of Christ Church Cathedral. The present cathedral was built in the 13th century and nothing was thought to remain of the original site until 1985 when a Saxon cemetery was discovered under the Cathedral cloisters. Oxford is commonly known as the 'City of Dreaming Spires' because of the domes, spires and towers of the buildings of England's first university which was established in about 1200. The oldest building in the city is the 11th century Saxon tower of St Michael at Northgate Church, Cornmarket. The first Morris Oxford was produced at a garage in Longwall Street in 1913 starting a tradition of motor manufacture which continues to this day.

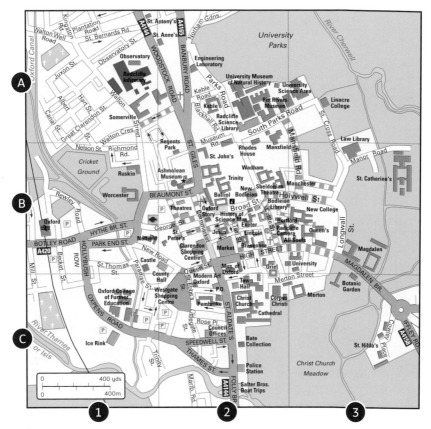

Index to street names

Radcliffe Camera

Stratford-upon-Avon

Beautifully sited on the River Avon, Stratford is a small Tudor market town and Britain's most visited tourist attraction outside London. It is internationally renowned as the birthplace of William Shakespeare in 1564 and home to the Royal Shakespeare Company. The house where it is thought that Shakespeare was born is in Henley Street and the cottage of his wife, Anne Hathaway is a beautiful and typical English country cottage and garden. The foundations of New Place, the house where he died, are beneath the garden at Nash's House and his grave is at Holy Trinity Church. The 14 arch Clopton Bridge dates from the late 15th century on the south side of which is Alveston Manor which is said to be the site of the very first performance of 'A Midsummer Night's Dream'.

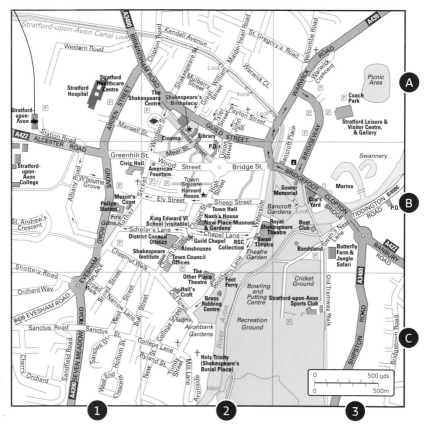

Index to street names

Swan Theatre

Photo © www.heritagecities.com

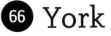

York

The city of York is rich in history, splendour and variety. The Romans, who founded the city in AD71, the Vikings, the Normans, and the Georgians have all left their mark. There are many museums reflecting on the changing times and they display various archaeological finds, including York Castle Museum, Jorvik Viking Centre, the Yorkshire Museum and the more chilling York Dungeon.

The ancient walls still surrounding the city are largely medieval but there are still remnants of the walls of the original Roman Fortress. The Multangular Tower in the Museum Gardens was the western corner of the Roman Fort and is the most intact structure remaining from

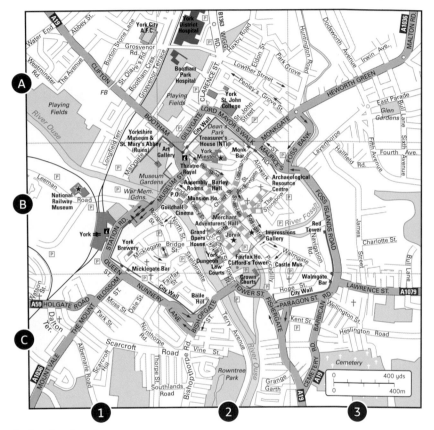

Index to street names

this time. It was built on the orders of the Emperor Septimius Severus, who lived in York from AD209 to AD211. Within the walls are narrow medieval streets and alleyways, including York's oldest street, 'Shambles' and cars are banned from the city centre. Micklegate Bar is the southern gatehouse through which monarchs traditionally entered the city. It contains a museum over four floors looking at the history of York and includes several severed heads on the second floor.

The Merchants Adventurers' Hall is evidence of York's prosperous times, during the Middle Ages, as a trading city operating under Guilds. With the Victorian Age came an

York Centre from City Walls   Photo © Yorkshire Tourist Board

Micklegate Bar   Photo © www.heritagecities.com

economic revival for York through the Railways, and the National Railway Museum celebrates over 200 years of railway history.

The Mansion House is in St Helen's Square and is the home of the Lord Mayor of York while in office. It underwent considerable restoration on 1998 to bring it back to its former glory and contains a wide variety of exhibits. It was built in 1732 to designs of an unknown architect. Behind the Mansion House is the Guildhall. First mention is made of a Guildhall in York in 1256 although it was not until 1378 that reference is made to the current site on the banks of the River Ouse. The current building is a recreation of the 15th century building that stood until it was gutted by German bombs in 1942. It is now in use as council offices.

The Shambles

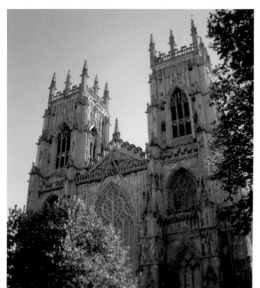

York Minster

Whip-ma-whop-ma-gate is the shortest street in York at 35m (115ft) and has the longest name. It was originally Whitnourwhatnourgate but evolved to its current form in the 16th century after public floggings were performed here. It means 'neither one thing nor the other'.

The Archaeological Resource Centre (ARC) in St Saviourgate is a museum housed in a restored medieval church and looks at how archaeological digs have contributed to discovering the history of York. There are hands-on exhibits as well as computer aided displays for all ages.

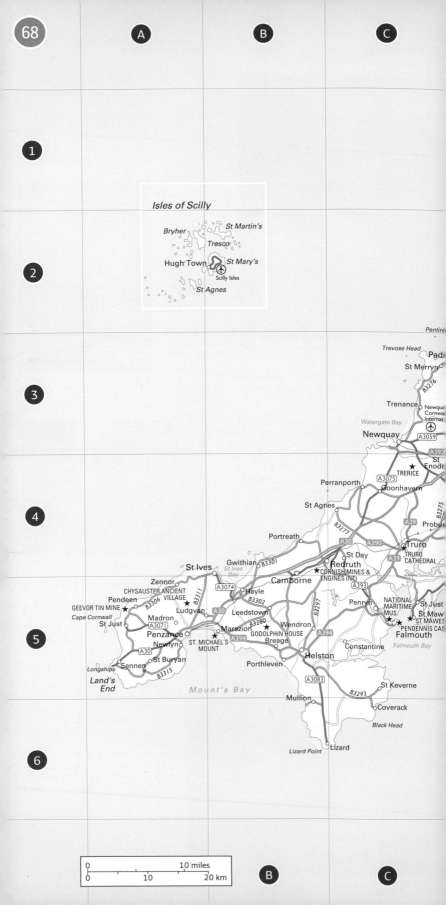

★ **JURASSIC COAST**
The Dorset and East Devon coast is designated a World Heritage Site between Exmouth in the west and Studland in the east.

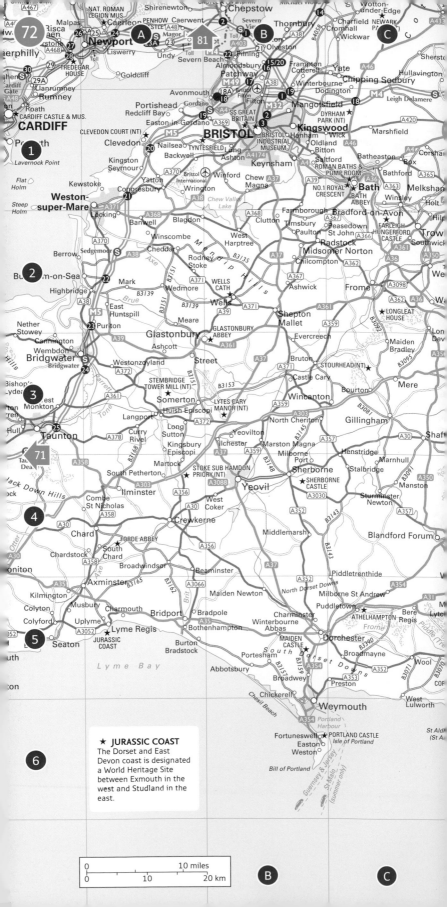

A S B 81 C

NAT. ROMAN
LEGION MUS.
Caerleon
PENHOW Caerwent
STLE A48
A48
Magor
Undy
Severn View
Toll
Shirenewton
Chepstow
Thornbury
Wotton-
under-Edge
Charfield NEWARK
Cromhall
Wickwar
A4058
A38
A403
Malpas
Risca
Newport
Lisworth
Liswerry
Severn Beach
Pilning
Almondsbury
Patchway
Frampton
Cotterell
Yate
Chipping Sodbury
A46
Hullavington
Sherston
Caerphilly
TREDEGAR
HOUSE
Goldcliff
Avonmouth
Gordano
M49
Filton
Winterbourne
Dodington
Leigh Delamere
M4
Llanrumney
Rumney
Portishead
Redcliff Bay
Easton-in-Gordano
SS GREAT
BRITAIN
BRISTOL
BRISTOL
INDUSTRIAL
MUSEUM
Mangotsfield
DYRHAM
PARK (NT)
Marshfield
A420
CARDIFF
CARDIFF CASTLE & MUS.
Penarth
Lavernock Point
CLEVEDON COURT (NT)
Clevedon
Nailsea
Backwell
Long
Ashton
TYNTESFIELD
Kingswood
Hanham
Oldland
Bitton
Wick
Salford
ROMAN BATHS &
PUMP ROOM
Batheaston
Bathford
Box
Corsham
A4
Kingston
Seymour
Bristol
International
Winford
Chew
Magna
Keynsham
A4
NO.1 ROYAL
CRESCENT
BATH
ABBEY
Bath
A363
A365
Melksham
Flat
Holm
Steep
Holm
Weston-
super-Mare
Congresbury
Wrington
Chew Valley
Lake
A38
Farmborough
A367
Peasedown
St John
Bradford-on-Avon
Winsley
Holt
Trow
Berrow
Sedgemoor
Locking
Banwell
Winscombe
Blagdon
West
Harptree
Clutton
Timsby
Paulton
Radstock
Midsomer Norton
FARLEIGH
HUNGERFORD
CASTLE
Southwick
Kewstoke
Cheddar
Rodney
Stoke
Chilcompton
A362
Berrow
Mark
Wedmore
WELLS
CATH
Ashwick
Frome
A362
A36
LONGLEAT
HOUSE
Maiden
Bradley
Lon
Dev
Burnham-on-Sea
Highbridge
East
Huntspill
Meare
Wells
Shepton
Mallet
A361
A359
Puriton
Glastonbury
GLASTONBURY
ABBEY
Evercreech
Bruton
STOURHEAD(NT)
Mere
Bridgwater
Westonzoyland
Ashcott
Street
Castle Cary
Wincanton
Bourton
Gillingham
A30
Shaf
Taunton
Somerton
Huish Episcopi
STEMBRIDGE
TOWER MILL (NT)
LYTES CARY
MANOR (NT)
North Cheriton
Monkton
Langport
Long
Sutton
A372
Yeovilton
Marston Magna
Milborne
Port
Henstridge
Marnhull
Stalbridge
Manston
71
Taunton
Dea
Curry
Rivel
Kingsbury
Episcopi
Ilchester
Sherborne
SHERBORNE
CASTLE
Sturminster
Newton
Martock
STOKE SUB HAMDON
PRIORY (NT)
Yeovil
Combe
St Nicholas
Ilminster
West
Coker
Middlemarsh
Blandford Forum
Chard
FORDE ABBEY
South
Chard
Crewkerne
A37
Chardstock
Broadwindsor
Beaminster
Piddletrenthide
A354
Honiton
Axminster
A3066
Maiden Newton
North Dorset Downs
Milborne St Andrew
A31
Kilmington
Colyton
Colyford
Musbury
Charmouth
Uplyme
Bridport
Bradpole
Charminster
Winterbourne
Abbas
Puddletown
ATHELHAMPTON
Bere
Regis
Lytc
Seaton
Lyme Regis
JURASSIC
COAST
Burton
Bradstock
Bothenhampton
A35
MAIDEN
CASTLE
Dorchester
Broadmayne
Wool
Abbotsbury
Portesham
Broadwey
Preston
A352
West
Lulworth
Lyme Bay
Chickerell
Chesil Beach
Weymouth
Portland
Harbour
★ JURASSIC COAST
The Dorset and East
Devon coast is designated
a World Heritage Site
between Exmouth in the
west and Studland in the
east.
Fortuneswell
Easton
Weston
PORTLAND CASTLE
Isle of Portland
St Ald
(St A
Bill of Portland

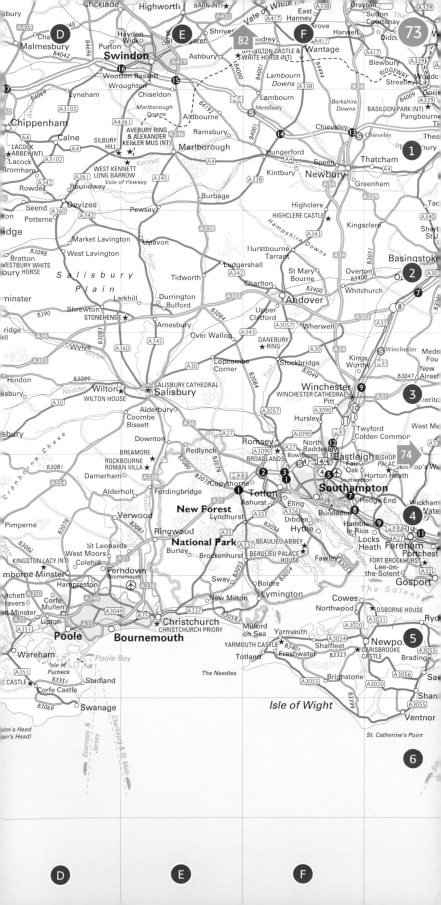

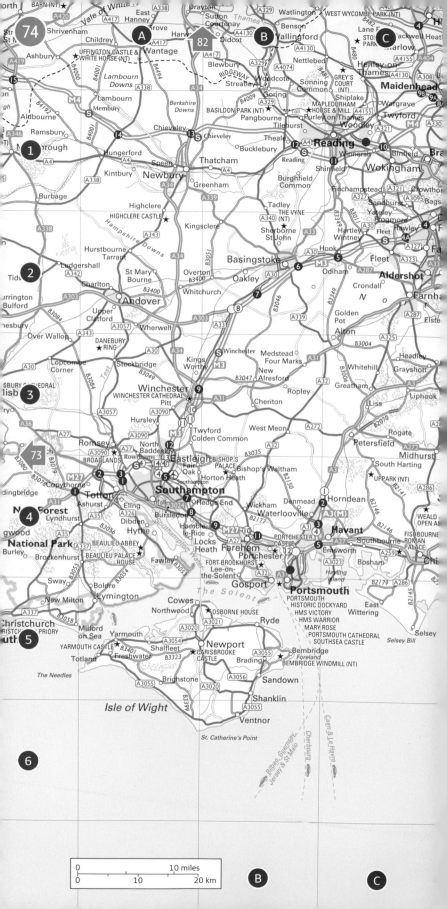

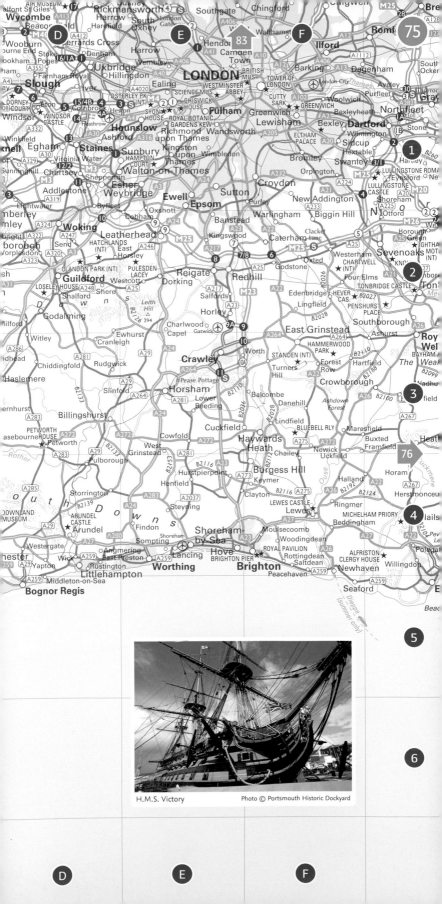

H.M.S. Victory

Photo © Portsmouth Historic Dockyard

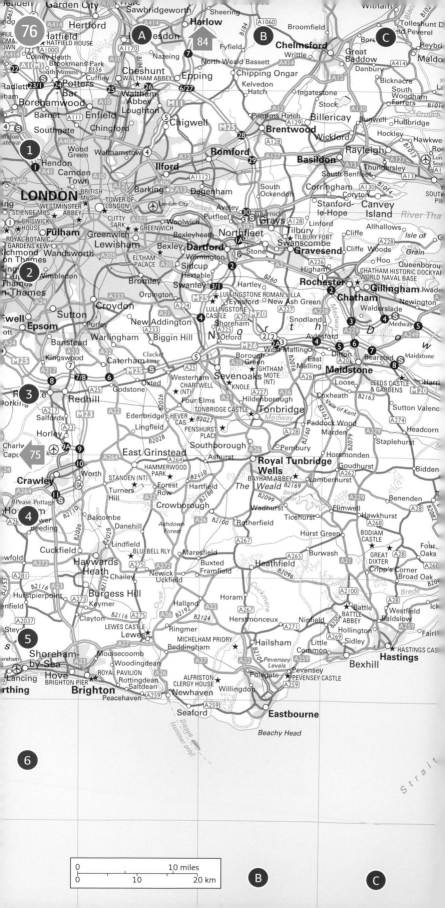

Leeds Castle
Photo © Sylvia Gray

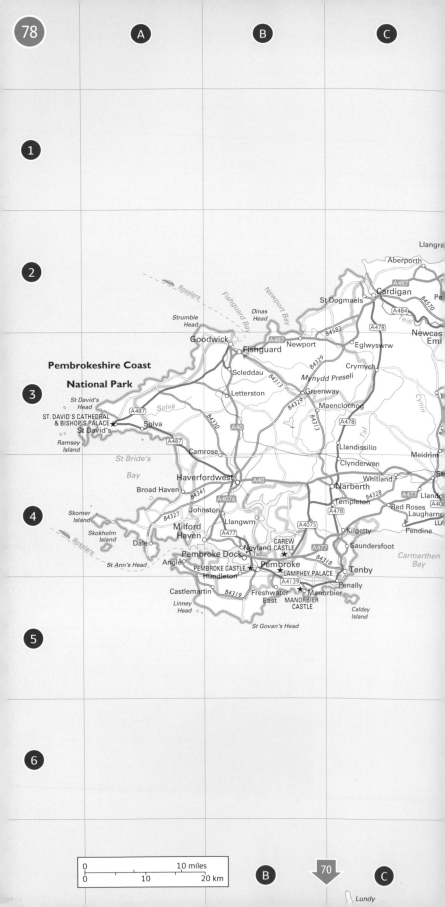

A   B   C

1

2

Pembrokeshire Coast

National Park

3

4

5

6

0 ——————— 10 miles
0 —— 10 —— 20 km

70

B   C

Lundy

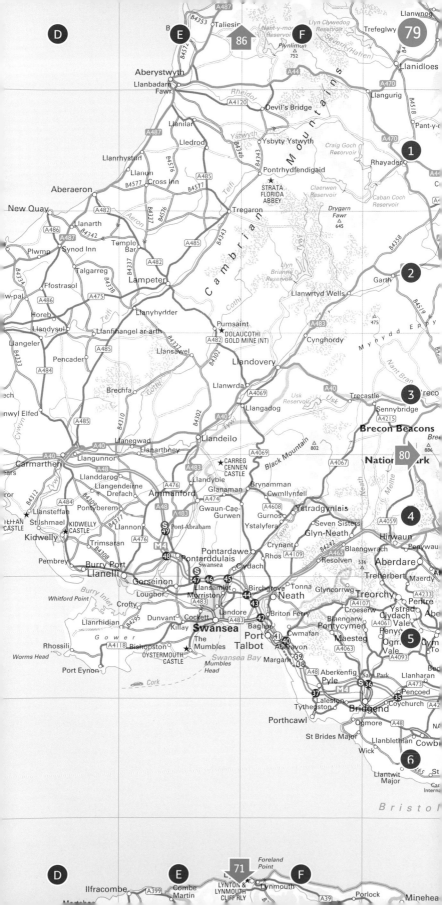

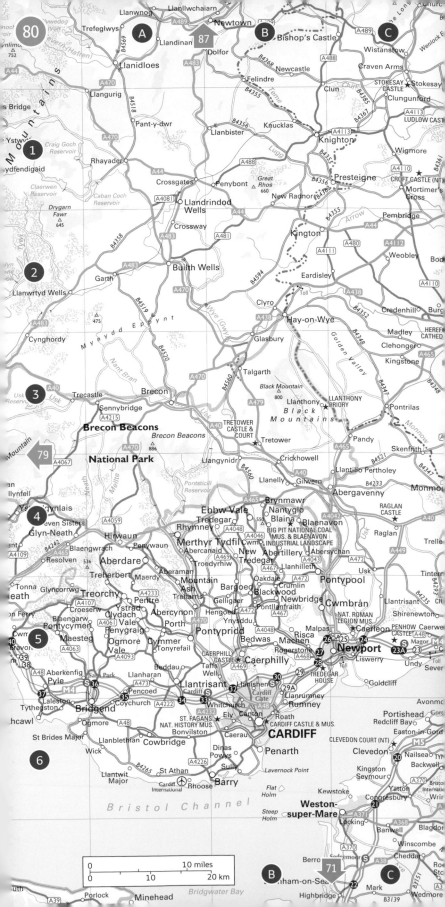

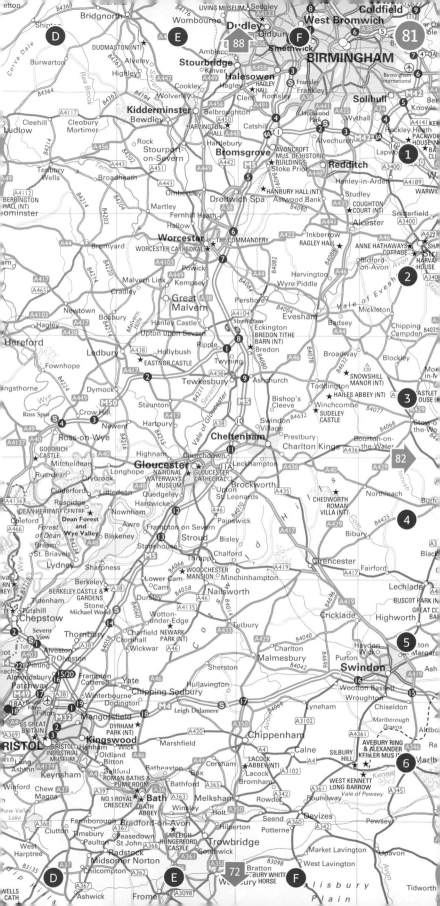

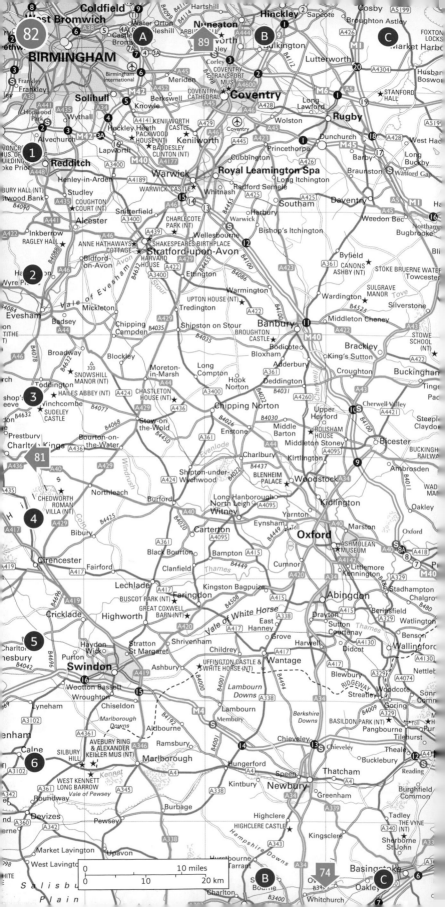

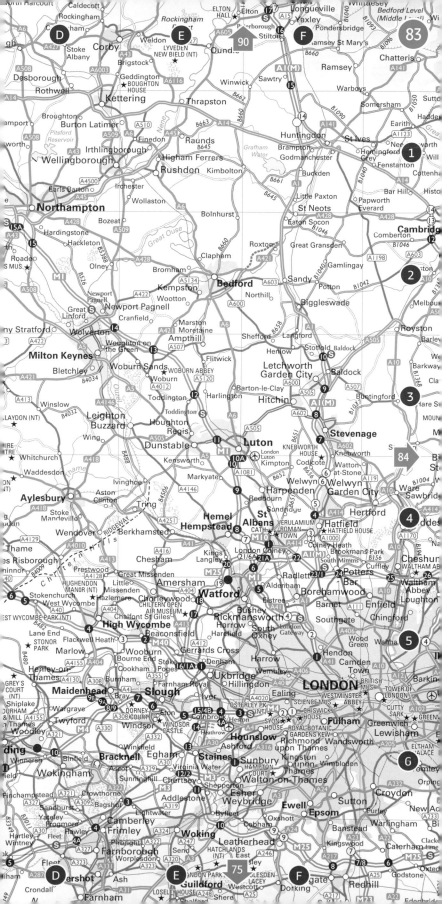

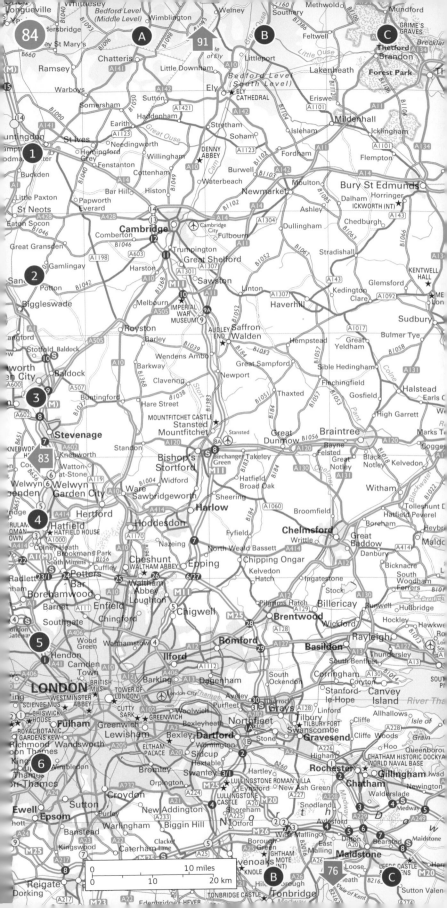

Caernarfon Castle
Photo © Welsh Tourist Board

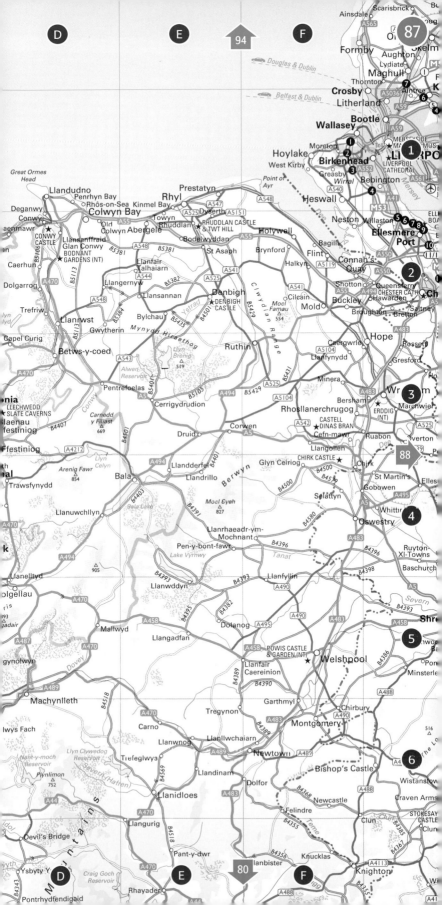

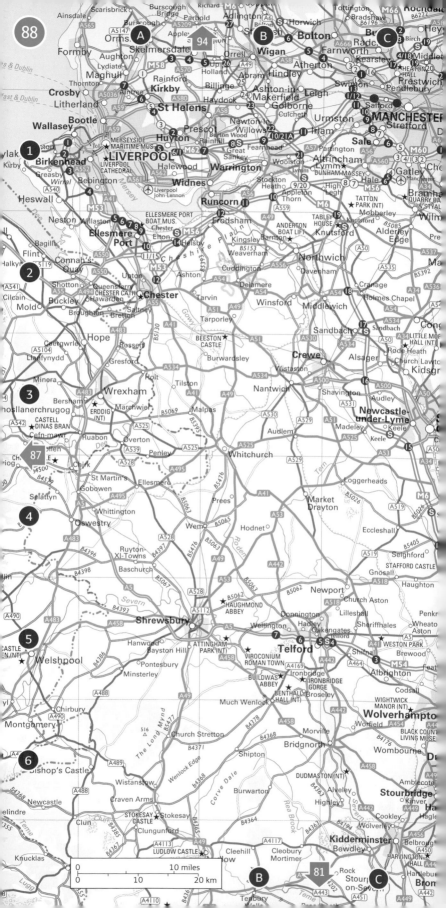

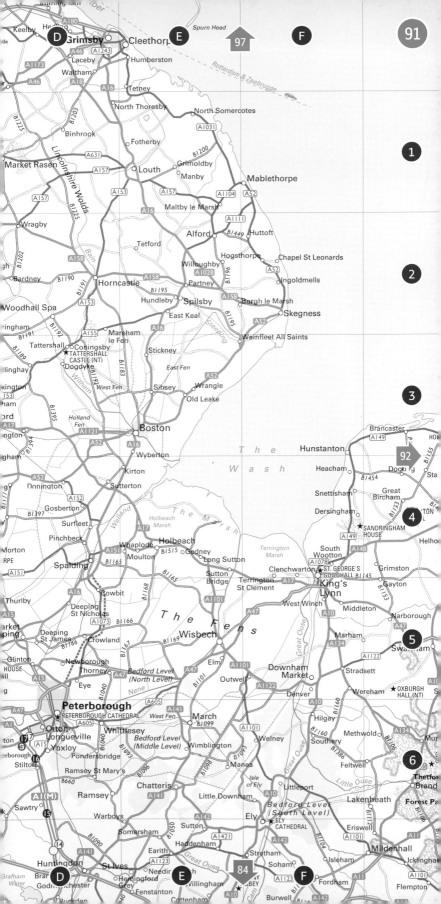

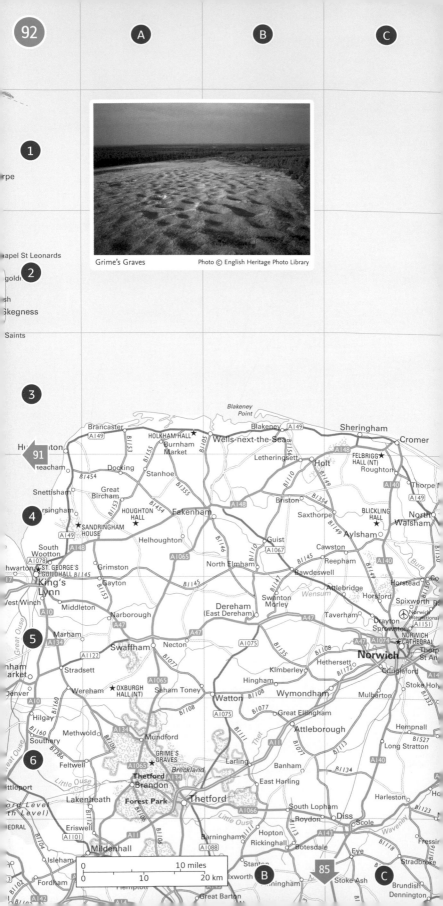

Grime's Graves   Photo © English Heritage Photo Library

1

rpe

apel St Leonards

goldⁱ

sh

Skegness

Saints

2

3

Blakeney Point

Brancaster   HOLKHAM HALL ★   Wells-next-the-Sea   Blakeney   A149   Sheringham
                  Burnham   Cromer
91
Hu   ton   Market   Letheringsett   Holt   FELBRIGG ★
Heacham   HALL (NT) Roughton
              Docking   Stanhoe   Thorpe
      B1454   B1355   B1110   A148   A149
Snettisham   Great   Briston   B1354
              Bircham   Saxthorpe   BLICKLING   North
rsingham ○   HOUGHTON   Fakenham   HALL ★   Walsham
              HALL ★   Aylsham
★ SANDRINGHAM   B1146   Guist   A140
  HOUSE   Helhoughton   A1067   Cawston   Reepham
South   North Elmham   Bawdeswell   Horstead
Wootton   Grimston   Spixworth
★ ST. GEORGE'S   B1145   Swanton   Attlebridge Horsford
  GUILDHALL B1145   Morley Wensum   Taverham ○ Drayton
King's   Gayton   Sprowston Norwich
Lynn B1153   Dereham   A1074 NORWICH
West Winch Middleton Narborough (East Dereham)   A47   CATHEDRAL ★
        A10   A47   NORWICH   Thorp
Marham   Swaffham   Necton   A1075   B1135 B1108   St An
A134   Kimberley Hethersett B1172
A1122   Hingham   Cringleford
nham Stradsett Wereham ★ OXBURGH   Saham Toney   Stoke Holy
arket   Denver   HALL (NT)   Watton B1108 Wymondham   Mulbarton
Hilgay   A1065   A1075   B1077 Great Ellingham
        B1160 Methwold   Mundford   Attleborough   Hempnall
Southery B1386   Breckland   Larling Banham   B1113 Long Stratton
6 Feltwell A1065 GRIME'S   A140
              GRAVES Thetford   East Harling   B1134 Harleston
ttleport Lakenheath Brandon Thetford   South Lopham   Diss
ord Level   Forest Park   A1066   Roydon ○ Scole
th Level) Eriswell   Little Ouse   Waveney
EDRAL   A1101   Barningham Hopton   B1118
    Mildenhall   A11   B1106 Rickinghall Botes.dale Eye   Fressi
Isleham   Stan.ton   Stradbroke
Fordham   lxworth ningham   **B**   Stoke Ash **C** Brundish
                                        Great Barton   Dennington

0   10 miles
0   10   20 km

85

Houghton Hall

Photo © Houghton Hall

Marble Hall, Holkham Hall

Photo © Holkham Hall

Mundesley

ket

Happisburgh

Stalham

Low A149 Hickling
Street A1151

shall Martham West Somerton
Hoveton The Hemsby
Horning A1062 Broads Filby Ormesby St Margaret
heath Broad A1064
Salhouse Billockby Caister-on-Sea
Little
Plumstead Acle Bure
Brundall A47
sw Great
Yarmouth

Bradwell
cross A143 Hopton
Thurton Corton
rooke Loddon B1074
Hales B1136 Haddiscoe Oulton
Woodton A1117 Lowestoft
B1532
Beccles A146 Carlton Colville
Bungay A12
s A145 Kessingland
B1127
ersfield A144 Brampton
etfield B1124 A12

Reydon
Halesworth B1125 Southwold
field B1117 Blyth B1387 Walberswick

85 Westleton

A1120 Yoxford

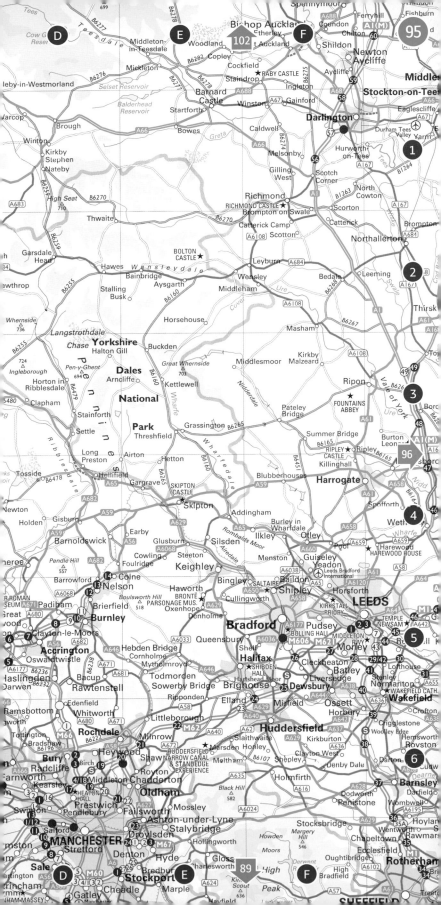

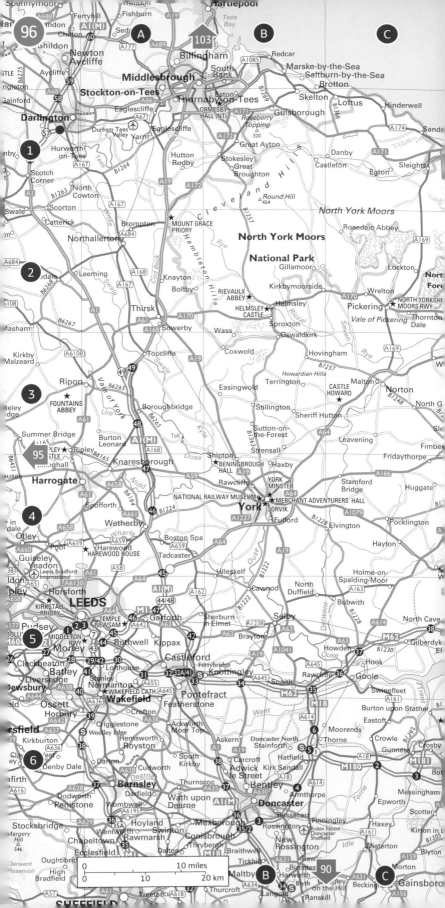

1

2

3

4

5

6

itby
WHITBY ABBEY
High
Hawsker
Robin
Hood's Bay
Steintondale
A171
Cloughton
Burniston
Hackness
Scalby
A165 Scarborough
SCARBOROUGH CASTLE
Park
iding
A170
Eastfield
Seamer
Snainton
Cayton
erwent
Filey
A1039
A64
Staxton
Knapton
Hunmanby
Wold
Newton
Butterwick
B1249
B1229
Bempton
Flamborough Head
B1253
Flamborough
A165
SEWERBY HALL & GARDENS
Langtoft
Rudston
Bridlington
B1252
Kilham
Hilderthorpe
A614
B1249
A165
Bridlington
Bay
Driffield
B1249
Skipsea
Bainton
Hutton
Cranswick
Beeford
B1248
Middleton-
on-the-Wolds
Brandesburton
B1244
Hornsea
A164
B1243
Leven
Sigglesthorne
A1035
Molescroft
A165
Skirlaugh
Aldbrough
A1079
Beverley
BURTON
CONSTABLE
HALL
B1238
B1242
034
B1230
Woodmansey
Sproatley
Cottingham
Bilton
South Cave
A1079
Preston
Hedon
Withernsea
A164
Anlaby
A165
B1362
ghton
Swanland
KINGSTON
Thorngumbald
North
A1105 A63
UPON HULL
A1033
Keyingham
A1033
rough
Ferriby
Barton-
upon-Humber
Patrington
Easington
B1445
A1077
Goxhill
A15
B1206
Barrow
upon Humber
Winterton
B1204
A1077
ORMANBY HALL
A160
Ulceby
Immingham
Spurn Head
B1204
A180
Scunthorpe
A18
Keelby
Healing
sford
Broughton
Humberside
Grimsby
Cleethorpes
A4
Brigg
A46
A1243
Humberston
A1084
Laceby
B1398
A1173
Hibaldstow
Caistor
A46
Waltham
A18
Rotterdam & Zeebrugge
B1434
A16
Tetney
A15
B1225
South Kelsey
North Thoresby
B1434
North Somercotes
B1398
Binbrook
A1031
Fotherby
91
B1200
D
A1103
E
A631
F
gh
A631
Middle Rasen
Market Rasen
A157
Louth
Grimoldby

Peel Castle & Round Tower, Isle of Man

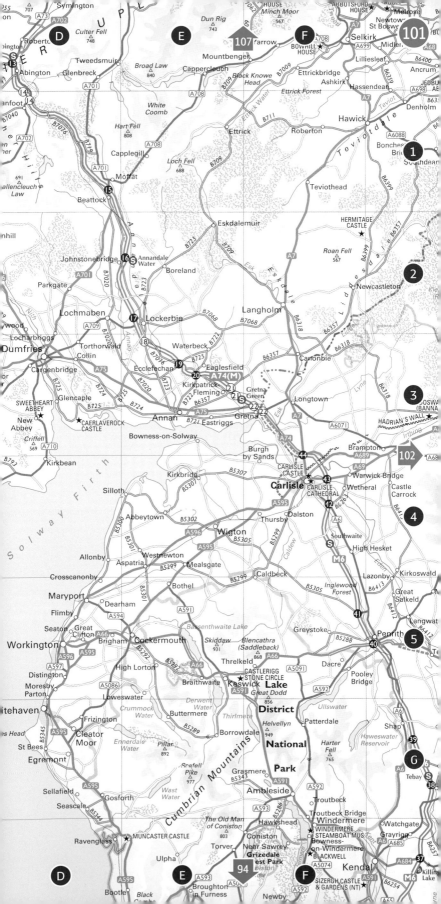

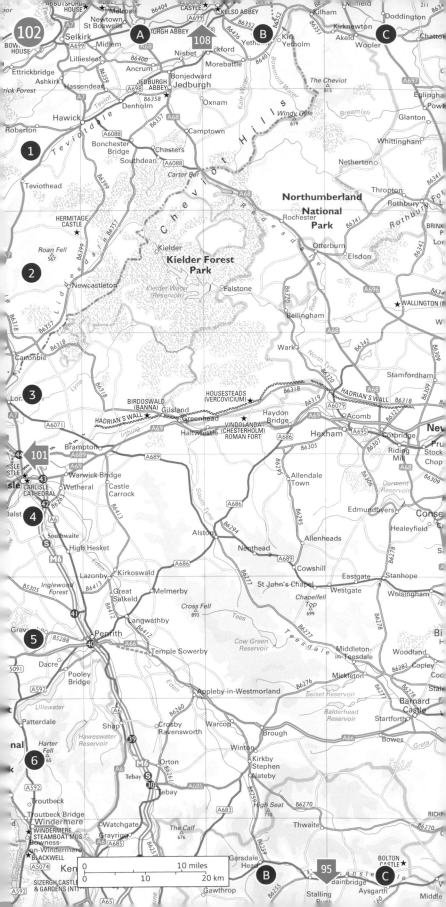

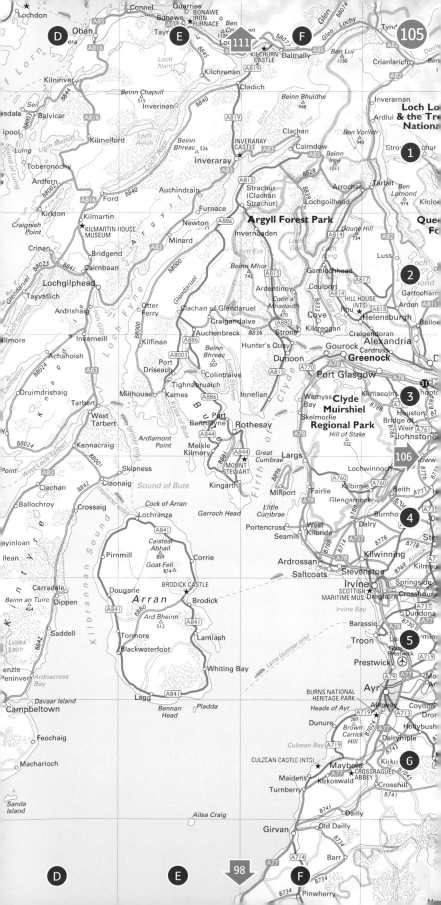

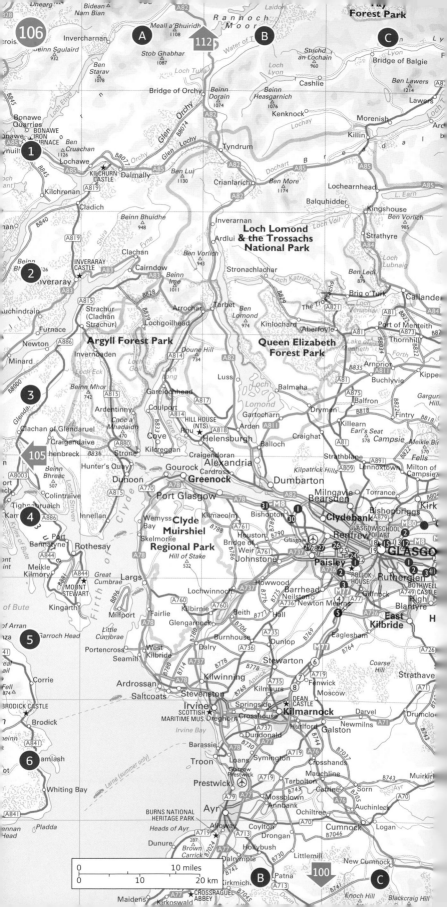

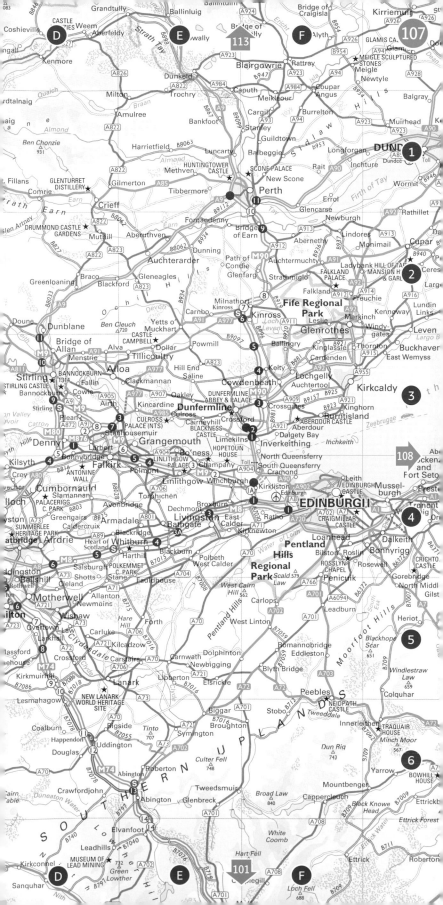

Mellerstain

Photo © Mellerstain Trust

BENBECULA
(nn na Faoghla)

orry

Wiay

A

116

Boreraig

Miloraig

B

Dunvegan

Roskhill

Borve

Kensaleyre

Bernisd

Carbost

C

A850

B884

Healabhal
Bheag
488

Skye

B885

Portree

865

B8909

Loch Sgioport

OUTH UIST
hist a' Deas)

Beinn Mhòr

1

Loch Eynor

Bracadale

Portnalong

A863

A87

Talisker

B8009

Carbost

Sligachan

Beinn Bhreac
445

Cuillin
Hills

Loch Bracadale

Glenbrittle

Sgurr
Alasdair

993

Lochboisdale (Loch Baghasdail)

Loch Baghasdail

Soay

Ludag

Loch
Scav

2

(Eriosgaigh)

Sea of the Hebrides

Canna

124

Sound of Canna

Kilmory

Rum
(Rhum)

Kinloch

Cuillin Sound

3

Askival
812

Sound of Rum

Rubha nam
Meirleach

Eigg

An
393

Eilean
nan Each

Sound of Eigg

Muck

I
N
N
E
R

H
E
B
R
I
D
E
S

4

Castlebay

Lochboisdale

Point of
Ardnamurchan

Achosr

A
d

Eilean Mòr

Sorisdale

B8007

Kilchoa

B8072

Clabhach

Coll

Ardmore Point

Arinagour

Caliach
Point

Tobermo

B8070

Loch
Eatharna

Calgary

Gunna

Crossapol
Bay

Dervaig

B880

5

Hough Bay

B8068

B8069

Caolas

Calgary Bay

Kilninian

Tiree

Tiree

Scarinish

Loch Tuath

Barrapoll

B8065

Hynish Bay

Treshnish Isles

Gometra

Lagganulva

Ulva

Balephuil

Balemartine

Little
Colonsay

Staffa

Loch

Balnahard

B80

6

IONA (NTS)

Baile Mòr
Iona

Fionnphort

Loch Scridain

A849

Ross of Mull

Bunessan

Soa Island

Sound of Iona

Ardchiavaig

Mal
P

0   10 miles

0   10   20 km

B

104

C

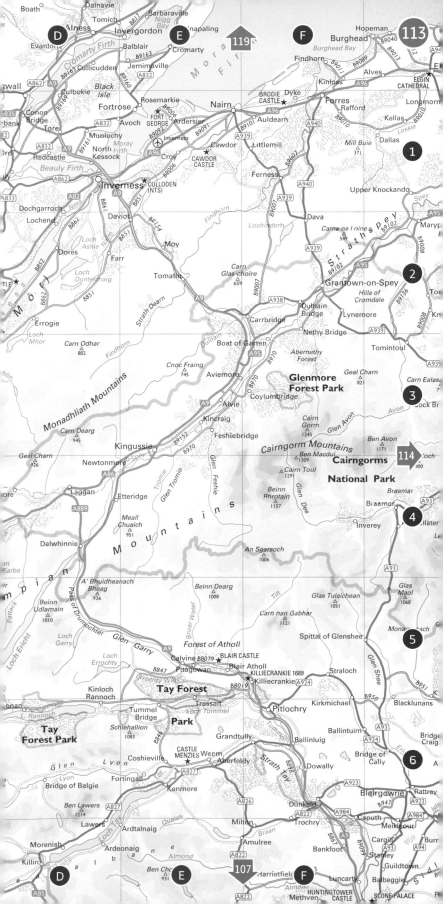

Troup Head
Rosehearty
Macduff
Gardenstown
Fraserburgh
Inverallochy
off
Longmanhill
New
Aberdour
Mid Ardlaw
B9031
Memsie
St Combs
A947
A98
Ladysford
A981
A90
B9033
Loch of Strathbeg
Rattray
Head
New
Pitsligo
Strichen
Crimond
New Byth
B9105
New Leeds
A90
St Fergus
Turriff
B9021
B9170
Maud
Mintlaw
Longside
Peterhead
Darra
New Deer
B9029
A950
B9170
Stuartfield
Auchnagatt
A948
A952
Boddam
Kirkton of Auchterless
FYVIE
CASTLE
Hill of
Dudwick
174
A90
E
B9005
Fyvie
Methlick
Hatton
Cruden Bay
B9001
HADDO HOUSE &
COUNTRY PARK
Ythan
A948
Toll of
Birness
A975
Bay of Cruden
20
A947
B9170
B9005
Tarves
Ellon
B999
Oldmeldrum
B9000
Inverurie
A920
A920
Pitmedden
A920
Collieston
Whiterashes
Newburgh
B993
A947
B999
Newmachar
B979
A90
Balmedie
nay
Kintore
B977
Aberdeen
Dyce
CASTLE
FRASER
Blackburn
B997
Bridge of Don
of Skene
A96
A90
A944
Bucksburn
Kirkton of Skene
Westhill
Aberdeen
Echt
B9119
B9125
Cults
977
Peterculter
Charlestown
Cove Bay
DRUM CASTLE
A93
Dee
Portlethen
CRATHES
CASTLE
B9077
Banchory
Kirkton of
Durris
Netherley
Newtonhill
B979
Mongour
376
A957
Rickarton
Muchalls
Dye
Drumlithie
Stonehaven
DUNNOTTAR CASTLE
A90
A92
rae
B967
Roadside of Kinneff
rdoun
Bervie Water
Inverbervie
Laurencekirk
Gourdon
B9120
A92
rykirk
St Cyrus
OF
S)
Montrose
Ferryden
nan Bay
lor

North Ugie
Kirkwall & Lerwick

Balmoral Castle   Photo © Aberdeen & Grampian Tourist Board

ss

tland
rries

1

Elgin Cathedral   Photo © Aberdeen & Grampian
Tourist Board

2

Dunrobin Castle   Photo © Highlands of Scotland
Tourist Board

3

4

5

6

tknockie
Cullen   Portsoy   Whitehills   Troup Head   Rosehearty   Fraserburgh
Fordyce   A98   B9139   Macduff   Gardenstown   B9031   Inverallochy
199   Durn   Banff   New   Mld Ardlaw   Memsie   St Combs
Hill   B9121   Longmanhill   B9031   Aberdour   A98   B9033   Loch of Strathbeg
A95   B9025   A97   Ladysford   A981   A90
Cornhill   B9022   Deveron   A98   Rattray
430   Finnygaud   A947   New   Strichen   Crimond   Head
B9105   Pitsligo   B9093   New Leeds   A90
B9022   Aberchirder   New Byth   B9021   St Fergus
D   Turriff   E   minestown   115   F   Mintla   Longside
Milltown of   B9024   Darra   B9170   New Dear   Maud   B9029   A950

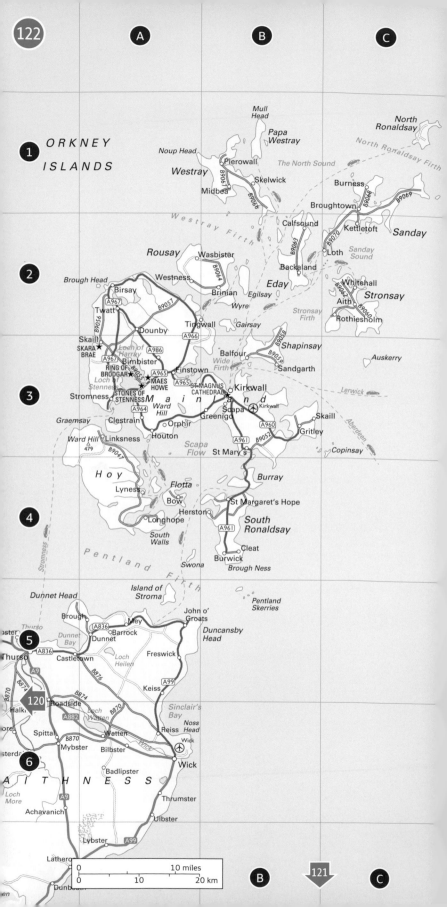

A
B
C

1

*ORKNEY
ISLANDS*

Mull
Head

Papa
Westray

*North
Ronaldsay*

North Ronaldsay Firth

Noup Head

B9070

Pierowall

The North Sound

Burness

B9068

Westray

Skelwick

Broughtown

B9069

Midbea

B9068

Calfsound

Kettletoft

Sanday

B9070

Loth

Westray Firth

B9065

B9063

*Sanday
Sound*

2

Rousay

Wasbister

Backaland

Whitehall

Stronsay

Brough Head

Birsay

Westness

Brinian

Egilsay

Eday

B9064

B9061

Aith

B9060

A967

B9057

Twatt

B9056

Dounby

Tingwall

Wyre

Gairsay

Rothiesholm

*Stronsay
Firth*

Skaill

SKARA
BRAE ★

*Loch of
Harray*

A986

Bimbister

Balfour

Shapinsay

B9058

Sandgarth

B9059

Auskerry

A967

RING OF
BRODGAR ★

Finstown

A965

3

Stromness

*Loch of
Stenness*

STONES OF
STENNESS ★

A964

★MAES
HOWE

A965

ST MAGNUS
CATHEDRAL ★

*Wide
Firth*

Lerwick

M a i n l a n d

Kirkwall

Kirkwall

Aberdeen

Graemsay

Clestrain

Ward
Hill

Orphir

Greenigo

Scapa

A960

Skaill

Gritley

Houton

A961

B9052

Ward Hill
△
479

Linksness

*Scapa
Flow*

St Mary's

Copinsay

B9047

St Margaret's Hope

Burray

4

Hoy

Lyness

Flotta

Bow

Herston

*South
Ronaldsay*

A961

Longhope

*South
Walls*

Cleat

Stromness

Pentland Firth

Swona

Burwick

Brough Ness

Dunnet Head

Island of
Stroma

*Pentland
Skerries*

Brough

John o'
Groats

Thurso

*Dunnet
Bay*

A836

Mey

Duncansby
Head

5

oster

Thurso

A836

Castletown

Barrock

Dunnet

Freswick

*Loch
Heilen*

B876

A9

B874

120

Roadside

B874

Keiss

A99

*Sinclair's
Bay*

Halkirk

A882

Watten

B870

Reiss

*Noss
Head*

B870

ore

Spittal

B870

Wick

6

sterd

Mybster

Bilbster

Badlipster

Wick

C A I T H N E S S

*Loch
More*

Thrumster

A9

Achavanich

Ulbster

Lybster

A99

Lathero

0 — 10 miles
0 — 10 — 20 km

Dunbeath

B

121

C

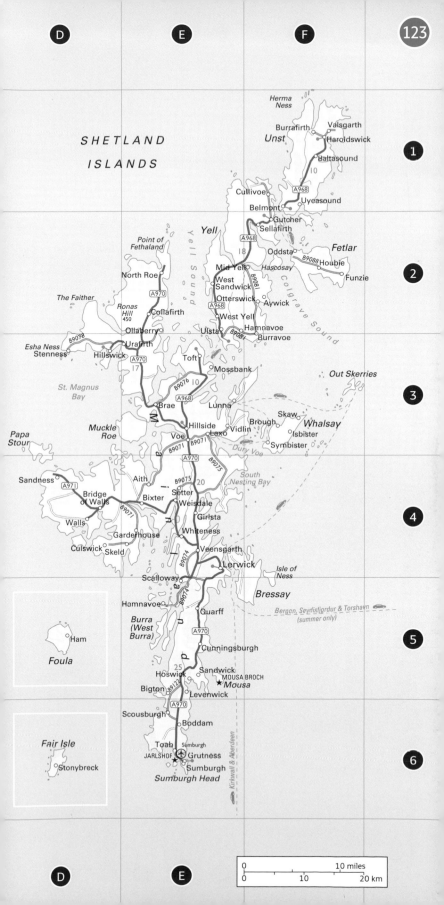

The following is a comprehensive listing of all named places and heritage sites which appear in this atlas. The heritage sites are in purple type and they are also listed and described in the separate guide section.

Administrative area abbreviations

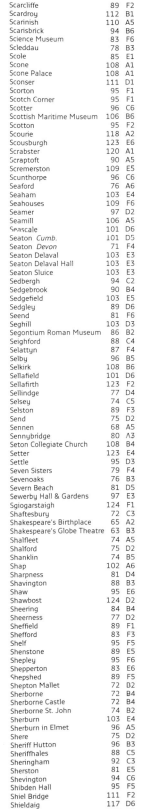